T0140161

Advances in Information Security

Volume 57

Series Editor

Sushil Jajodia, Center for Secure Information Systems, George Mason University, Fairfax, VA, 22030-4444, USA

More information about this series at http://www.springer.com/series/5576

Giovanni Livraga

Protecting Privacy in Data Release

 Springer

Giovanni Livraga
Universita degli Studi di Milano
Crema, Italy

ISSN 1568-2633
Advances in Information Security
ISBN 978-3-319-35525-2   ISBN 978-3-319-16109-9   (eBook)
DOI 10.1007/978-3-319-16109-9

Springer International Publishing AG Switzerland is part of Springer Science+Business Media (www.springer.com)

To my family
To Cesare

Preface

Data sharing and dissemination play a key role in our information society. Not only do they prove to be advantageous to the involved parties, but they can also be fruitful to the society at large: for instance, new treatments for rare diseases can be discovered with real clinical trials shared by hospitals and pharmaceutical companies. The advancements in the Information and Communication Technology (ICT) make the process of releasing a data collection simpler than ever. The availability of novel computing paradigms, such as data outsourcing and cloud computing, makes scalable, reliable, and fast infrastructures a dream come true at reasonable costs. As a natural consequence of this scenario, data owners often rely on external servers for releasing their data collections, thus delegating the burden of data storage and management to the service provider. Unfortunately, the price to be paid is in terms of unprecedented privacy and security risks. Data collections often include sensitive information, not intended for disclosure, that should be properly protected. The problem of protecting privacy in data release has been under the attention of the research and development communities for a long time. However, the richness of released data, the large number of available sources, and the emerging outsourcing/cloud scenarios raise novel problems, not addressed by traditional approaches, which call for enhanced solutions.

In this book, we propose a comprehensive approach for protecting sensitive information when large collections of data are publicly or selectively released by their owners. In a nutshell, this requires protecting data explicitly included in the release, as well as protecting information not explicitly released but that could be exposed by the release, and ensuring that access to released data be allowed only to authorized parties according to the data owners' policies. More specifically, these three aspects translate to three requirements, addressed by this book, which can be summarized as follows. The first requirement is the *protection of data explicitly included in a release*. While intuitive, this requirement is complicated by the fact that privacy-enhancing techniques should not prevent recipients from performing legitimate analysis on the released data but, on the contrary, should ensure sufficient visibility over non sensitive information. We therefore propose a solution, based on a novel formulation of the fragmentation approach, that vertically fragments a data collection so to satisfy requirements for both information protection and visibility, and we complement it with an effective technique for enriching the utility of the released data. The second requirement is the *protection of data not explicitly included in a release*. As a matter of fact, even a collection of non sensitive data might enable recipients to infer (possibly sensitive) information not explicitly disclosed but that somehow depends on the released information (e.g., the release of the treatment with which a patient is being cared can leak information about his/her disease). To address this requirement, starting from a real case study, we propose a solution for counteracting the inference of sensitive information that can be drawn observing peculiar value distributions in a released data collection. The third requirement is *access control enforcement*. Available solutions fall short in emerging computing paradigms for a variety of reasons. Traditional access control mechanisms are in fact typically based on a reference monitor mediating access requests, and do not fit outsourcing/cloud scenarios where neither data owners are willing nor cloud providers are trusted, to enforce the authorization policy. Recent solutions applicable to outsourcing scenarios assume outsourced data to be read-only and cannot easily manage (dynamic) write authorizations. We therefore propose an approach for efficiently supporting grant and revoke of write authorizations, building upon the selective encryption approach, and we also define a subscription-based authorization policy, to fit real-world scenarios where users pay for a service and access the resources made available during their subscriptions.

The main contributions of this book can therefore be summarized as follows.

- With respect to the protection of data explicitly included in a release, our original results are: (1) a novel modeling of the fragmentation problem; (2) an efficient technique for computing a fragmentation, based on reduced Ordered Binary Decision Diagrams (OBDDs) to formulate the conditions that a fragmentation must satisfy; (3) the computation of a minimal fragmentation not fragmenting data more than necessary, with the definition of both an exact and a heuristics algorithm providing faster computational time while well approximating the exact solutions; (4) the definition of loose associations, a sanitized form of the sensitive associations broken by fragmentation, specifically designed to operate on arbitrary fragmentations; and (5) the definition of a heuristic algorithm for the computation of arbitrary loose associations, experimentally proved to enhance precision of queries executed over different fragments.
- With respect to the protection of data not explicitly included in a release, our original results are: (1) the definition of a novel and unresolved inference scenario, raised from a real case study where data items are incrementally released upon request; (2) the definition of several metrics to assess the inference exposure due to a data release, based upon the concepts of mutual information, Kullback–Leibler distance between distributions, Pearson's cumulative statistic, and Dixon's coefficient; (3) the identification of a safe release with respect to a given inference channel; and (4) the definition of the controls to be enforced to guarantee that no sensitive information be leaked releasing non sensitive data items.

- With respect to the access control enforcement, our original results are: (1) the management of dynamic write authorizations, by defining a solution based on selective encryption for efficiently and effectively supporting grant and revoke of write authorizations; (2) the definition of an effective technique to guarantee data integrity, so to allow the data owner and the users to verify that modifications to a resource have been produced only by authorized users; and (3) the modeling and enforcement of a subscription-based authorization policy, to support scenarios where both the set of users and the set of resources change frequently over time, and users' authorizations to access resources are based on their subscriptions.

Milan, Italy   Giovanni Livraga
November 2014

Acknowledgements

This book is the result of the publication of my Ph.D. thesis, and there is a long list of people I am indebted to and to which I want to express my gratitude.

I must first sincerely thank my advisor Prof. Pierangela Samarati, for having dedicated her time to follow me in my work with constant presence and valuable and fruitful supervision. I am particularly grateful for the many opportunities I got from her, among which the possibility of preparing this book is just a little example.

I am grateful to Prof. Sabrina De Capitani di Vimercati, for her valuable guidance, profitable comments on the work, and optimistic spin I have always got from her, which helped to find the right track in many occasions.

I am also indebted to Dr. Sara Foresti, for always having her office door open when I knock, and being ready to provide help and many corrections to my work.

I would like to express my gratitude to Prof. Sushil Jajodia, who first envisioned the opportunity to publish this book based on my Ph.D. thesis. I am grateful to him also for the opportunity to visit the Center for Secure Information Systems at George Mason University, USA, where I could find a stimulating and pleasant environment.

I thank Dr. Michele Bezzi, Dr. Valentina Ciriani, Prof. Stefano Paraboschi, and Dr. Roberto Sassi, for the valuable discussions and their support on different aspects of the work I present in this book. I would like to thank Prof. Vijay Atluri, Prof. Sushil Jajodia, and Prof. Javier Lopez, for providing precious comments and suggestions that improved the presentation of this work.

My gratitude goes also to Susan Lagerstrom-Fife and Jennifer Malat, for their support in the preparation of this book.

A special mention to my family: mum and dad, for bringing me up the way I am and for being two examples that have motivated me to reach this goal; Chiara, for the lovely chats on Tuesday lunch breaks; Matteo, for the help I can have when I need it.

Cesare: Your support is and has been fundamental to me, also in reaching this goal. You are always right next to me when I need it, and this is just priceless to me. And thanks, for patiently caring about me and, more patiently, teaching me to care about myself. Having you by my side makes me a lucky man.

In random order, The Brooke's inner circle: Gemma, Plitz, Soult, Vitti, Ilaria, Marta and Claudio. Riki and Stefi. Alice and Michele and our coffee breaks. Ruggero, Angelo, Paolo, Gerson, and the other (present and past) Ph.D. students and colleagues at the department. Chiara and Nora, wonderful *quasi*-flatmates, and helpful friends in troublesome occasions. Federico, Francesca, Erika, and all the other guys, for having opened their Gran Sasso door to me.

A last, special, though to my grandmothers Augusta and Alice who, I am sure, are the most proud of all.

Contents

Chapter 1
Introduction

Private companies, public organizations and final users are more and more releasing, sharing, and disseminating their data, to take reciprocal advantage of the great benefits they can obtain by making their data available, publicly or selectively, to others. Unfortunately, these benefits come at the price of unprecedented privacy risks: large collections of data often include sensitive information, possibly related to users, which should be properly protected. The availability of effective means for protecting data against privacy violations is then emerging as one of the key issues to be addressed in such an open and collaborative scenario.

In this book, we define a comprehensive approach for protecting sensitive information when large collections of data are publicly or selectively released by their owners. In the remainder of this chapter, we discuss the motivations behind the work, our objectives and our contributions. We finally illustrate the outline of the book.

1.1 Motivation

The advancements in the Information and Communication Technology (ICT) have revolutionized our lives in a way that was unthinkable until few years ago. We live in the Globalization era, where everything we need to do is available within "one mouse click". Global infrastructure, digital infrastructure, digital society are only few examples of terms used to refer to our society. The term that better represents our society is however *information society* (or *information age*) since information plays a key role in the daily life activities of everyone. Every time we browse Internet, perform online transactions, fill in forms to, for example, pay bills, taxes or participate in online games, and spend our time in online social networks, information about us is collected, stored, and analyzed. At the same time, public and private organizations need to share and disseminate their information, also due to the

© Springer International Publishing Switzerland 2015
G. Livraga, *Protecting Privacy in Data Release*, Advances in Information
Security 57, DOI 10.1007/978-3-319-16109-9_1

benefits that such information sharing brings to them and to their end users. Such advantages are easy to understand: as an example, consider how medical research can advance, to the benefits of the entire humanity, thanks to hospitals sharing health information about their patients with pharmaceutical companies to the aim of improving known treatments–or even discovering new ones–based on real-world clinical trials. As another example, public, private, and governmental organizations might disclose or share their data collections for research or statistical purposes, for providing services more efficiently and effectively, or because forced by laws and regulations. Medical, financial, census or demographic, and scientific data are only few examples of information whose release and exchange can be fruitful to the involved parties and the society at large. The process of releasing a collection of data can be either *public* (i.e., data are published and restrictions are enforced neither on accessing nor on using them) or *selective* (i.e., different portions of the released collection can be accessed by different parties). The emerging paradigms of data outsourcing and cloud computing indeed facilitate data release. Giving to users and companies the opportunity to benefit from the lower costs, higher availability, and larger elasticity that are offered by the rapidly growing market of cloud providers, data owners can easily release large data collections without the burden of further managing them. As witnessed, for example, by the seemingly never-ending success of services like Amazon S3 and EC2, enjoying the benefits of the highly scalable, reliable, fast, and inexpensive infrastructure such providers offer, users and companies are more and more resorting to *honest-but-curious* external servers (i.e., trusted for managing data but not for accessing their content) to store their data and make them available to others.

The complexity and variety of our information society introduce however new risks, and pose new research challenges. The vast amount of personal (possibly user-generated) data collected, stored, and processed, the unclear data ownership, and the lack of control of the users on their own data are creating unprecedented risks of privacy breaches. The problem of properly protecting the privacy of the users is clearly not new and has received considerable attention from the research and industrial communities. In the past, the restricted access to information and its expensive processing represented a basic form of protection that does not hold anymore: with the rate at which technology is developing, it is now becoming easier and easier to access huge amounts of data by using, for example, portable devices (e.g., PDAs, mobile phones) and ubiquitous network resources. Moreover, the advancements of the ICT make us available powerful techniques and technological resources for analyzing and correlating data coming from different sources, and resorting to cloud/outsourcing solutions makes data owners inevitably lose direct control over their own data.

Considering that large collections of data often include sensitive information, whose confidentiality must be safeguarded, it is clear that the protection of data against improper disclosure is a key factor in our information society, and yet a problem far from having a well-defined solution. The efforts of the scientific community in this direction, and the media coverage on privacy issues, testify how data protection is a sine-qua-non condition for our society to fully enjoy the benefits of data sharing and dissemination. However, serious privacy incidents can be right behind the corner: two well-known examples of privacy violations are the America OnLine (AOL) and Netflix incidents [7, 85]. AOL is an Internet services and media company that in 2006 released around 20 millions of search records of 650,000 of its customers. To protect the privacy of its customers, AOL de-identified such records by substituting personal identifiers with numerical identifiers, which were therefore released together with the term(s) used for the search, the timestamp, whether the user clicked on a result, and the corresponding visited website. With these data, two reporters of the New York Times newspaper were able to identify AOL customer no. 4417749 as Thelma Arnold, a 62 years old widow living in Lilburn [7]. In the same year, the on-line movies renting service Netflix publicly released 100 millions records, showing the ratings given by 500,000 users to the movies they rented. The records were released within the "Netflix Prize" competition that offered $1 million to anyone who could improve the algorithm used by Netflix to suggest movies to its customers based on their previous ratings. Also in this case, records were de-identified by replacing personal identifiers with numerical identifiers. However, some researchers were able to de-anonymize the data by comparing the Netflix data against publicly available ratings on the Internet Movie Database (IMDb). For instance, the release of her movie preferences damaged a lesbian mother since she was re-identified, and her sexual orientation disclosed against her own will [85].

1.2   Objectives

There are mainly three key aspects to be considered when designing a system for ensuring that no sensitive information be leaked when releasing a data collection, as briefly outlined in the following.

- *Protection of data explicitly involved in a release.* Large data collections often-times include sensitive data that should be protected (e.g., medical information about diseases suffered from patients, financial details about the income of employees, personal information of individuals such as religious, sexual, or polit-ical preferences). However, protecting privacy of sensitive information should not prevent recipients from performing legitimate analysis on the released data. In other words, privacy-enhancing techniques should balance between privacy protection, on one hand, and information visibility, on the other hand. Recent proposals considering confidentiality and visibility constraints (i.e., requirements on privacy and visibility) have put forward the promising idea of computing vertical fragments over the original data structure so that all the constraints are satisfied. To further enrich the utility of the released data, fragments can be complemented with a sanitized form of the broken sensitive associations among attributes. To ensure proper protection to data privacy, while maximizing the visibility over non sensitive information, it is therefore necessary to define novel formulations of the fragmentation problem, to efficiently and effectively satisfy

confidentiality and visibility constraints. Also, it is important to enrich the utility
of released data, independently from the number of released fragments.

- *Protection of data not explicitly involved in a release.* The release of non
sensitive data (and thus the exclusion of sensitive data from the release), in
some scenarios, might only at a first sight be a safe approach to protect data
confidentiality. In fact, sensitive information that is not published, and should
remain protected, may become indirectly available when it is somehow related
to, and deducible from, released non sensitive data (as an example, the release of
the treatment with which a patient is being cared reduces the uncertainty about
the possible disease she suffers from, due to the correlation existing between
an illness and its treatments). Such a problem has been extensively studied
in multilevel database management systems, with solutions that however do
not fit the data release scenario. Some attempts have recently been done in
this context offering solutions to block or limit the exposure of sensitive or
private information. However, new scenarios of data publication, coupled with
the richness of published data and the large number of available data sources,
raise novel problems that still need to be addressed. It is therefore of primary
importance the design of novel privacy-preserving techniques able to capture,
and protect, sensitive information not explicitly included in a release that might
be exposed as consequence of the release itself.
- *Access control enforcement.* When the data release process is selective, besides
protecting data privacy, another requirement is that of implementing an access
control mechanism, to ensure that users can access only the data allowed by the
access policy. Traditional access control architectures are based on the presence
of a trusted component, called *reference monitor*, in charge of enforcing the
policy defined by the data owner. However, as already mentioned, users and
companies are more and more resorting to cloud storage systems to make their
data selectively available to others. In these scenarios, unfortunately, neither the
data owner is willing, nor the cloud storage server is trusted, to enforce the access
control policy. Existing solutions for access control enforcement in outsourcing
scenarios have mainly focused on read access restrictions, while few efforts have
been devoted to the management of write privileges, which becomes a key factor
in emerging applicative scenarios (e.g., document sharing) where the data owner
may wish to grant other users the privilege to modify some of her resources. In
addition, we need to consider the proliferation of subscription-based services,
where users dynamically join and leave the system, and access resources based
on their subscriptions. We need therefore to re-consider the current understanding
of how access control is enforced in outsourcing scenarios, to take into account
both the management of write privileges and dynamic subscription-based access
policies.

This book focuses on the three high-level objectives mentioned above, to the aim
of defining a comprehensive solution to protect data privacy in release scenarios. In
the remainder of this chapter, we discuss in more details the specific contributions
of this work.

1.3 Contributions of the Book

This book addresses the problems related to privacy and security when a data owner wants to (publicly or selectively) release a large collection of data. The specific contributions of the book focus on the three privacy and security aspects illustrated above, that is, the protection of data explicitly involved in a release, the protection of data not explicitly involved but possibly exposed by a release, and the enforcement of access restrictions. In the remainder of this section, we illustrate the contributions in more details.

1.3.1 Protection of Data Explicitly Involved in a Release

The first contribution of this book is related to the protection of the privacy of data explicitly included in a release, while satisfying the needs for information availability of the recipients [29, 30, 42, 45]. The original contribution of our work can be summarized as follows.

Problem Modeling Data release must find a good balance between the need for making certain information available to others, and the equally strong need to ensure proper protection to sensitive information. The (vertical) fragmentation of the original data collection can effectively satisfy both *confidentiality constraints*, modeling the need for protecting confidential information, and *visibility constraints*, modeling the need for information of data recipients [3, 27, 28, 38]. In this book, we build upon the fragmentation approach to define our privacy-enhancing technique for protecting information confidentiality in data release, while satisfying visibility constraints. The peculiarity of our solution consists of a novel modeling of the fragmentation problem, which exploits the representation of confidentiality and visibility constraints as Boolean formulas and that interprets fragments as truth assignments over the Boolean variables representing the attributes in the original relation. This modeling is at the basis of the definition of an efficient solution to the fragmentation problem.

Efficient Fragmentation Computation Thanks to the Boolean formulation of the problem, the computation of a fragmentation that satisfies a set of confidentiality and visibility constraints can rely on the efficiency with which Boolean formulas are represented and manipulated. To this aim, we take advantage of reduced Ordered Binary Decision Diagrams (OBDDs), a canonical form for representing and efficiently manipulating Boolean formulas [80]. OBDDs are used in practical applications more often than other classical representations of Boolean formulas because they have a canonical form that uniquely characterizes a given function, and because operations on Boolean formulas can be performed efficiently in time and space [68]. We take advantage of our OBDDs-based formulation to efficiently formulate the correctness conditions that a fragmentation must satisfy.

The efficiency of our proposed OBDDs-based approach is testified by the promising experimental results illustrated in this book.

Minimality Given a set of confidentiality and visibility constraints, our goal is that of computing a fragmentation that does not split attributes among fragments when it is not necessary for satisfying confidentiality constraints. The rationale is that maintaining a set of attributes in the same fragment releases, besides their values, also their associations. Therefore, the utility of released data for final recipients is higher when releasing a fragmentation composed of fewer fragments, since they also provide recipients with visibility over associations among attributes. To this aim, we define an exact algorithm for computing a *minimal* fragmentation (i.e., composed of the minimum number of fragments). In addition, we define a heuristic algorithm that, as proved by our experimental results, provides faster computational time while well approximating the minimal fragmentations computed by the exact algorithm.

Extended Loose Associations To enrich the utility of the published fragments, it is possible to complement them with *loose associations*, a sanitized form of the sensitive associations broken by fragmentation [38]. The original definition of loose associations however considers fragmentations composed of two fragments only. If a fragmentation is composed of more than two fragments, the naive approach of releasing multiple associations between the different pairs of fragments can potentially expose sensitive associations, as we show in this book. To this aim, we define loose associations that operate among an arbitrary set of fragments. After illustrating the privacy risks related to publishing multiple loose associations, we describe an approach for supporting the more general case of publishing a single loose association among an arbitrary set of fragments. By defining a heuristic algorithm to compute safe loose associations and analyzing experimental results, which prove the efficacy of the approach in terms of more precise responses to queries posed by users, we provide a general solution, applicable to real-world scenarios to further fulfill the needs of data recipients while not compromising on data privacy.

1.3.2   Protection of Data Not Explicitly Involved in a Release

The second contribution of this book is the definition of a technique for capturing and counteracting the privacy risks that the release of a collection of non sensitive data can cause. Sensitive information, despite not appearing in the released dataset, might in fact be derived observing peculiar distribution of the values of the released data [13, 14]. The original contribution of our work can be summarized as follows.

Inference Model We identify and model a novel inference scenario, raised from a real case study that needed consideration where data items are incrementally released upon request. We address a specific problem related to inferences arising from the dependency of sensitive (not released) information referred to some entities on other (released) properties regarding such entities. In particular, we are concerned with the possible inferences that can be drawn by observing the distribution of values of non sensitive information associated with these entities. Such a problem of sensitive information derivation becomes more serious as the amount of released data increases, since external observations will tend to be more representative of the real situations and the confidence in the external observations will increase.

Inference Metrics We introduce several metrics to assess the inference exposure due to a data release. Our metrics are based on the concepts of *mutual information*, which has been widely used in several security areas ranging from the definition of distinguishers for differential side-channel analysis (e.g., [8, 17, 57, 105]) to data-hiding and watermarking security (e.g., [20]), and of *distance* between the expected and the observed distribution of values of non sensitive information. More precisely, we evaluate the inference exposure as the mutual information, the Kullback-Leibler distance between distributions, the Pearson's cumulative statistic, and the Dixon's coefficient that, as proved by our experimental results, particularly fit our scenario.

Release Regulation Based on the identified metrics, we formally define a safe release with respect to the modeled inference channels. We also describe the controls to be enforced in a scenario where data items are released one at a time, upon request. The process is regulated so that the release of data to the external world be safe with respect to inferences. Our experimental results evaluate the inference exposure (computed as the mutual information, Kullback-Leibler distance between distributions, Pearson's cumulative statistic, or Dixon's coefficient), and the information loss (i.e., the number of requests not fulfilled) caused by our privacy protection technique, and compare the results obtained adopting the different metrics, identifying pros and cons of the proposed metrics, and of their (possible) joint adoption.

1.3.3 Access Control Enforcement

The third and last contribution of this book is a solution for enforcing write access restrictions and a subscription-based access control policy in data release scenarios. To fit the emerging cloud computing paradigm, we align our scenario to the current trend toward data outsourcing, and we assume the owner to rely on honest-but-curious external storage servers to selectively share her data. According to this, our techniques are based on selective encryption, so that released resources self-enforce the access restrictions [40, 41]. The original contribution of our work can be summarized as follows.

Dynamic Write Authorizations Traditional solutions for access control enforcement in outsourcing scenarios assume data to be read-only, implying write authorizations to be a specific privilege of the owner. Such an assumption can result restrictive in several scenarios where the data owner outsourcing the data to an external server may also want to authorize other users to write and update the outsourced resources (e.g., document sharing scenarios). We address this limitation by proposing an approach for efficiently and effectively supporting grant and revoke of write authorizations. Our solution nicely complements existing techniques for access control enforcement in outsourcing scenarios, providing a general solution, applicable to scenarios where read and write authorizations can dynamically change over time. Our solution relies on selective encryption for enforcing read and write access restrictions having efficiency and manageability as primary goal, and results appealing for its efficiency and flexibility, as it avoids expensive re-keying and re-encryption operations.

Data Integrity When managing write authorizations, providing the data owner with a means for verifying that the server and users are behaving properly (i.e., they do not tamper with resources) has a double advantage: (1) it allows detecting resource tampering, due to the server not performing the required access control or directly tampering with resources, and (2) it discourages improper behavior by the server and by the users since they know that their improper behavior can be easily detected, and their updates recognized as invalid and discarded. We therefore complement our solution with an integrity check technique to verify that modifications to a resource have been produced only by authorized users. Our solution is based on HMAC functions, and allows both the data owned and the users to detect misbehavior (or laziness) by the server as well as misbehavior by users that can happen with the help of the server (not enforcing the required controls since it is either colluding with the user herself or just behaving lazily) or without the help of the server (if the user improperly acquires write privilege for a resource by others).

Subscription-Based Policy Traditional solutions for access control enforcement over outsourced data cannot easily support a scenario where both the set of users who can access a resource and the set of resources change frequently over time. Therefore, they do not fit emerging real-world scenarios where users pay for a service and then can freely access the resources made available during their subscriptions such as, for instance, movie rental services. In fact, to access resources also after the expiration of their subscriptions, users should download the resources for which they are authorized to their local machine. To address this limitation, we complement our selective encryption-based solution with the definition of a subscription-based authorization policy. Our solution avoids the burden of downloading resources to the users, allowing them to maintain the right to access such resources without the worry that they will lose this right after the expiration of their subscriptions. Our proposal to enforce the subscription-based authorization policy relies once again on selective encryption, to guarantee both continuous data availability, and *forward* and *backward* protection requirements, meaning that users can access resources released neither before the beginning of their subscriptions, nor after their expiration.

1.4 Organization of the Book

In this chapter, we discussed the motivations behind the work proposed in this book, and we illustrated our high-level objectives and main contributions. The remaining chapters are organized as follows.

Chapter 2 presents the state of the art techniques available for counteracting privacy and security issues arising in data release scenarios. It focuses on the context of privacy-preserving data publishing, inference control, and access control enforcement in outsourcing scenarios.

Chapter 3 illustrates our fragmentation-based solution for protecting data privacy while ensuring adequate information visibility in data release scenarios. We provide both a heuristic and an exact algorithm for computing a minimal fragmentation, based on a novel OBDDs-based formulation. By providing experimental results comparing the execution time and the fragmentations returned by the exact and heuristic algorithms, we show that the heuristic algorithm has low computation cost and determines a fragmentation close to optimum. To further enrich the utility of the released fragments, we propose to release loose associations among fragmentations composed of arbitrary sets of fragments. Experimental results witness how our solution allows for more precise query answers.

Chapter 4 focuses on the problem of sensitive information leakage deriving from the release of a collection of non sensitive data. The chapter illustrates our model capturing this inference problem, where sensitive information is characterized by peculiar value distributions of non sensitive released data. It then describes how, leveraging on different statistical metrics applied on released data, the data owner can counteract possible inferences that an observer might otherwise draw. Finally, it also shows the results of an experimental evaluation of our solution, showing its efficacy and discussing the applicability of the different metrics in different scenarios.

Chapter 5 addresses the problem of enforcing access restrictions in data release in cloud/outsourcing scenarios. It first extends selective encryption approaches to the support of write privileges, proposing a technique able to efficiently enforce updates in the write access policy. It then illustrates a subscription-based authorization policy, also enforced by means of selective encryption.

Chapter 6 summarizes the contributions of this book, provides our final remarks, and outlines directions for future works.

Chapter 2
Related Work

This chapter illustrates research proposals related to this book, which are mainly devoted to the protection of data and user privacy and to the enforcement of access restrictions in data release scenarios. We will discuss recent proposals for private data publishing based on syntactic and semantic privacy definitions, as well as techniques exploiting data fragmentation and solutions for counteracting inferential disclosure of sensitive information. We will then illustrate available techniques for enforcing access control in outsourcing scenarios, with particular attention to the recently proposed strategy of selective encryption.

The remainder of this chapter is organized as follows. Section 2.1 presents syntactic data protection techniques. Section 2.2 illustrates recent semantic data protection techniques. Section 2.3 discusses fragmentation-based approaches for privacy protection. Section 2.4 presents techniques developed for counteracting inferential disclosure of sensitive information. Section 2.5 discusses recent approaches for enforcing access control in data release in outsourcing/cloud scenarios. Finally, Sect. 2.6 concludes the chapter.

2.1 Syntactic Data Protection Techniques

In this section, we present some of the most important data protection techniques applicable in data release scenarios based on a syntactic privacy requirement.

Basic Concepts and Assumptions Syntactic data protection techniques aim at satisfying a syntactic privacy requirement, such as "each release of data must be indistinguishably related to no less than a certain number of individuals in the population". These techniques assume data to be released to be in the form of a *microdata* table (i.e., a table containing detailed information related to specific respondents) defined on a set of attributes that can be classified as: *identifiers* (attributes that uniquely identify a respondent, such as SSN); *quasi-identifiers*

© Springer International Publishing Switzerland 2015
G. Livraga, *Protecting Privacy in Data Release*, Advances in Information
Security 57, DOI 10.1007/978-3-319-16109-9_2

(*QI*, attributes that, in combination, can be linked with external information to reduce the uncertainty over the identities to which data refer, such as DoB, Sex, and ZIP); and *confidential* and *non-confidential attributes*. Data privacy is protected by applying microdata protection techniques on the QI, typically guaranteeing data truthfulness [55], while not modifying the sensitive attributes. Syntactic techniques can counteract either *identity disclosure*, protecting respondents' identities, or *attribute disclosure* protecting respondents' sensitive information.

Syntactic data protection techniques are based on the assumption that the release of a microdata table can put at risk only the privacy of those individuals contributing to the data collection. The first step for protecting their privacy consists in removing (or encrypting) explicit identifiers before releasing the table. However, a de-identified microdata table does not provide any guarantee of anonymity, since the quasi-identifier can still be linked to publicly available information to re-identify respondents. A study performed on 2000 U.S. Census data showed that 63 % of the U.S. population can be *uniquely identified* combining their gender, ZIP code, and complete date of birth [59]. As an example, consider the de-identified table in Fig. 2.1a, including the medical information of a set of hospitalized patients, and the list of teachers in Sacramento made available by the local schools in Fig. 2.1b. Quasi-identifying attributes DoB, Sex, and ZIP can be exploited for linking the tuples in the medical table with the teachers' list, possibly re-identifying individuals and revealing their illnesses. In this example, the de-identified medical data include only one male patient, born on 1958/07/09 and living in 94232 area.

a

SSN	Name	DoB	Sex	ZIP	Disease
		1970/09/02	M	94152	Hepatitis
		1970/09/20	F	94143	Cardiomyopathy
		1970/09/12	F	94148	Eczema
		1970/09/05	M	94155	Pneumonia
		1960/08/01	F	94154	Stroke
		1960/08/02	F	94153	Stroke
		1960/08/10	M	94140	Stroke
		1960/08/20	M	94141	Stroke
		1970/08/07	F	94141	High Cholesterol
		1970/08/05	F	94142	Erythema
		1958/07/09	*M*	*94232*	Diabetes
		1970/08/25	M	94153	High Cholesterol
		1970/08/30	M	94156	Angina Pectoris
		1960/09/02	M	94147	Hepatitis
		1960/09/05	M	94145	Flu
		1960/09/10	F	94158	Angina Pectoris
		1960/09/30	F	94159	Cardiomyopathy

b

Name	Address	City	ZIP	DoB	Sex	Course	School
...	...	...	...	...	...	...	...
John Doe	100 Park Ave.	Sacramento	*94232*	*58/07/09*	*male*	Maths	High School
...	...	...	...	...	...	...	...

Fig. 2.1 An example of de-identified microdata table (**a**) and of publicly available non de-identified dataset (**b**)

This combination, if unique in the external world as well, uniquely identifies the corresponding tuple as pertaining to *John Doe*, 100 Park Ave., Sacramento, revealing that he suffers from diabetes.

In the following, we present syntactic data protection techniques developed for counteracting identity and attribute disclosure in data release. We first describe the k-anonymity proposal [94], one of the most popular syntactic privacy definitions developed for protecting a released dataset against identity disclosure. We then present solutions that protect released data against attribute disclosure, and overview some enhancements to traditional syntactic techniques introduced to remove assumptions characterizing traditional approaches.

k-Anonymity Samarati [94] proposes the k-anonymity approach, enforcing the well-known protection requirement, typically applied by statistical agencies, demanding that any released information should be *indistinguishably related* to no less than a certain number of respondents. Since re-identification is assumed to occur exploiting quasi-identifying attributes only, this general requirement has been translated into the k-anonymity requirement: *Each release of data must be such that every combination of values of quasi-identifiers can be indistinctly matched to at least k respondents* [94]. As each respondent is assumed to be represented by at most one tuple in the released table and vice-versa (i.e. each tuple includes information related to one respondent only), a microdata table satisfies the k-anonymity requirement if and only if: (1) each tuple in the released table cannot be related to less than k individuals in the population; and (2) each individual in the population cannot be related to less than k tuples in the table.

To verify whether a microdata table satisfies the k-anonymity requirement, the data holder should know in advance any possible external source of information that an observer could exploit for re-identification. Since this assumption is unfeasible in practice, the k-anonymity requirement is enforced by taking a safe approach and requiring each respondent to be indistinguishable from at least $k - 1$ respondents of the table itself. A table is therefore said to be k-anonymous if each combination of values of the quasi-identifier appears with either zero or at least k occurrences in the released table. For instance, the table in Fig. 2.1a is 1-anonymous if we assume the quasi-identifier to be composed of DoB, Sex, and ZIP, since different combinations of values appear only once in the table. The definition of k-anonymous table represents a sufficient (but not necessary) condition for the k-anonymity requirement. In fact, since each combination of values of quasi-identifying attributes appears with at least k occurrences: (1) each respondent cannot be associated with less than k tuples in the released table; and (2) each tuple in the released table cannot be related to less than k respondents in the population.

k-Anonymity is typically achieved by applying *generalization* and *suppression* over quasi-identifying attributes, while leaving sensitive and non sensitive attributes unchanged. Generalization substitutes the original values with more general values. For instance, the date of birth can be generalized by removing the day, or the day and the month of birth. Suppression consists in removing information from the microdata table. The combination of generalization and suppression has the advantage of reducing the amount of generalization required to satisfy k-anonymity, thus releasing more precise (although non-complete) information. Intuitively, if a limited number of outliers (i.e., quasi-identifying values with less than k occurrences in the table) would force a large amount of generalization to satisfy k-anonymity, these outliers can be more conveniently removed from the table, improving the quality of released data. For instance, consider the table in Fig. 2.1a and assume that the quasi-identifier is composed of attribute ZIP only. Since there is only one person living in 94232 area (11th tuple), attribute ZIP should be generalized removing the last three digits to guarantee 4-anonymity. However, if the 11th tuple in the table is suppressed, 4-anonymity can be achieved by generalizing the ZIP code removing only the last digit.

The approaches proposed in the literature to enforce k-anonymity can be classified on the basis of the granularity at which generalization and suppression operate [24]. More precisely, generalization can be applied at the *cell* level (substituting the cell value with a more general value) or at the *attribute* level (generalizing all the cells in the column). Suppression can be applied at the *cell*, *attribute*, or *tuple* level (removing a single cell, a column, or a row, respectively). Most of the solutions adopt attribute generalization and tuple suppression [9, 69, 94]. Figure 2.2 reports a 4-anonymous version of the table in Fig. 2.1a, obtained adopting attribute-level generalization (attributes DoB, Sex, and ZIP have been generalized by hiding the day of birth, the sex, and the last two digits of the ZIP code, respectively) and tuple-level suppression (the 11th tuple related to *John Doe* has been removed). Note that symbol ∗ represents any value in the attribute domain. Solutions adopting cell generalization have recently been investigated, since they cause a reduced information loss with respect to attribute generalization [70]. These approaches have however the drawback of producing tables where the values in the cells of the same column may be heterogeneous (e.g., some tuples report the complete date of birth, while other tuples only report the year of birth).

Regardless of the different level at which generalization and suppression are applied to enforce k-anonymity, information loss is inevitable due to the reduction in the details of the released data. To minimize the loss of information (and

Fig. 2.2 An example of 4-anonymous table

SSN	Name	DoB	Sex	ZIP	Disease
		1970/09/**	*	941**	Hepatitis
		1970/09/**	*	941**	Cardiomyopathy
		1970/09/**	*	941**	Eczema
		1970/09/**	*	941**	Pneumonia
		1960/08/**	*	941**	Stroke
		1960/08/**	*	941**	Stroke
		1960/08/**	*	941**	Stroke
		1960/08/**	*	941**	Stroke
		1970/08/**	*	941**	High Cholesterol
		1970/08/**	*	941**	Erythema
		1970/08/**	*	941**	High Cholesterol
		1970/08/**	*	941**	Angina Pectoris
		1960/09/**	*	941**	Hepatitis
		1960/09/**	*	941**	Flu
		1960/09/**	*	941**	Angina Pectoris
		1960/09/**	*	941**	Cardiomyopathy

maximize the utility of released data for final recipients), it is necessary to compute a k-anonymous table that minimizes generalization and suppression. The computation of an optimal k-anonymous table is however NP-hard. Therefore, both exact and heuristic algorithms have been proposed [24].

ℓ-**Diversity** Two attacks that may lead to attribute disclosure in a k-anonymous table are the *homogeneity attack* [75, 94] and the *external knowledge attack* [75].

- *Homogeneity attack.* The homogeneity attack occurs when, in a k-anonymous table, all the tuples in an equivalence class (i.e., all the tuples with the same value for the quasi-identifier) assume also the same value for the sensitive attribute. If a data recipient knows the quasi-identifier value of an individual represented in the microdata table, she can identify the equivalence class representing the target respondent, and then infer the value of her sensitive attribute. For instance, consider the 4-anonymous table in Fig. 2.2 and suppose that *Alice* knows that her friend *Gary* is a male, born on 1960/08/10 and living in 94140 area. Since all the tuples in the equivalence class with quasi-identifier ⟨1960/08/**,*,941**⟩ have *Stroke* as a value for attribute Disease, *Alice* can infer that *Gary* had a stroke.
- *External knowledge attack.* The external knowledge attack occurs when the data recipient can reduce her uncertainty about the value of the sensitive attribute of a target respondent, exploiting some additional (external) knowledge about the respondent. As an example, consider the 4-anonymous table in Fig. 2.2 and suppose that *Alice* knows that her friend *Ilary* is a female, living in 94141 area and born on 1970/08/07. Observing the 4-anonymous table, *Alice* can infer that *Ilary* suffers from either *High Cholesterol, Erythema*, or *Angina Pectoris*. Suppose now that *Alice* sees *Ilary* running in the park every day. Since a person suffering from *Angina Pectoris* does not run every day, *Alice* can infer that *Ilary* suffers from *High Cholesterol* or *Erythema*.

Machanavajjhala et al. [75] propose the definition of ℓ-diversity to counteract homogeneity and external knowledge attacks, by requiring the presence of at least ℓ *well-represented* values for the sensitive attribute in each equivalence class. Several definitions for "well-represented" values have been proposed. A straightforward approach is to consider ℓ values well-represented if they are different. Therefore, the simplest formulation of ℓ-diversity requires that each equivalence class be associated with at least ℓ different values for the sensitive attribute. For instance, consider the 4-anonymous and 3-diverse table in Fig. 2.3 and suppose that *Alice* knows that her neighbor *Ilary* is a female, living in 94141 area and born on 1970/08/07. Observing the table in Fig. 2.3, *Alice* can infer that *Ilary* suffers from either *Cardiomyopathy, Eczema, High Cholesterol*, or *Erythema*. Since *Alice* knows that *Ilary* goes running every day, *Alice* can exclude the fact that *Ilary* suffers from *Cardiomyopathy*, but she cannot precisely determine whether *Ilary* suffers from *Eczema, High Cholesterol*, or *Erythema*.

The problem of computing an ℓ-diverse table minimizing the loss of information caused by generalization and suppression is computationally hard. It is interesting to note that any algorithm proposed to compute a k-anonymous table that minimizes

Fig. 2.3 An example
of 4-anonymous and
3-diverse table

SSN	Name	DoB	Sex	ZIP	Disease
		1970/**/**	M	9415*	High Cholesterol
		1970/**/**	M	9415*	Angina Pectoris
		1970/**/**	M	9415*	Hepatitis
		1970/**/**	M	9415*	Pneumonia
		1970/**/**	F	9414*	Cardiomyopathy
		1970/**/**	F	9414*	Eczema
		1970/**/**	F	9414*	High Cholesterol
		1970/**/**	F	9414*	Erythema
		1960/**/**	F	9415*	Stroke
		1960/**/**	F	9415*	Stroke
		1960/**/**	F	9415*	Angina Pectoris
		1960/**/**	F	9415*	Cardiomyopathy
		1960/**/**	M	9414*	Stroke
		1960/**/**	M	9414*	Stroke
		1960/**/**	M	9414*	Hepatitis
		1960/**/**	M	9414*	Flu

loss of information can be adapted to guarantee also ℓ-diversity, controlling if the condition on the diversity of the sensitive attribute values is satisfied by all the equivalence classes [75].

t-**Closeness**   Although ℓ-diversity represents a first step in counteracting attribute disclosure, this solution may still produce a table that is vulnerable to privacy breaches caused by *skewness* and *similarity attacks* [72].

- *Skewness attack.* The skewness attack exploits the possible difference in the frequency distribution of the sensitive attribute values within an equivalence class, with respect to the frequency distribution of sensitive attribute values in the population (or in the released microdata table). In fact, differences in these distributions highlight changes in the probability with which a respondent in the equivalence class is associated with a specific sensitive value. As an example, consider the 3-diverse table in Fig. 2.3 and suppose that *Alice* knows that her friend *Gary* is a male living in 94140 area and born on 1960/08/10. In the equivalence class with quasi-identifier ⟨1960/**/**,M,9414*⟩, two out of four tuples have value *Stroke* for attribute Disease. *Alice* can infer that *Gary* had a stroke with probability 50 %, compared to a probability of 12.5 % of the respondents of the released table.
- *Similarity attack.* The similarity attack occurs when, in an ℓ-diverse table, the values for the sensitive attribute associated with the tuples in an equivalence class are semantically similar, although syntactically different. For instance, consider the 3-diverse table in Fig. 2.3 and suppose that *Alice* knows that her friend *Olivia* is a female, living in 94158 area, and born on 1960/09/10. In the equivalence class with quasi-identifier ⟨1960/**/**,F,9415*⟩, attribute Disease assumes values *Stroke*, *Angina Pectoris*, and *Cardiomyopathy*. As a consequence, *Alice* can discover that *Olivia* suffers from a cardiovascular disease.

Li et al. [72] propose the definition of t-closeness to counteract skewness and similarity attacks, requiring that the frequency distribution of the sensitive values in each equivalence class be close (i.e., with distance smaller than a fixed threshold t)

to that in the released microdata table. In this way, the skewness attack has no effect since the knowledge of the quasi-identifier value for a target respondent does not change the probability for a malicious recipient of correctly guessing the sensitive value associated with the respondent. t-Closeness reduces also the effectiveness of the similarity attack, because the presence of semantically similar values in an equivalence class can only be due to the presence, with similar relative frequencies, of the same values in the microdata table.

The enforcement of t-closeness requires to evaluate the distance between the frequency distribution of the sensitive attribute values in the released table and in each equivalence class. Such distance can be computed adopting different metrics, such as the Earth Mover Distance used by t-closeness [72].

Other Approaches k-Anonymity, ℓ-diversity, and t-closeness are based on some restrictive assumptions that make them not always suitable for specific scenarios. Some of these (limiting) assumptions can be summarized as follows: (1) each respondent is represented by a single tuple in the microdata table; (2) all data to be released are stored in a single table; (3) once released, data are not further modified; (4) all the data that need to be released are available to the data holder before their release; (5) the same degree of privacy is guaranteed to all data respondents; (6) the released microdata table has a single quasi-identifier, known in advance; and (7) no external knowledge (except for that behind linking attacks counteracted by k-anonymity) is available to recipients. Recently, the scientific community has started to extend the pioneering techniques illustrated so far in this chapter removing these assumptions, proposing solutions specifically tailored for supporting, among other scenarios: (1) multiple tuples per respondent (e.g., [101, 107]); (2) release of multiple tables (e.g., [86, 107]); (3) data republication (e.g., [113]); (4) continuous data release (e.g., [71, 109, 118]); (5) personalized privacy preferences (e.g., [56, 112]); (6) multiple and/or non-predefined quasi-identifiers (e.g., [89, 101]); (7) adversarial external knowledge (e.g., [21, 76, 79]). Figure 2.4 summarizes some notable solution recently proposed to extend the definitions of k-anonymity, ℓ-diversity, and t-closeness removing the above-illustrated assumptions.

2.2   Semantic Data Protection Techniques

In this section, we present some of the most important data protection techniques applicable in data release scenarios based on a semantic privacy requirement.

Basic Concepts and Assumptions   Semantic techniques satisfy a semantic privacy requirement [50, 67] that must be enforced by the mechanism chosen for releasing the data, such as "the result of an analysis carried out on a released dataset must be insensitive to the insertion or deletion of a tuple in the dataset". These protection techniques have recently been proposed to protect the privacy of both data respondents and individuals who are not included in data undergoing release. To illustrate, consider the release of a dataset that can be used to compute the average

Fig. 2.4 Syntactic techniques removing traditional assumptions

Assumption	Available techniques
multiple tuples per respondent	(X,Y)-Privacy [112] k^m-Anonymity [106]
multiple tables	(X,Y)-Privacy [112] MultiR k-anonymity [90]
microdata re-publication	m-Invariance [117]
data streams	Correlation tracking [76] Stream k-anonymity [122] ℓ-Eligibility [113]
personalized privacy preferences	(α_i,β_i)-Closeness [58] Personalized privacy [116]
multiple quasi-identifiers	Butterfly [93]
non-predefined quasi-identifiers	k^m-Anonymity [106]
external knowledge	Privacy Skyline [21] ε-Privacy [79] (c,k)-Safety [83]

amount of taxes annually paid by the citizens of Sacramento for each profession, and suppose that this information was not publicly available before the release. Assume that *Alice* knows that the taxes paid by *Bob* are 1,000$ less than the average taxes paid by *teachers* living in Sacramento. Although this piece of information alone does not permit *Alice* to gain any information about the taxes paid by *Bob*, if combined with the released dataset, it allows *Alice* to infer the taxes paid by *Bob*. Note that this leakage does not depend on whether *Bob* is represented in the released dataset. Differently from syntactic techniques, semantic data protection approaches typically guarantee data protection by adding noise to the released data. Noise addition perturbs the original content of the dataset, thus achieving privacy at the price of data truthfulness.

Semantic techniques operate in both the *non-interactive* scenario (i.e., consisting in the release of a privacy-preserving data collection), and the *interactive* scenario (i.e., consisting in evaluating queries over a private data collection managed by the data holder, without revealing any sensitive information). In the first scenario, protection techniques are used to compute a privacy-preserving dataset, which is representative of the original data collection. In the latter scenario, protection techniques are used to guarantee that the query result (also when possibly combined with other results collected by data recipients) cannot be exploited to gain information that should be kept secret.

In this section we illustrate the *differential privacy* approach [50], a recent semantic data protection technique, and present some relaxed definitions and enhanced formulations proposed to address specific data release scenarios.

Differential Privacy One of the first definitions of privacy states that *anything that can be learned about a respondent from the statistical database should be learnable without access to the database* [33]. Although originally stated for statistical databases, this definition is also well suited for data release scenario. Unfortunately, only an empty dataset can guarantee absolute protection against information leakage [50] since, besides exposing the privacy of data respondents, the release of a microdata table may also compromise the privacy of individuals who are *not* represented by a tuple in the released table (as illustrated in the beginning of this section).

Dwork [50] proposes *differential privacy* to guarantee that the release of a microdata table does not disclose sensitive information about *any* individual who may or may not be represented by a tuple in the table. Differential privacy aims at releasing a dataset that allows data recipients to learn properties about the population as a whole, while protecting the privacy of single individuals. The semantic privacy guarantee provided by differential privacy is that the probability that a malicious recipient correctly infers the sensitive attribute value associated with a target respondent is not affected by the presence/absence of the corresponding tuple in the released table. Formally, given two datasets T and T' differing only for one tuple, an arbitrary randomized function $\mathcal{K}$ (typically, the release function) satisfies ϵ-*differential privacy* if and only if $P(\mathcal{K}(T) \in S) \leq \exp(\epsilon) \cdot P(\mathcal{K}(T') \in S)$, where S is a subset of the possible outputs of function $\mathcal{K}$ and ϵ is a public privacy parameter. Intuitively, the released dataset satisfies ϵ-differential privacy if the removal (insertion, respectively) of one tuple from (into, respectively) the dataset does not significantly affect the result of the evaluation of function $\mathcal{K}$. As an example, consider an insurance company that consults a medical dataset to decide whether an individual is eligible for an insurance contract. If differential privacy is satisfied, the presence or absence of the tuple representing the individual in the dataset does not significantly affect the final decision taken by the insurance company. It is important to note that the external knowledge that an adversary may possess cannot be exploited for breaching the privacy of individuals. In fact, the knowledge that the recipient gains looking at the released dataset is bounded by the multiplicative factor $\exp(\epsilon)$, for any individual either represented or not in the released microdata table. In other words, the probability of observing a result in S for the evaluation of function $\mathcal{K}$ over T is close to the probability of observing a result in S for the evaluation of function $\mathcal{K}$ over T' (i.e., the difference between $P(\mathcal{K}(T) \in S)$ and $P(\mathcal{K}(T') \in S)$ is negligible). Note that the definition of ϵ-differential privacy does not depend on the computational resources of adversaries, and therefore it protects a data release against computationally-unbounded adversaries.

The techniques proposed to enforce the ϵ-differential privacy definition traditionally *add noise* to the released data. The magnitude of the noise is computed as a function of the difference that the insertion/removal of one respondent may cause on the result of the evaluation of function $\mathcal{K}$. Differential privacy can be enforced in both the interactive and non-interactive scenarios, possibly adopting different approaches for noise addition [50, 53]. In the *interactive scenario*, ϵ-differential privacy is ensured by adding *random noise* to the query results evaluated on the original dataset [52]. The typical distribution considered for the random noise is *Laplace distribution* $Lap(\Delta(f)/\epsilon)$ with probability density function $P(x) = exp(-|x|/b)/2b$, where $b = \Delta(f)/\epsilon$ and $\Delta(f)$ is the maximum difference between the query result evaluated over T and over T' (which, for example, is equal to 1 for count queries, since T and T' differ for at most one tuple). In the *non-interactive scenario*, the data holder typically releases a *frequency matrix*, with a dimension for each attribute and an entry in each dimension for each value in the attribute domain. The value of a cell in the matrix is obtained counting the tuples in the table that assume, for each attribute, the value represented by the entry associated with the cell. Since each cell in the frequency matrix is the result of the evaluation of a count query on the original dataset, the techniques proposed to guarantee ϵ-differential privacy in the interactive scenario can also be adopted to protect the entries of the released frequency matrix (i.e., to protect the result of the count queries).

Extending Differential Privacy The original definition of ϵ-differential privacy is strict and imposes very tight constraints on the data that can be released. However, there are different scenarios where an increased flexibility, to be achieved at the price of a relaxed privacy requirement, may be accepted by the data holder to provide data recipients with information of higher interest. Examples of extended techniques, relaxing the original definition of ϵ-differential privacy, are (ϵ,δ)-differential privacy [51] and *computational differential privacy* [83].

The definition of differential privacy has also been specifically refined to address peculiar data release scenarios. Figure 2.5 summarizes some recent refinements of differential privacy, which have been proposed for managing the release of the result of count queries, synthetic data, and sparse frequency matrices. In the figure, the considered refinements have been classified according to the scenario in which they operate (i.e., interactive, non-interactive, or both), and the goal they achieve in data release.

Solution	Objective	Scenario	
		interactive	non interactive
matrix mechanism [75]	minimize noise addition, consistent query answers	×	
Privlet [118]	reduce error in the result of range-count queries	×	×
universal histogram [65]	satisfy consistency constraints in different query results	×	
diff. private synthetic data [123]	preserve statistical characteristics of synthetic datasets		×
data summaries [32]	reduce time in computing frequency matrices		×

Fig. 2.5 Semantic techniques for specific release scenarios

2.3   Data Fragmentation and Privacy-Preserving Associations

The adoption of generalization and suppression (syntactic data protection techniques) results in tables that are less complete and less detailed than the original microdata tables. On the other hand, exploiting noise addition (semantic data protection techniques) perturbs the original data, compromising their truthfulness. An alternative approach that permits the release of the exact distribution of the quasi-identifier values and does not compromise data truthfulness, while guaranteeing to preserve the privacy of the respondents, is based on *fragmentation*. In a nutshell, fragmentation consists in splitting the original microdata table in vertical fragments, such that the attributes composing the quasi-identifier and the sensitive attribute (or, more generally, attributes that should not be visible in association) are not represented in the same fragment. To prevent the possibility of reconstructing the sensitive associations broken by fragmentation, fragments should clearly be disjoint, meaning that no recipient can compute their join. Several strategies have been proposed in the literature for defining a fragmentation whose fragments cannot be joined. For instance, the *two can keep a secret* approach [3] assumes the existence of two non-communicating servers storing a pair of fragments defined over the original data collection. Since collusion among servers can compromise the protection of sensitive data, Ciriani et al. [23, 26, 28] propose a joint adoption of fragmentation and encryption to possibly store *multiple* fragments on the same server. The *departing from encryption* approach [27] is based on the assumption that the data owner is willing to store a limited portion of the data to protect sensitive associations among them.

In this section, we illustrate *Anatomy* [111] and *loose associations* [38], two notable solutions adopting a fragmentation-based approach to protect privacy in data release while aiming at releasing useful information to the recipients.

Anatomy   Xiao and Tao [111] first proposed a group-based approach to guarantee ℓ-diversity in microdata release, to avoid resorting to generalization. Anatomy first partitions the tuples in the microdata table in groups that satisfy the ℓ-diversity principle (i.e., each group includes at least ℓ well-represented values for the sensitive attribute). Each group is then associated with a unique group identifier and the microdata table is split into two fragments, F_1 and F_2, including the attributes composing the quasi-identifier and the sensitive attribute, respectively. For each tuple, both F_1 and F_2 report the identifier of the group to which it belongs. For simplicity, each group in the fragment storing the sensitive attribute has a tuple for each sensitive value appearing in the group, and reports the frequency with which the value is represented in the group. For instance, consider the microdata table in Fig. 2.6a and assume that the data holder is interested in releasing a 3-diverse table. Figure 2.6b illustrates the two fragments F_1 and F_2 obtained by partitioning the tuples in the table in Fig. 2.6a in groups that satisfy 3-diversity. Although a malicious recipient may know the quasi-identifier value of a target respondent, she can only infer that the respondent belongs to one group (say, g_1) in F_1, and that the sensitive value of the target respondent is one of the values in the group

a

DoB	Sex	ZIP	Disease
1950/06/02	F	94141	H1N1
1950/06/20	M	94132	Gastritis
1950/06/12	M	94137	Dyspepsia
1950/06/05	F	94144	Pneumonia
1940/04/01	M	94143	Peptic Ulcer
1940/04/02	M	94142	Peptic Ulcer
1940/04/10	F	94139	Peptic Ulcer
1940/04/20	F	94130	Peptic Ulcer
1940/06/07	M	94130	Broken Leg
1940/06/05	M	94131	Short Breath
1940/06/25	F	94142	Broken Leg
1940/06/30	F	94145	Stomach Cancer
1950/05/02	F	94136	H1N1
1950/05/05	F	94134	Flu
1950/05/10	M	94147	Stomach Cancer
1950/05/30	M	94148	Gastritis

b

F_1

DoB	Sex	ZIP	GroupID
1940/04/01	M	94143	1
1940/04/02	M	94142	1
1940/06/07	M	94130	1
1940/06/05	M	94131	1
1950/06/02	F	94141	2
1950/06/05	F	94144	2
1950/05/02	F	94136	2
1950/05/05	F	94134	2
1940/04/10	F	94139	3
1940/04/20	F	94130	3
1940/06/25	F	94142	3
1940/06/30	F	94145	3
1950/06/20	M	94132	4
1950/06/12	M	94137	4
1950/05/10	M	94147	4
1950/05/30	M	94148	4

F_2

GroupID	Disease	Count
1	Peptic Ulcer	2
1	Broken Leg	1
1	Short Breath	1
2	H1N1	2
2	Pneumonia	1
2	Flu	1
3	Peptic Ulcer	2
3	Broken Leg	1
3	Stomach Cancer	1
4	Gastritis	2
4	Dyspepsia	1
4	Stomach Cancer	1

Fig. 2.6 An example of microdata table (**a**) and of two fragments F_1 and F_2 (**b**) satisfying 3-diversity obtained adopting the Anatomy approach

in F_2 that is in relation with g_1. To illustrate, assume that *Alice* knows that her friend *Barbara* is a female living in 94139 area and born on 1940/04/10. *Alice* can easily infer that her friend is represented by the ninth tuple of table F_1 in Fig. 2.6b. However, since the tuples in the third group of F_1 are in relation with the tuples in the third group of F_2 in Fig. 2.6b, *Alice* can only infer that *Barbara* suffers from either *Peptic Ulcer*, *Broken Leg*, or *Stomach Cancer*. Note that the privacy guarantee offered by Anatomy is exactly the same offered by traditional generalization-based approaches. In fact, a malicious data recipient cannot associate less than ℓ different sensitive values with each respondent in the released table. However, by releasing the exact distribution of the values of the attributes composing the quasi-identifier, the evaluation of aggregate queries can be more precise [111].

Loose Associations Building on a similar idea, De Capitani di Vimercati et al. [38] propose a more flexible solution, called *loose associations*, to guarantee privacy in data publication without adopting generalization. Loose associations have been proposed to protect generic sensitive associations among the attributes in a data collection. For instance, consider the microdata table in Fig. 2.6a and suppose that attributes SSN, Name, and Treatment are also represented in the table. A possible set of sensitive associations defined among attributes {SSN,Name,DoB, Sex,ZIP,Disease,Treatment} could include: (1) both the associations between the values of attributes SSN and Disease, and between the values of Name and Disease; (2) the association between the values of quasi-identifying attributes DoB, Sex, ZIP and the values of sensitive attribute Disease; (3) the association between the values of attributes Disease and Treatment. Given a set of sensitive associations defined among the attributes included in a microdata table, they are broken by publishing a set of different fragments. It is easy to see that the problem of protecting the association of a sensitive attribute with the respondents' quasi-identifier, tackled by Anatomy, can be modeled through the definition of a sensitive association among the sensitive attribute and quasi-identifying attributes. Like Anatomy, the original microdata table can then be split in different fragments in such a way that the sensitive attribute is not stored together with all the attributes composing the quasi-identifier. It is in fact sufficient to store a subset of the quasi-identifying attributes in a fragment F_1, and all the other quasi-identifying attributes in another fragment F_2, together with the sensitive attribute. For instance, consider the microdata table in Fig. 2.6a. A fragmentation that would protect against identity and attribute disclosures could be composed of the following two fragments: F_1(DoB,Sex,ZIP) and F_2(Disease). Note that a fragmentation is not unique: F_1(DoB,Sex) and F_2(ZIP,Disease) is another solution that still protects the association between the sensitive attribute and the quasi-identifier (as well as the other sensitive associations mentioned above).

To provide the data recipient with some information on the associations in the original relation broken by fragmentation, provided a given privacy degree of the association is respected, in [38] the authors propose to publish a *loose association* between the tuples composing F_1 and F_2. The tuples in F_1 and in F_2 are independently partitioned in groups of size at least k_1 and k_2, respectively. Each group in F_1 and in F_2 is then associated with a different group identifier. For each tuple, both F_1 and F_2 report the identifier of the group to which the tuple belongs. The group-level relationships between the tuples in F_1 and in F_2 are represented by an additional table A that includes, for each tuple t in the original microdata table, a tuple modeling the relationship between the group where t appears in F_1 and the group where t appears in F_2. For instance, Fig. 2.7a represents two fragments F_1 and F_2 for the microdata table in Fig. 2.6a. Both the fragments have been partitioned into groups of 2 tuples each and the lines between the tuples in F_1 and F_2 represent their relationships in the original microdata table. Figure 2.7b illustrates the three relations, F_1, A, and F_2 that are released instead of the original microdata. It is easy to see that, even if a malicious recipient knows the quasi-identifier of a respondent, she can only identify the tuple related to the target respondent in F_1, but not the corresponding Disease in F_2. For instance, assume that *Alice* knows that her

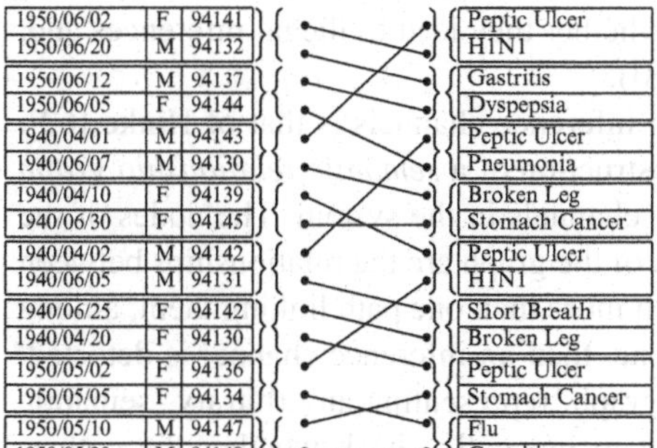

Fig. 2.7 An example of a 4-loose association (**a**) and released relations F_1, A_{12}, and F_2 (**b**) defined on the microdata in Fig. 2.6a

friend *Barbara* is a female living in 94139 area and born on 1940/04/10. By looking at the released tables, *Alice* discovers that her friend is represented by the seventh tuple in F_1, which belongs to group *dsz4*. However, since group *dsz4* is associated in A with two different groups in F_2 (i.e., *d4* and *d5*) *Alice* cannot identify the illness *Barbara* suffers from, since it could be either *Peptic Ulcer*, *Broken Leg*, *Stomach Cancer*, or *H1N1*. It is easy to see that also the other sensitive associations mentioned above are not exposed by the release of the loose association.

The partitioning of the tuples in the two fragments should be carefully designed to guarantee an adequate protection degree. In fact, a loose association enjoys a degree k of protection if every tuple in A indistinguishably corresponds to at least k distinct associations among tuples in the two fragments (i.e., it could have been generated starting from k different tuples in the microdata table). The release of F_1, F_2, and A satisfies k-*looseness*, with $k \leq k_1 \cdot k_2$, if for each group g_1 in F_1 (group g_2 in F_2, respectively), the union of the tuples in all the groups with which g_1 (g_2, respectively) is associated in A is a set of at least k different tuples. Figure 2.7b represents an example of a 4-loose association. This implies that it is not possible, for a malicious data recipient, to associate with each quasi-identifier value in F_1 less than 4 different diseases in F_2.

We note that loose associations are limited to the consideration of fragmentations composed of a single pair of fragments. In Chap. 3, besides proposing a novel and efficient fragmentation strategy operating in the multiple fragments scenario, we also extend the loose association definition to operate on arbitrary sets of fragments.

2.4 Inference Control

Inference problems have been extensively studied in the context of multilevel database systems (e.g., [34, 66, 74, 78]). Most inference research addresses detection of inference channels within a stored database or at query processing time. In the first case, inference channels are removed by upgrading selected schema components or redesigning the schema (e.g., [91]). In the second case, database transactions are evaluated to determine whether they lead to illegal inferences and, if so, deny the query (e.g., [58, 63, 84, 98]).

One of the first attempts to deal with inference channels is that of Hinke [62], proposing an approach based on the construction of a *semantic relationship graph* among data, in order to locate inference channels in the system. The nodes of the graph are the data items, while the edges of the graph are the relationships between data. If the graph includes two nodes with more than one path linking them, among which a user is cleared to follow only one, then an inference channel is detected. The generic definition of an arc in the graph, representing an arbitrary 'semantic relationship', requires a security analyst to manually check whether the path is really exploitable by an attacker. When, after the manual analysis, a discovered arc is proved to be a real inference channel, the next step is to raise the security level of one of the edges of the path leading to the channel. Smith [98] refines Hinke's work [62] on semantical relationships graphs, allowing users to express different types of relationships. In this approach a number of possible types of data items and relationships between them is identified. Every relationship can be labeled with a security level. Thuraisingham [102] proposes a more general logic-based framework dealing with inference problems.

In recent years, many other proposals have been presented to deal with inference channels, aiming to a general and strong formulation of the problem in order to find formal and automated models and frameworks to provide protection [18, 34, 36, 47, 64, 77]. Hinke and Delugach [47, 63–65] propose a solution for an automated analysis of inferences in general purpose databases, addressing the representation of external knowledge as well. The proposed method is based on a graph representation to locate inference channels, representing the knowledge needed for the problem, such as data items, relationships between them, domain knowledge and data sensitivity. The basic idea is that there is an inference channel if there exists a path going from a low-level piece of information to a high-level one in the graph representing the system. Brodsky et al. [18] adopt logic-based techniques to identify inference channels, and propose a way to represent the database and domain knowledge. In their proposal, they present a security framework called DiMon (Disclosure Monitor), built upon an access control model based on a security lattice. Their proposal can be applied in data-dependent mode as well as in data-independent mode (i.e., depending on the actual data values or not). Another approach is the one proposed by Dawson et al. [34], focusing on the problem of classifying existing databases. The information is classified by enforcing explicit data classification as well as inference and association constraints. The computed classification is guaranteed to be optimal, that is, it ensures satisfaction of the constraints (free from inference) and guarantees that the information is not overclassified. The approach is not limited to specific forms of security lattices, but security classes (security labels) can be taken from any generic lattice. This proposal allows the definition of *lower bound* security constraints, whose aim is to prevent unauthorized downward information flows, and the definition of *upper bound* security constraints, whose aim is to set an upper limit for the security level of an attribute, for visibility purposes.

All the solutions mentioned so far operate in the multilevel database scenario. Some solutions have recently been designed to deal with inference channels in data publishing scenarios. These more recent proposals aim, for example, at destroying the correlation between two disjoint and pre-defined subsets of attributes before their publication [100]. The solution in [108] instead aims at guaranteeing k-anonymity when publicly releasing a microdata table, assuming that the adversarial knowledge includes functional dependencies among attributes. The first solution investigating privacy breaches that data dependencies may cause to fragmented data considers the non-communicating servers scenario [15]. The authors specifically analyze how the possible a-priori knowledge of dependencies among the data may cause violations to confidentiality constraints, when data are stored at two non-communicating servers. The authors propose a solution for computing a safe fragmentation w.r.t. inference channels exploiting an integer programming approach. A different analysis of the privacy risks possibly caused by inferences based on observers' knowledge has been illustrated in [16], where the authors prove that, for solutions that depart from encryption, no information can be inferred by an adversary who knows Equality and Tuple Generating Dependencies (which include both functional and join dependencies).

Despite the above-mentioned attempts to define solutions to counteract inferential disclosure in data publishing, some scenarios remain unsolved and need further consideration. In Chap. 4, we consider a scenario where data are incrementally released and sensitive (non released) information depend on (and can therefore be inferred from) non sensitive released data. We propose a model capturing and a solution counteracting this inference problem, where sensitive information is characterized by peculiar value distributions of non sensitive released data.

2.5   Access Control in Data Outsourcing

When the data release process is selective, different users may have different access privileges on the released data. Traditional access control architectures are based on the presence of a trusted component, called *reference monitor*, that is in charge of enforcing the access control policy defined by the data owner. However, as already mentioned, users and companies are more and more resorting to cloud storage systems to make their data and resources selectively available to others. In these scenarios, unfortunately, neither the data owner (for efficiency reasons) nor the cloud server storing the data (for privacy reasons) can enforce the access control policy.

In this section we illustrate two approaches, based on selective encryption and attribute-based encryption respectively, recently proposed for enforcing access control in cloud/outsourcing scenarios.

2.5.1   Selective Encryption

One of the solutions recently investigated to provide access control enforcement to outsourced data without relying on the cloud provider and/or on the data owner is based on selective encryption. The intuition is, given a relation R to be outsourced, to use different encryption keys for different tuples and to selectively distribute these keys to authorized users. Each user can decrypt and have visibility over subsets of tuples, depending on the keys she knows. The authorization policy regulating which users can read which tuples is defined by the data owner before outsourcing R (e.g., [37, 40]). The authorization policy can be represented as an binary *access matrix* $\mathcal{M}$ with a row for each user u, and a column for each tuple t, where: $\mathcal{M}[u_i, t_j] = 1$ iff u_i can access t_j; $\mathcal{M}[u_i, t_j] = 0$ otherwise. To illustrate, consider the relation in Fig. 2.8a. Figure 2.8b illustrates an example of access matrix regulating access to the tuples in the relation by users A, B, C, and D. The jth column of the

a

	SSN	Name	ZIP	MarStatus	Illness
t_1	123456789	Ann	22010	single	gastritis
t_2	234567891	Barbara	24027	divorced	neuralgia
t_3	345678912	Carl	22010	married	gastritis
t_4	456789123	Daniel	20100	married	gastritis
t_5	567891234	Emma	21048	single	neuralgia
t_6	678912345	Fred	23013	married	hypertension
t_7	789123456	Gary	22010	widow	gastritis
t_8	891234567	Harry	24027	widow	hypertension

b

	t_1	t_2	t_3	t_4	t_5	t_6	t_7	t_8
A	1	1	0	1	1	1	1	0
B	1	1	1	1	1	0	0	0
C	1	1	1	0	1	1	0	0
D	0	0	0	1	1	1	0	1

Fig. 2.8 An example of relation (**a**) and of related access matrix (**b**)

matrix represents the access control list $acl(t_j)$ of tuple t_j, for each $j = 1, \ldots, |R|$. As an example, with reference to the matrix in Fig. 2.8b, $acl(t_1) = ABC$. Since the storing server is not trusted to access the plaintext data the owner wants to outsource, tuples are encrypted before being stored according to an *encryption policy*, which translates and reflects the authorization policy. The encryption policy, which defines and regulates the set of keys used to encrypt tuples and manages the key distribution to the users, must be *equivalent* to the authorization policy, meaning that they must authorize each user to access the same subset of tuples.

The first attempt to enforce access control through selective encryption was aimed at protecting access to XML documents (e.g., [81]). Different authorizations for different portions of the XML document, defined by the document creator, are enforced by using different keys to encrypt portions of the document regulated by different authorizations. Each user of the system is then communicated the set of keys used for encrypting the document portions she is authorized to access. More recent selective encryption approaches rely on key derivation techniques to reduce the key management overhead at both the data owner and users side (e.g., [37]). These solutions aim at defining a translation of the authorization policy into an equivalent encryption policy that guarantees that each user has to manage only one key and that each tuple is encrypted with only one key. To fulfill these two requirements, selective encryption approaches rely on *key derivation techniques* that permit to compute the value of an encryption key k_j starting from the knowledge of another key k_i and (possibly) a piece of publicly available information. To determine which keys can be derived from which other key, key derivation methods require the preliminary definition of a *key derivation hierarchy*. A key derivation hierarchy can be graphically represented as a graph with a vertex v_i for each key k_i in the system and an edge (v_i, v_j) from key k_i to key k_j iff k_j can be directly derived from k_i. Note that key derivation can be applied in chain, meaning that key k_j can be computed starting from key k_i if there exists a path (of arbitrary length) from v_i to v_j in the key derivation hierarchy.

A key derivation hierarchy can have different forms, as follows.

- *Chain of vertices* (e.g., [96]): the key k_j associated with a vertex is computed by applying a one-way function to the key k_i of its predecessor in the chain. No public information is needed.

- *Tree hierarchy* (e.g., [97]): the key k_j associated with a vertex is computed by applying a one-way function to the key k_i of its direct ancestor and a publicly available label l_j associated with k_j. Public labels are necessary to guarantee that different children of the same node in the tree have different keys.
- *DAG hierarchy* (e.g., [4–6, 32, 46]): keys in the hierarchy can have more than one direct ancestor. The derivation process is therefore based on techniques that assign a piece of publicly available information, called *token*, to edge in the key derivation hierarchy [5, 6]. Given two keys k_i and k_j, and the public label l_j of k_j, token $d_{i,j}$ allows for the computation of k_j from k_i and l_j. Token $d_{i,j}$ is computed as $d_{i,j} = k_j \oplus f(k_i, l_j)$, where $\oplus$ is the bitwise XOR operator, and f is a deterministic cryptographic function. By means of $d_{i,j}$, all users knowing (or able to derive) key k_i can also derive key k_j.

Each of the proposed key derivation hierarchies has advantages and disadvantages. However, adopting token-based key derivation seems to best fit the outsourcing scenario since it minimizes the need of re-encryption and/or key re-distribution in case of updates to the authorization policy (for more details, see Chap. 5).

To satisfy the desiderata of limiting the key management overhead, De Capitani di Vimercati et al. [37] propose to adopt the set containment relationship $\subseteq$ over the set $\mathcal{U}$ of users to define a DAG key derivation hierarchy suited for access control enforcement. Such a hierarchy has a vertex for each of the elements of the power-set of $\mathcal{U}$, and a path from v_i to v_j iff the set of users represented by v_i is a subset of that represented by v_j. The correct enforcement of the authorization policy defined by the data owner is guaranteed iff: (1) each user u_i is communicated the key associated with the vertex v_i representing it; and (2) each tuple t_j is encrypted with the key associated with the set of users in $acl(t_j)$. With this strategy, each user has to manage one key only, and each tuple is encrypted with one key only. Moreover, tuples characterized by the same access control list are encrypted with the same key. For instance, Fig. 2.9a illustrates the key derivation hierarchy induced by the set $\mathcal{U} = \{A,B,C,D\}$ of users and the subset containment relationship over it (in the figure, vertices are labeled with the set of users they represent). Figures 2.9b and c illustrate the keys assigned to users in the system and the keys used to encrypt the tuples in the relation in Fig. 2.8a, respectively. The encryption policy in the figure enforces the access control policy in Fig. 2.8b as each user can derive, from her own key, the keys of the vertices to which she belongs and hence decrypt the tuples she is authorized to read. For instance, user C can derive the keys used to encrypt tuples t_1, t_2, t_3, t_5, and t_6, and then access their content. Since, as previously mentioned, a path represents a set of tokens, it is easy to see that the encryption policy induced by such a key derivation hierarchy is equivalent to the authorization policy defined by the data owner: each tuple can be decrypted and accessed by all and only the users in its access control list.

Even though this approach correctly enforces an authorization policy and enjoys ease of implementation, it defines more keys and more tokens than necessary. Since tokens are stored in a publicly available token catalog at the server side, when a user

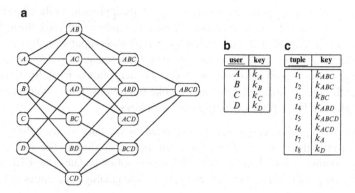

Fig. 2.9 An example of encryption policy equivalent to the access control policy in Fig. 2.8b

u wants to access a tuple t she needs to interact with the server to visit the path in the key derivation hierarchy from the vertex representing u to the vertex representing $acl(t)$. Therefore, keeping the number of tokens low increases the efficiency of the derivation process (and the response time to users). The problem of minimizing the number of tokens, while guaranteeing equivalence between the authorization and the encryption policies, is however NP-hard (it can be reduced to the set cover problem) [37]. It is however interesting to note that: (1) the vertices needed for correctly enforcing an authorization policy are only those representing singleton sets of users (corresponding to user keys) and the access control lists of the tuples (corresponding to keys used to encrypt tuples) in R; (2) when two or more vertices have more than two common direct ancestors, the insertion of a vertex representing the set of users corresponding to these ancestors reduces the total number of tokens. Elaborating on these two intuitions to reduce the number of tokens of the system, in [37] the authors propose a heuristic approach, proved to efficiently provide good results, to define a key derivation hierarchy.

2.5.2   Policy Updates

In case of changes to the authorization policy, the encryption policy must be updated accordingly, to guarantee that equivalence is preserved. Since the key used to encrypt each tuple t in R depends on the set of users who can access it, it might be necessary to re-encrypt the tuples involved in the policy update with a different key that only the users in its new access control lists know or can derive. A trivial approach to enforce a grant/revoke operation on tuple t requires the data owner to: (1) download the encrypted version of t from the server; (2) decrypt it; (3) update the key derivation hierarchy if it does not include a vertex representing the new set of users in $acl(t)$; (4) encrypt t with the key k' associated with the vertex representing $acl(t)$; (5) upload the new encrypted version of t on the server; and (6) possibly update the public catalog containing the tokens. This approach, while effective and correctly enforcing authorization updates, leaves the burden to manage the update at the data owner's side. Also, re-encryption operations are computationally expensive. To limit the data owner's overhead, De Capitani di Vimercati et al. [37] propose an over-encryption approach, adopting two layers of encryption to partially delegate to the server the management of grant and revoke operations. Each layer has its key derivation hierarchy, defined on a different set of keys.

- The *Base Encryption Layer* (BEL) is applied by the data owner before storing the dataset at the server, and encrypts each tuple according to the authorization policy existing at initialization time. In case of policy updates, the BEL is only updated by possibly inserting tokens in the public catalog (i.e., edges in the key derivation hierarchy).
- The *Surface Encryption Layer* (SEL) is applied by the server over the tuples that have already been encrypted by the data owner at the BEL. It dynamically enforces the authorization policy updates by possibly re-encrypting tuples and changing the SEL key derivation hierarchy to correctly reflect the updates.

Intuitively, with the over-encryption approach, a user can access a tuple t only if she knows both the keys used to encrypt t at BEL and the key used to encrypt it at SEL. At initialization time, the key derivation hierarchies and the encryption of resources at BEL and SEL coincide, but they immediately change and become different at each policy update. Grant and revoke operations operate as follows.

- *Grant.* When user u is granted access to tuple t, she needs to know the key used to encrypt t at both BEL and SEL. Hence, the data owner adds a token in the BEL key derivation hierarchy from the vertex representing u to the vertex whose key is used to encrypt t (i.e., to the vertex representing $acl(t)$ at initialization time). The owner then asks the server to update the key derivation hierarchy at SEL and to possibly re-encrypt tuples. Tuple t in fact needs to be encrypted, at SEL, with the key of the vertex representing $acl(t) \cup \{u\}$ (which is possibly inserted into the hierarchy). Besides t, also other tuples may need to be re-encrypted at SEL to guarantee the correct enforcement of the policy update. In fact, the tuples that are encrypted with the same key as t at BEL and that user u is not allowed to read must be encrypted at SEL with a key that u does not know (and cannot derive). The data owner must then make sure that each tuple t_i sharing the BEL encryption key with t are encrypted at SEL with the key of the vertex representing $acl(t_i)$.
- *Revoke.* When user u loses the privilege of accessing tuple t, the data owner simply asks the server to re-encrypt (at SEL) the tuple with the key associated with the set $acl(t) \setminus \{u\}$ of users. If the vertex representing this group of users is not represented in the SEL key derivation hierarchy, the server first updates the hierarchy inserting the new vertex, and then re-encrypts the tuple.

Since the management of (re-)encryption operations at the SEL is delegated to the server, there is the risk of collusions with a user. In fact, by combining their knowledge, a user and the server can possibly decrypt tuples that neither the server nor the user can access. Collusion represents a risk to the correct enforcement of the authorization policy, but this risk is limited, well defined, and can be reduced at the price of using a higher number of keys at BEL.

2.5.3 Alternative Approaches

An alternative solution to selective encryption for access control enforcement is represented by *Attribute-Based Encryption* (ABE [60]). ABE is a particular type of public-key encryption that regulates access to tuples on the basis of descriptive attributes, associated with tuples and/or users, and on policies defined over them regulating access to the data. ABE can be implemented either as *Ciphertext-Policy ABE* (CP-ABE [110]) or as *Key-Policy ABE* (KP-ABE [60]), depending on how attributes and authorization policies are associated with tuples and/or users. Both the strategies have been recently widely investigated, and several solutions have been proposed in the literature, as briefly illustrated in the following.

- *CP-ABE* associates with each user u a key and a set of attributes describing her. Each tuple t in R is encrypted using a key k, associated with an *access structure* modeling the access control policy regulating accesses to the tuple content. The access structure associated with tuple t represents the sets of attributes that users must possess to derive the key k used to encrypt t (and then to decrypt and read the tuple content). Graphically, an access structure is a tree whose leaves represent attributes and whose internal nodes represent logic gates, such as conjunctions and disjunctions. For instance, suppose that access to a tuple of a relation should be granted only to doctors specialized in neurology or cardiology. Figure 2.10 illustrates the access structure associated with such tuple, representing the Boolean formula (*role* = 'doctor') ∧ (*specialty* = 'cardiology' ∨ *specialty* = 'neurology'). A user u can access a tuple t only if the set of attributes associated with her key satisfies the access policy regulating access to t (similarly to traditional role-based access control). Although CP-ABE effectively and efficiently enforce access control policies, one of the main concerns in the wide adoption of this technique is related with the management of attribute revocation. In fact, when a user loses one of her attributes, she should not

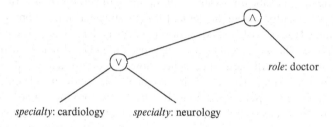

Fig. 2.10 An example of access structure

be able to access tuples that require the revoked attribute for the access. The trivial approach to manage this update is computationally expensive as it implies re-encryption. Yang et al. [115] address this problem proposing an efficient encryption scheme able to manage attribute revocation, ensuring the satisfaction of both backward security (i.e., a revoked user cannot decrypt the tuples requiring the attribute revoked to the user) and forward security (i.e., a newly joined user with sufficient attributes can access all the tuples outsourced before her join). Zhiguo et al. [106] define instead a hierarchical attribute-based solution based on CP-ASBE, an extended version of CP-ABE in which attributes associated with users are organized in a recursive set structure, and propose a flexible and scalable approach to support user revocation.

• *KP-ABE* associates, in contrast to CP-ABE, access structures with users' keys and sets of attributes with tuples. User u can decrypt tuple t if the attributes associated with t satisfy the access structure of the user. To minimize the overhead cause by asymmetric encryption, the tuple content can be encrypted with a symmetric key. Access to the symmetric key k used to encrypt t is then protected through KP-ABE [116]. Only authorized users can remove the KP-ABE encryption layer to retrieve the symmetric key use to encrypt tuples and access their content. This solution also supports policy updates, and couples ABE with proxy re-encryption to delegate to the storing server most of the re-encryption operations necessary to enforce policy updates.

All the solutions described in this section, be them based on selective encryption or on ABE, focus only on the enforcement of read access privileges and do not support restrictions on write operations, which are assumed to be an exclusive privilege of the data owner. In the literature, few works have addressed this issue. Raykova et al. [92] adopt selective encryption to enforce the data owner's authorization policy on outsourced data, relying on asymmetric encryption to enforce both read and write privileges and defining two key derivation hierarchies: one for private keys (to enforce read privileges) and one for public keys (to enforce write privileges). This solution also proposes to replicate resources and perform updates on a different copy of the data, to prevent unauthorized write operations from destroying valuable data content. De Capitani di Vimercati et al. [39] adopt selective encryption and write tags to enforce static write privileges on outsourced data. Zhao et al. [117] combine CP-ABE and Attribute-Based Signature (ABS) techniques to enforce read and write access privileges, respectively. This approach, although effective, has the disadvantage of requiring the presence of a trusted party for correct policy enforcement. Ruj et al. [93] investigate a similar approach based on the combined use of ABE and ABS for supporting both read and write privileges. This solution has the advantage over the approach in [117] of being suited also to distributed scenarios. All these approaches, however, do not address the problem of efficiently supporting changes to the authorization policy, which may require expensive data re-encryption operations. In Chap. 5, we propose an access control solution, based on selective encryption, able to efficiently enforce updates in the write access policy, and we complement it with an effective data integrity control mechanism and a subscription-based authorization policy.

2.6 Chapter Summary

The needs for privacy protection and access control enforcement in data release scenarios have recently been widely recognized by the research community, which have proposed different models and techniques to ensure appropriate protection of sensitive information not intended for disclosure. In this chapter, we illustrated some of these well-known approaches, focusing on data protection techniques (syntactic, semantic and fragmentation-based), on solutions for counteracting inferential disclosure of sensitive information not explicitly included in the release, and on recent access control mechanisms suited to cloud/outsourcing scenarios. In the remainder of this book, we will study more in depth the fragmentation-based approach for preserving privacy in data release, proposing a novel model of the problem and also illustrating a possible way to enhance the utility of the released data to the recipients. We will then consider a novel, unsolved scenario of inferential disclosure by proposing a model characterizing the problem and a solution for counteracting possible privacy breaches. Finally, we will focus on access control enforcement and, leveraging on the selective encryption approach, we will define a flexible access control model that both enforces dynamic write privileges, and supports novel subscription-based scenarios.

Chapter 3
Enforcing Confidentiality and Visibility Constraints

The most straightforward understanding of, and the first requirement for, protecting privacy when releasing a data collection is indeed the protection of the sensitive data included in the release. However, privacy protection should not prevent recipients from performing legitimate analysis on the released dataset, and should ensure adequate visibility over non sensitive information. In this chapter, we illustrate a solution allowing a data owner to publicly release a dataset while satisfying confidentiality and visibility constraints over the data, expressing requirements for information protection and release, respectively, by releasing vertical views (*fragments*) over the original dataset. We translate the problem of computing a fragmentation composed of the minimum number of fragments into the problem of computing a maximum weighted clique over a fragmentation graph. The fragmentation graph models fragments, efficiently computed using Ordered Binary Decision Diagrams (OBDDs), which satisfy all the confidentiality constraints and a subset of the visibility constraints defined in the system. To further enrich the utility of the released fragments, our solution complements them with *loose associations* (i.e., a sanitized form of the sensitive associations broken by fragmentation), specifically extended to safely operate on multiple fragments. We define an exact and a heuristic algorithm for computing a minimal and a locally minimal fragmentation, respectively, and a heuristic algorithm to efficiently compute a safe loose association

Part of this chapter is reprinted from Journal of Computer Security, vol. 20, no. 5: V. Ciriani, S. De Capitani di Vimercati, S. Foresti, G. Livraga, and P. Samarati, "An OBDD Approach to Enforce Confidentiality and Visibility Constraints in Data Publishing", pp. 463–508 [30], ©2012, with permission from IOS Press.

Part of this chapter is reprinted from Journal of Computer Security, vol. 23, no. 1: S. De Capitani di Vimercati, S. Foresti, S. Jajodia, G. Livraga, S. Paraboschi, and P. Samarati, "Loose Associations to Increase Utility in Data Publishing", pp. 59–88 [45], ©2015, with permission from IOS Press.

© Springer International Publishing Switzerland 2015
G. Livraga, *Protecting Privacy in Data Release*, Advances in Information
Security 57, DOI 10.1007/978-3-319-16109-9_3

among multiple fragments. We also prove the effectiveness of our proposals by means of extensive experimental evaluations.

3.1 Introduction

Information sharing and dissemination are typically selective processes. While on one side, there is a need-or demand-for making certain information available to others, there is on the other side an equally strong need to ensure proper protection of sensitive information. It is therefore important to provide data holders with means to express and enforce possible constraints over their data, modeling the need for information of the data recipients (*visibility* constraints) and the need for protecting confidential information against improper disclosures (*confidentiality* constraints).

Recent proposals considering confidentiality and visibility constraints have put forward the idea of computing vertical fragments over the original data structure (typically a relation) so that all constraints are satisfied [3, 27, 28, 38]. While such proposals have been introduced as a way of departing from data encryption when relying on external servers for data storage, data fragmentation results appealing also in data release scenarios. In fact (regardless of whether the data owner relies on external service providers for data management), data fragments can be seen as different (vertical) views that a data holder can release to external parties to satisfy their demand for information, while at the same time guaranteeing that confidential information is not disclosed. The problem of computing data views taking into consideration both privacy needs and visibility requirements makes however the data fragmentation problem far from trivial. In particular, ensuring some meaningful form of minimality of the fragments to be released (to the aim of avoiding unnecessary fragmentation of attributes), makes the problem NP-hard [38].

To further enrich the utility of the released fragments, a data owner can complement them with *loose associations* [38], which permit to partially reconstruct the association between sub-tuples in fragments, while not precisely disclosing the association among attribute values that are considered sensitive. Loose associations partition the tuples in fragments in groups and release the associations between sub-tuples in fragments at the granularity of group (instead of the precise tuple-level association). Loose associations can then be used for evaluating aggregate queries, with limited errors in the result, and for data mining. The existing approach operates under the assumption that a fragmentation includes two fragments only, and produces a single loose association between this pair of fragments. A fragmentation may however include an arbitrary number of fragments, and the definition of a loose associations should then consider the presence of multiple fragments.

The contributions of this chapter are multi-fold. First, we propose a new modeling of the fragmentation problem that exploits the representation of confidentiality and visibility constraints as Boolean formulas, and of fragments as truth assignments over Boolean variables corresponding to attributes in the original relation. In this way, the computation of a fragmentation that satisfies the given constraints relies on the efficiency with which Boolean formulas are represented and manipulated. Since the classical methods for operating on Boolean formulas are impractical for large-scale problems, we adopt reduced Ordered Binary Decision Diagrams (OBDDs), which are a canonical form for representing and efficiently manipulating Boolean formulas [80]. OBDDs are used in practical applications more often than other classical representations of Boolean formulas because they have a canonical form that uniquely characterizes a given function, and because operations on Boolean formulas can be performed quite efficiently in time and space [68]. The size of an OBDD does not directly depend on the size of the corresponding formula and even though, in the worst case, it could be exponential in the number of variables in the formula, the majority of Boolean formulas can be represented by compact OBDDs. Our approach then transforms all the inputs of the fragmentation problem into Boolean formulas, and takes advantage of their representation through OBDDs to process different constraints simultaneously and to easily check whether a fragmentation satisfies all the given confidentiality and visibility constraints. Our solution is based on a graph modeling of the fragmentation problem that permits to reformulate it as the (NP-hard) problem of computing a maximum weighted clique. Based on this modeling, we then define an exact and a heuristic algorithm for computing a fragmentation composed of the minimum number of fragments. We formally analyze the correctness and computational complexity of both our exact and heuristic algorithms and present a set of experiments for assessing their efficiency (in terms of computational time) and the effectiveness of the heuristics (in terms of number of fragments of the computed fragmentation). The experimental results prove that our heuristics, while providing faster computational time, well approximates the minimal fragmentations computed by the exact algorithm. We also propose to adopt loose associations to further enrich the utility of the released fragments. We first show that the direct adoption of loose associations to generic fragmentations composed of more than two fragments opens the door to harmful privacy breaches. Moved by this consideration, we then propose a solution for the definition of loose associations among arbitrary sets of fragments, and define a heuristic algorithm for computing safe loose associations. The experimental results prove that our approach is effective in allowing for more accurate responses to the queries posed by users and operating on fragmentations.

By proposing two efficient techniques for fragmenting a dataset, and a general method to enrich the utility of the computed fragmentation not limited to any specific number of fragments, we make a further step toward the realization of concrete privacy-enhancing techniques, easily applicable in real-world scenarios to balance privacy needs of data owners and visibility needs of data recipients.

3.1.1 Chapter Outline

The remainder of this chapter is organized as follows. Section 3.2 introduces confidentiality and visibility constraints, and describes the fragmentation problem. Section 3.3 presents our modeling of the problem, defining OBDDs corresponding to constraints, and illustrating how the truth assignments that satisfy the constraints can be composed for computing a solution to the fragmentation problem. Section 3.4 uses the truth assignments extracted from OBDDs and their relationships to reformulate the fragmentation problem in terms of the maximum weighted clique problem over a fragmentation graph. Section 3.5 describes an exact algorithm for computing a minimal fragmentation, based on the graph modeling of the problem. Section 3.6 illustrates a heuristic approach that computes a locally minimal fragmentation by iteratively building a clique. Section 3.7 presents the experimental results comparing the exact and heuristic algorithms. Section 3.8 introduces the concept of loose association, and illustrates the privacy risks caused by the release of multiple loose associations over fragmentations composed of more than two fragments. Section 3.9 presents our definition of loose association, taking into account an arbitrary number of fragments. This section also introduces the properties that need to be guaranteed to ensure that a loose association satisfies a given privacy degree, and provides some observations on loose associations. Section 3.10 discusses the utility of loose associations in terms of providing better response to queries. Section 3.11 illustrates our heuristic algorithm for the computation of a loose association. Section 3.12 presents our experimental analysis, on synthetic as well as on real datasets, showing the efficiency of our approach and the utility provided in query execution. Finally, Sect. 3.13 gives our final remarks and concludes the chapter.

3.2 Preliminary Concepts

We consider a scenario where, consistently with other proposals (e.g., [3, 28, 38, 94]), the data undergoing possible external release are represented with a single relation r over a relation schema $R(a_1, \ldots, a_n)$, and there are no dependencies among the attributes in R. We use standard notations of relational database theory and, when clear from the context, we use R to denote either the relation schema R or the set $\{a_1, \ldots, a_n\}$ of attributes in R. We consider two kinds of constraints on data: *confidentiality constraints*, imposing restrictions on the (joint) visibility of values of attributes in R, and *visibility constraints*, expressing requirements on data views [28, 38].

Definition 3.1 (Confidentiality Constraint). Given a relation schema $R(a_1, \ldots, a_n)$, a *confidentiality constraint* c over R is a subset of $\{a_1, \ldots, a_n\}$.

Confidentiality constraints state that the values of an attribute (*singleton constraint*) or the associations among the values of a given set of attributes (*association constraint*) are sensitive and should not be visible. More precisely, a singleton constraint $\{a\}$ states that the values of attribute a should not be visible. An association constraint $\{a_{i_1}, \ldots, a_{i_m}\}$ states that the values of attributes $a_{i_1}, \ldots, a_{i_m}$ should not be visible in association. For instance, Fig. 3.1b illustrates one singleton (c_1) and four association ($c_2, \ldots, c_5$) constraints for relation PATIENTS in Fig. 3.1a.

a

PATIENTS

SSN	Name	Birth	Race	ZIP	Job	InsRate	Disease
123-45-6789	Alice	74/01/17	white	24201	nurse	5K	diabetes
234-56-7654	Barbara	49/02/21	white	24223	clerk	9K	stomach ulcer
345-67-8123	Carol	55/10/01	asian	25273	manager	7K	hearth attack
456-78-9876	Donna	68/12/29	white	26134	lawyer	8K	gastritis
567-89-0534	Emma	81/10/02	black	24343	chef	6K	asthma

b

$\mathcal{C}$

$c_1 = \{\text{SSN}\}$
$c_2 = \{\text{Name, InsRate}\}$
$c_3 = \{\text{Name, Disease}\}$
$c_4 = \{\text{Birth, Race, ZIP}\}$
$c_5 = \{\text{Job, Disease}\}$

c

$\mathcal{V}$

$v_1 = \text{Name} \lor (\text{Birth} \land \text{ZIP})$
$v_2 = \text{Job} \land \text{InsRate}$
$v_3 = \text{Disease} \land (\text{Birth} \lor \text{Race})$

Fig. 3.1 Example of relation (**a**) and of confidentiality (**b**) and visibility constraints (**c**) over it

The satisfaction of a confidentiality constraint c_i clearly implies the satisfaction of any confidentiality constraint c_j such that $c_i \subseteq c_j$, making c_j redundant. A set $\mathcal{C}$ of confidentiality constraints is *well defined* if $\forall c_i, c_j \in \mathcal{C}$, $i \neq j$, $c_i \not\subseteq c_j$, that is, $\mathcal{C}$ does not contain redundant constraints. Note that, while previous approaches assume that a pre-processing phase removes redundant constraints from $\mathcal{C}$, the solution proposed in this chapter implicitly transforms $\mathcal{C}$ into a well defined set of confidentiality constraints (see Sect. 3.3).

Visibility constraints are defined as follows.

Definition 3.2 (Visibility Constraint). Given a relation schema $R(a_1, \ldots, a_n)$, a *visibility constraint* v over R is a monotonic Boolean formula over attributes in R.

Intuitively, a visibility constraint imposes the release of an attribute or the joint release of a set of attributes. Visibility constraint $v = a$ states that the values of attribute a must be visible. Visibility constraint $v = v_i \land v_j$ states that v_i and v_j must be jointly visible (e.g., constraint v_2 in Fig. 3.1c requires the joint release of attributes Job and InsRate since the associations between their values must be visible). Visibility constraint $v = v_i \lor v_j$ states that at least one between v_i and v_j must be visible (e.g., constraint v_1 in Fig. 3.1c requires that the values of attribute Name or the association between the values of attributes Birth and ZIP be released). Note that negations are not used in the definition of visibility constraints since they model requirements of non-visibility, which are already captured by confidentiality constraints.

Confidentiality and visibility constraints can be enforced by partitioning (fragmenting) attributes in R in different sets (*fragments*). A fragmentation of relation R is a set of fragments, as formally captured by the following definition.

Definition 3.3 (Fragmentation). Given a relation schema $R(a_1, \ldots, a_n)$, a *fragmentation* $\mathscr{F}$ of R is a set $\{F_1, \ldots, F_l\}$ of fragments, where each fragment F_i, $i = 1, \ldots, l$, is a subset of $\{a_1, \ldots, a_n\}$.

Consistently with the proposal in [38], a fragmentation is not required to be complete, that is, it does not need to include all the attributes of the original relation. If the data holder is interested in releasing all the (non sensitive) attributes in R [3, 27], it is sufficient to include an additional visibility constraint $v=a$ for each attribute $a{\in}R$ such that there does not exist a constraint $c{\in}\mathscr{C}$ with $c=\{a\}$. Given a relation R, a set $\mathscr{C}$ of confidentiality constraints, and a set $\mathscr{V}$ of visibility constraints, a fragmentation $\mathscr{F}$ of R is *correct* if it satisfies: (1) all the confidentiality constraints in $\mathscr{C}$, and (2) all the visibility constraints in $\mathscr{V}$. Formally, a correct fragmentation is defined as follows.

Definition 3.4 (Correct Fragmentation). Given a relation schema $R(a_1, \ldots, a_n)$, a set $\mathscr{C}$ of confidentiality constraints over R, and a set $\mathscr{V}$ of visibility constraints over R, a fragmentation $\mathscr{F}$ of R is *correct* with respect to $\mathscr{C}$ and $\mathscr{V}$ iff:

1. $\forall c{\in}\mathscr{C}, \forall F{\in}\mathscr{F}: c \not\subseteq F$ (confidentiality);
2. $\forall v{\in}\mathscr{V}, \exists F{\in}\mathscr{F}: F$ satisfies v (visibility);
3. $\forall F_i, F_j{\in}\mathscr{F}, i \neq j : F_i \cap F_j = \emptyset$ (unlinkability).

Condition 1 ensures that neither sensitive attributes nor sensitive associations are visible in a fragment. Condition 2 ensures that all the visibility constraints are satisfied. Condition 3 ensures that fragments do not have common attributes and therefore that association constraints cannot be violated by joining fragments. We note that singleton constraints can be satisfied only by not releasing the involved sensitive attributes. Association constraints can be satisfied either by not releasing at least one of the attributes in each constraint, or by distributing the attributes among different (unlinkable) fragments. Visibility constraints are satisfied by ensuring that each constraint is satisfied by at least one fragment. Figure 3.2 illustrates an example of correct fragmentation of relation PATIENTS in Fig. 3.1a with respect to the confidentiality and visibility constraints in Fig. 3.1b and in Fig. 3.1c, respectively.

Given a set of confidentiality and visibility constraints, we are interested in a fragmentation that does not split attributes among fragments when it is not necessary for satisfying confidentiality constraints. The rationale is that maintaining a set of attributes in the same fragment releases, besides their values, also their associations. The utility of released data for final recipients is higher when releasing a fragmentation composed of fewer fragments, since they also have visibility of

Fig. 3.2 Example of fragmentation of relation PATIENTS in Fig. 3.1a satisfying the constraints in Figs. 3.1b and c

F_1			F_2	
Birth	**ZIP**	**Disease**	**Job**	**InsRate**
74/01/17	24201	diabetes	nurse	5K
49/02/21	24223	stomach ulcer	clerk	9K
55/10/01	25273	hearth attack	manager	7K
68/12/29	26134	gastritis	lawyer	8K
81/10/02	24343	asthma	chef	6K

the associations among the attributes. Our goal is then to compute a *minimal* fragmentation, that is, a fragmentation with the minimum number of fragments. Formally, the problem of computing a minimal fragmentation is defined as follows.

Problem 3.1 (Minimal Fragmentation). Given a relation schema $R(a_1, \ldots, a_n)$, a set $\mathcal{C}$ of confidentiality constraints over R, and a set $\mathcal{V}$ of visibility constraints over R, determine (if it exists) a fragmentation $\mathcal{F} = \{F_1, \ldots, F_l\}$ of R such that:

1. $\mathcal{F}$ is a correct fragmentation of R with respect to $\mathcal{C}$ and $\mathcal{V}$ (Definition 3.4);
2. $\nexists \mathcal{F}'$ such that: (1) $\mathcal{F}'$ is a correct fragmentation of R with respect to $\mathcal{C}$ and $\mathcal{V}$, and (2) $\mathcal{F}'$ is composed of fewer fragments than $\mathcal{F}$.

The problem of computing a minimal fragmentation is NP-hard, since the minimum hypergraph coloring problem reduces to it in polynomial time [38]. We therefore adopt a definition of *locally minimal* fragmentation, which can be computed with an efficient heuristic. Such a definition is based on the following dominance relationship between the fragmentations of relation R.

Definition 3.5 (Dominance Relationship). Given a relation schema $R(a_1, \ldots, a_n)$ and two fragmentations $\mathcal{F}_i$ and $\mathcal{F}_j$ of R with $\bigcup_{F \in \mathcal{F}_i} F = \bigcup_{F \in \mathcal{F}_j} F$, $\mathcal{F}_i$ *dominates* $\mathcal{F}_j$, denoted $\mathcal{F}_i \succ \mathcal{F}_j$, iff $\mathcal{F}_i \neq \mathcal{F}_j$, and $\forall F_j \in \mathcal{F}_j$, $\exists F_i \in \mathcal{F}_i$ such that $F_j \subseteq F_i$, and $\forall F_i \in \mathcal{F}_i$, $\exists \{F_{j_h}, \ldots, F_{j_l}\} \in \mathcal{F}_j$ such that $F_{j_h} \cup \ldots \cup F_{j_l} = F_i$.

Definition 3.5 states that given two fragmentations $\mathcal{F}_i$ and $\mathcal{F}_j$ defined on the same set of attributes, $\mathcal{F}_i$ *dominates* $\mathcal{F}_j$ if $\mathcal{F}_i$ can be obtained by merging two (or more) fragments in $\mathcal{F}_j$. We note that fragmentations defined on different subsets of attributes in relation R cannot be compared with respect to the dominance relationship. As an example, consider relation PATIENTS in Fig. 3.1a, and fragmentation $\mathcal{F}_1 = \{\{\texttt{Birth},\texttt{ZIP},\texttt{Disease}\}, \{\texttt{Job},\texttt{InsRate}\}\}$ in Fig. 3.2. $\mathcal{F}_1$ dominates fragmentation $\mathcal{F}_2 = \{\{\texttt{Birth},\texttt{ZIP}\}, \{\texttt{Disease}\}, \{\texttt{Job},\texttt{InsRate}\}\}$ since $\mathcal{F}_1$ can be obtained by merging fragments $\{\texttt{Birth},\texttt{ZIP}\}$ and $\{\texttt{Disease}\}$ in $\mathcal{F}_2$.

A locally minimal fragmentation is defined as a correct fragmentation whose fragments cannot be merged without violating any confidentiality constraint (i.e., a locally minimal fragmentation cannot be dominated by a correct fragmentation). Note that all the visibility constraints satisfied by a fragmentation $\mathcal{F}$ are also satisfied by any fragmentation $\mathcal{F}'$ dominating it. The problem of computing a locally minimal fragmentation is formally defined as follows.

Problem 3.2 (Locally Minimal Fragmentation). Given a relation schema $R(a_1, \ldots, a_n)$, a set $\mathcal{C}$ of confidentiality constraints over R, and a set $\mathcal{V}$ of visibility constraints over R, determine (if it exists) a fragmentation $\mathcal{F} = \{F_1, \ldots, F_l\}$ of R such that:

1. $\mathcal{F}$ is a correct fragmentation of R with respect to $\mathcal{C}$ and $\mathcal{V}$ (Definition 3.4);
2. $\nexists \mathcal{F}'$ such that: (1) $\mathcal{F}'$ is a correct fragmentation of R with respect to $\mathcal{C}$ and $\mathcal{V}$, and (2) $\mathcal{F}' \succ \mathcal{F}$.

For instance, the fragmentation in Fig. 3.2 is locally minimal since merging F_1 with F_2 would violate confidentiality constraint c_5.

It is important to note that a locally minimal fragmentation may not be a minimal fragmentation, while a minimal fragmentation is also a locally minimal fragmentation. For instance, consider relation PATIENTS in Fig. 3.1a and the confidentiality and visibility constraints over it in Fig. 3.1b and in Fig. 3.1c, respectively. Fragmentation $\mathscr{F} = \{\{Name\}, \{Race,Disease\},\{Job,InsRate\}\}$ represents a locally minimal, but not a minimal, fragmentation for relation PATIENTS. Fragmentation $\mathscr{F}' = \{\{Birth,ZIP,Disease\}, \{Job,InsRate\}\}$ in Fig. 3.2 is both locally minimal and minimal since there does not exist a correct fragmentation of relation PATIENTS composed of one fragment only.

3.3   OBDD-Based Modeling of the Fragmentation Problem

We model the fragmentation problem as the problem of managing a set of Boolean formulas that are conveniently represented through *reduced and Ordered Binary Decision Diagrams* (OBDDs) [19]. OBDDs allow us to efficiently manipulate confidentiality and visibility constraints, and to easily compute a minimal (Sect. 3.5) or locally minimal (Sect. 3.6) fragmentation.

3.3.1   OBDD Representation of Constraints

In our modeling, attributes in R are interpreted as Boolean variables. Visibility constraints have already been defined as Boolean formulas (Definition 3.2). Each confidentiality constraint in $\mathscr{C}$ can be represented as the conjunction of the variables corresponding to the attributes in the constraint. For instance, Fig. 3.3 represents the Boolean interpretation of the relation schema (i.e., the set $\mathscr{B}$ of Boolean variables), and of the constraints over it in Fig. 3.1.

$\mathscr{B}$	$\mathscr{C}$	$\mathscr{V}$
SSN	$c_1 = SSN$	$v_1 = Name \lor (Birth \land ZIP)$
Name	$c_2 = Name \land InsRate$	$v_2 = Job \land InsRate$
Birth	$c_3 = Name \land Disease$	$v_3 = Disease \land (Birth \lor Race)$
Race	$c_4 = Birth \land Race \land ZIP$	
ZIP	$c_5 = Job \land Disease$	
Job		
InsRate		
Disease		

Fig. 3.3 Boolean interpretation of the relation schema and of the confidentiality and visibility constraints in Fig. 3.1

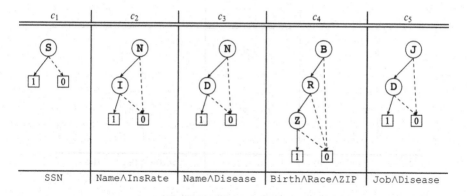

c_1	c_2	c_3	c_4	c_5
SSN	Name∧InsRate	Name∧Disease	Birth∧Race∧ZIP	Job∧Disease

Fig. 3.4 OBDDs representing the confidentiality constraints in Fig. 3.3

We use OBDDs as an effective and efficient approach for representing and manipulating Boolean formulas. An OBDD represents a Boolean formula as a rooted directed acyclic graph with two leaf nodes labeled 1 (true) and 0 (false), respectively, corresponding to the truth values of the formula. Each internal node in the graph represents a Boolean variable in the formula and has two outgoing edges, labeled 1 and 0, representing the assignment of values 1 and 0, respectively, to the variable. The variables occur in the same order on all the paths of the graph. Also, to guarantee a compact representation of the Boolean formula, the subgraphs rooted at the two direct descendants of each internal node in the graph are disjoint, and pairs of subgraphs rooted at two different nodes are not isomorphic. Figures 3.4 and 3.5 illustrate the OBDDs of the Boolean formulas in Fig. 3.3 that model the confidentiality and visibility constraints in Fig. 3.1b and in Fig. 3.1c, respectively. For simplicity, in these figures and in the following, attributes are denoted with their initials, edges labeled 1 are represented by solid lines, and edges labeled 0 are represented by dashed lines. A truth assignment to the Boolean variables in a formula corresponds to a path from the root to one of the two leaf nodes of the OBDD of the formula. The outgoing edge of a node in the path is the value assigned to the variable represented by the node. For instance, in the OBDD of v_1 in Fig. 3.5, the path traversing nodes N, B, Z, and 1 represents truth assignment [N = 0, B = 1, Z = 1] since the edge in the path outgoing from node N is labeled 0, and the edges in the path outgoing from nodes B and Z are labeled 1. We call *one-paths* (*zero-paths*, respectively) all the paths of an OBDD that reach leaf node 1 (0, respectively), which correspond to the assignments that satisfy (do not satisfy, respectively) the formula. For instance, path N, B, Z, and 1 is a one-path of the OBDD of v_1 in Fig. 3.5. Variables in the formula that do not occur in a path from the root to a leaf node are called *don't care* variables, since their values do not influence the truth value of the formula. For instance, with respect to one-path N and 1 of the OBDD of v_1 in Fig. 3.5, B and Z are don't care variables. In the remainder of the chapter, we use '-' as value for the don't care variables. If there is at least a don't care variable in a truth assignment, this assignment is *partial* (in contrast to *complete*), since not

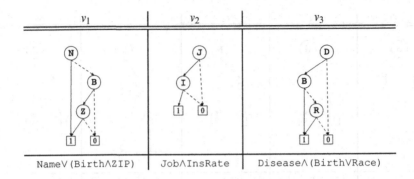

Fig. 3.5 OBDDs representing the visibility constraints in Fig. 3.3

all the variables in the formula have a value associated with them. We note that a partial truth assignment with k don't care variables is a compact representation of a set of 2^k complete truth assignments obtained by assigning to the don't care variables value 1 or 0. A complete truth assignment is *implicitly represented* by a partial truth assignment if, for each Boolean variable a in the formula, either a is a don't care variable for the partial truth assignment or the two truth assignments set a to the same value. For instance, the OBDD of v_1 in Fig. 3.5 has two one-paths, corresponding to truth assignments [N=1, B=-, Z=-] and [N=0, B=1, Z=1]. Partial truth assignment [N=1, B=-, Z=-] is a compact representation for [N=1, B=0, Z=0], [N=1, B=0, Z=1], [N=1, B=1, Z=0], and [N=1, B=1, Z=1].

3.3.2 Truth Assignments

In the Boolean modeling of the fragmentation problem, a fragment $F \in \mathscr{F}$ can be interpreted as a *complete* truth assignment, denoted I_F, over the set $\mathscr{B}$ of Boolean variables. Function I_F assigns value 1 to each variable corresponding to an attribute in F, and value 0 to all the other variables in $\mathscr{B}$. A fragmentation is then represented by a set of complete truth assignments, which is formally defined as follows.

Definition 3.6 (Set of Truth Assignments). Given a set $\mathscr{B}$ of Boolean variables, a *set $\mathscr{I}$ of truth assignments* is a set $\{I_1, \ldots, I_l\}$ of functions such that $I_i : \mathscr{B} \to \{0,1\}$, $i = 1, \ldots, l$.

With a slight abuse of notation, we use I to denote also the list of truth values assigned by I to variables in $\mathscr{B}$. For instance, fragmentation $\mathscr{F}$ in Fig. 3.2 corresponds to the set $\mathscr{I} = \{I_{F_1}, I_{F_2}\}$ of truth assignments, with $I_{F_1} = [S = 0, N = 0, B = 1, R = 0, Z = 1, J = 0, I = 0, D = 1]$ and $I_{F_2} = [S = 0, N = 0, B = 0, R = 0, Z = 0, J = 1, I = 1, D = 0]$. Given a Boolean formula f, defined over Boolean variables $\mathscr{B}$, and a truth assignment I, $I(f)$ denotes the result of the evaluation of f with respect to truth assignment I. A set $\mathscr{I}$ of truth assignments corresponds to a correct fragmentation (Definition 3.4) if it satisfies all the confidentiality and visibility constraints and each Boolean variable is set to 1 by at most one truth assignment in $\mathscr{I}$, as formally defined in the following.

Definition 3.7 (Correct Set of Truth Assignments). Given a set $\mathscr{B}$ of Boolean variables, a set $\mathscr{C}$ of confidentiality constraints over $\mathscr{B}$, and a set $\mathscr{V}$ of visibility constraints over $\mathscr{B}$, a set $\mathscr{I}$ of truth assignments is *correct* with respect to $\mathscr{C}$ and $\mathscr{V}$ iff:

1. $\forall c \in \mathscr{C}, \forall I \in \mathscr{I} : I(c) = 0$ (confidentiality);
2. $\forall v \in \mathscr{V}, \exists I \in \mathscr{I} : I(v) = 1$ (visibility);
3. $\forall I_i, I_j \in \mathscr{I}, i \neq j, \forall a \in \mathscr{B}$ with $I_i(a) = 1 : I_j(a) = 0$ (unlinkability).

Condition 1 ensures that the evaluation of any confidentiality constraint with respect to any truth assignment is false (i.e., all fragments satisfy confidentiality constraints). Condition 2 ensures that, for each visibility constraint, there is at least one truth assignment that makes the visibility constraint true (i.e., every visibility constraint is satisfied by at least one fragment). Condition 3 ensures that there is at most one truth assignment that sets a variable to true (i.e., fragments do not have common attributes). It is immediate to see that a set of truth assignments is correct with respect to $\mathscr{C}$ and $\mathscr{V}$ iff the corresponding fragmentation is correct with respect to $\mathscr{C}$ and $\mathscr{V}$ (i.e., Definition 3.7 is equivalent to Definition 3.4). OBDDs representing confidentiality and visibility constraints can be used to efficiently verify if a set $\mathscr{I}$ of truth assignments satisfies Condition 1 and Condition 2 in Definition 3.2: (1) each assignment $I \in \mathscr{I}$ must correspond to a zero-path in all the OBDDs of the confidentiality constraints; and (2) for each visibility constraint, at least one assignment $I \in \mathscr{I}$ must correspond to a one-path in the OBDD of the constraint. We also note that Condition 3 in Definition 3.2 can be efficiently verified by simply comparing the truth value assigned to each variable by the truth assignments in $\mathscr{I}$. For instance, consider the OBDDs of confidentiality and visibility constraints in Figs. 3.4 and 3.5, respectively, and the set $\mathscr{I} = \{I_{F_1}, I_{F_2}\}$, with $I_{F_1} = [\text{S} = 0, \text{N} = 0, \text{B} = 1, \text{R} = 0, \text{Z} = 1, \text{J} = 0, \text{I} = 0, \text{D} = 1]$ and $I_{F_2} = [\text{S} = 0, \text{N} = 0, \text{B} = 0, \text{R} = 0, \text{Z} = 0, \text{J} = 1, \text{I} = 1, \text{D} = 0]$, representing the fragmentation in Fig. 3.2. $\mathscr{I}$ is correct, since: (1) I_{F_1} and I_{F_2} correspond to zero-paths of the OBDDs of the confidentiality constraints (confidentiality); (2) I_{F_1} corresponds to a one-path of the OBDDs of v_1 and v_3, and I_{F_2} corresponds to a one-path of the OBDD of v_2 (visibility); and (3) each variable in $\mathscr{B}$ is set to 1 by at most one assignment between I_{F_1} and I_{F_2} (unlinkability).

Problem 3.1 (minimal fragmentation) can be reformulated as the problem of computing a correct set of truth assignments composed of the minimum number of truth assignments, which is formally defined as follows.

Problem 3.3 (Minimal Set of Truth Assignments). Given a set $\mathscr{B}$ of Boolean variables, a set $\mathscr{C}$ of confidentiality constraints over $\mathscr{B}$, and a set $\mathscr{V}$ of visibility constraints over $\mathscr{B}$, determine (if it exists) a set $\mathscr{I}$ of truth assignments such that:

1. $\mathscr{I}$ is a correct set of truth assignments (Definition 3.7);
2. $\nexists \mathscr{I}'$ such that: (1) $\mathscr{I}'$ is a correct set of truth assignments, and (2) $\mathscr{I}'$ is composed of fewer truth assignments than $\mathscr{I}$.

Analogously, the problem of computing a locally minimal fragmentation (Problem 3.2) can be reformulated as the problem of computing a correct set $\mathscr{I}$ of truth assignments such that no pair of truth assignments I_i and I_j in $\mathscr{I}$ can be combined producing a new assignment I_{ij} such that $\forall a \in \mathscr{B}, I_{ij}(a) = I_i(a) \vee I_j(a)$, and all the confidentiality constraints are satisfied. This condition can be formally formulated by first translating the dominance relationship between fragmentations into an equivalent dominance relationship between sets of truth assignments as follow.

Definition 3.8 (Dominance Relationship). Given a set $\mathscr{B}$ of Boolean variables and two sets of truth assignments $\mathscr{I}_i$ and $\mathscr{I}_j$ over $\mathscr{B}$, $\mathscr{I}_i$ dominates $\mathscr{I}_j$, denoted $\mathscr{I}_i \succ \mathscr{I}_j$, iff $\mathscr{I}_i \neq \mathscr{I}_j$ and $\forall I_j \in \mathscr{I}_j$, $\exists I_i \in \mathscr{I}_i$ such that $\forall a \in \mathscr{B}$, with $I_j(a) = 1$, $I_i(a) = 1$ and $\forall I_i \in \mathscr{I}_i$, $\exists \{I_{j_h}, \ldots, I_{j_l}\} \in \mathscr{I}_j$ such that $\forall a \in \mathscr{B}, I_i(a) = I_{j_h}(a) \vee \ldots \vee I_{j_l}(a)$.

The problem of computing a locally minimal fragmentation (Problem 3.2) can now be formally defined as the problem of computing a locally minimal set of truth assignments.

Problem 3.4 (Locally Minimal Set of Truth Assignments). Given a set $\mathscr{B}$ of Boolean variables, a set $\mathscr{C}$ of confidentiality constraints over $\mathscr{B}$, and a set $\mathscr{V}$ of visibility constraints over $\mathscr{B}$, determine (if it exists) a set $\mathscr{I}$ of truth assignments such that:

1. $\mathscr{I}$ is a correct set of truth assignments (Definition 3.7);
2. $\nexists \mathscr{I}'$ such that: (1) $\mathscr{I}'$ is a correct set of truth assignments, and (2) $\mathscr{I}' \succ \mathscr{I}$.

Our approach to solve the minimal and locally minimal set of truth assignments problems uses properties of the OBDDs to efficiently check if a set of truth assignments is correct. In principle, a set of truth assignments should be checked for correctness against each confidentiality constraint and each visibility constraint. We can cut down on such controls by noting that if a truth assignment I does not make true any confidentiality constraint, Boolean formula $c_1 \vee \ldots \vee c_m$ evaluates to false with respect to I. Also, if truth assignment I makes true at least one of the confidentiality constraints in $\mathscr{C}$, Boolean formula $c_1 \vee \ldots \vee c_m$ evaluates to true with respect to I. In other words, we can check all the confidentiality constraints together in a single step. Formally, this observation is expressed as follows.

Observation 1 *Given a set* $\mathscr{B} = \{a_1, \ldots, a_n\}$ *of Boolean variables, a set* $\mathscr{C} = \{c_1, \ldots, c_m\}$ *of confidentiality constraints over* $\mathscr{B}$, *and a truth assignment* I:

$$\forall c_i \in \mathscr{C}, I(c_i) = 0 \iff I(c_1 \vee \ldots \vee c_m) = 0.$$

To verify whether a truth assignment I satisfies the given confidentiality constraints, we can then simply check if I corresponds to a zero-path of the OBDD representing the disjunction of confidentiality constraints. For instance, consider the confidentiality constraints in Fig. 3.3, the OBDD representing their disjunction in Fig. 3.6, and truth assignment $I_{F_1} = [S = 0, N = 0, B = 1, R = 0, Z = 1, J = 0, I = 0, D = 1]$, representing fragment F_1 in Fig. 3.2. I_{F_1} corresponds to a zero-path of the OBDD in Fig. 3.6, implying that I_{F_1} does not violate any confidentiality constraint.

Fig. 3.6 OBDD representing
the disjunction of the
confidentiality constraints
in Fig. 3.3

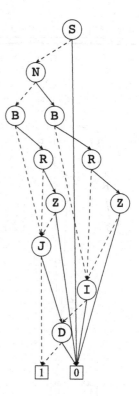

For each visibility constraint v, a correct set of truth assignments must include at least a truth assignment I satisfying v, while not violating confidentiality constraints (i.e., $I(v) = 1$ and $I(c_1 \vee \ldots \vee c_m) = 0$). This is equivalent to say that Boolean formula $v \wedge \neg(c_1 \vee \ldots \vee c_m)$ with respect to truth assignment I evaluates to true, as formally observed in the following.

Observation 2 *Given a set $\mathcal{B} = \{a_1, \ldots, a_n\}$ of Boolean variables, a set $\mathcal{C} = \{c_1, \ldots, c_m\}$ of confidentiality constraints over $\mathcal{B}$, a visibility constraint v over $\mathcal{B}$, and a truth assignment I:*

$$I(v) = 1 \text{ and } I(c_1 \vee \ldots \vee c_m) = 0 \iff I(v \wedge \neg(c_1 \vee \ldots \vee c_m)) = 1.$$

In other words, the set of one-paths of the OBDD of formula $v_i \wedge \neg(c_1 \vee \ldots \vee c_m)$ represents in a compact way all and only the truth assignments that satisfy v_i and that do not violate any confidentiality constraint. In the following, we will use O_i to denote the OBDD of Boolean formula $v_i \wedge \neg(c_1 \vee \ldots \vee c_m)$, and $\mathcal{P}_{v_i}$ to denote the set of one-paths in O_i, which can represent both complete and partial truth assignments. For instance, consider the confidentiality and visibility constraints in Figs. 3.4 and 3.5, respectively. Figure 3.7 illustrates the OBDDs of formulas $v_i \wedge \neg(c_1 \vee \ldots \vee c_5)$, $i = 1, \ldots, 3$, along with their one-paths. Note that all the variables in $\mathcal{B}$ not appearing in formula $v_i \wedge \neg(c_1 \vee \ldots \vee c_m)$ are considered as don't care variables for the one-paths in O_i, $i = 1, \ldots, k$.

$$v_1 \wedge \neg(c_1 \vee c_2 \vee c_3 \vee c_4 \vee c_5) \mid v_2 \wedge \neg(c_1 \vee c_2 \vee c_3 \vee c_4 \vee c_5) \mid v_3 \wedge \neg(c_1 \vee c_2 \vee c_3 \vee c_4 \vee c_5)$$

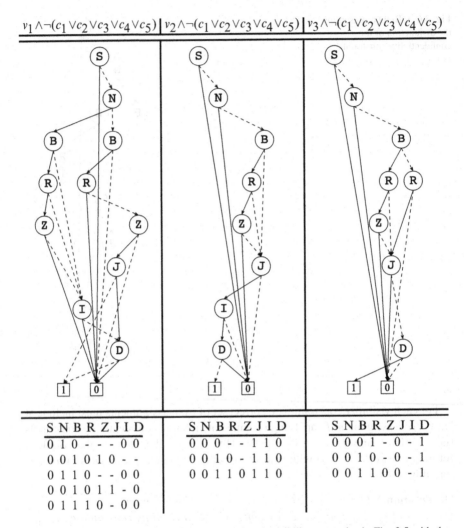

S N B R Z J I D
0 1 0 - - - 0 0
0 0 1 0 1 0 - -
0 1 1 0 - - 0 0
0 0 1 0 1 1 - 0
0 1 1 1 0 - 0 0

S N B R Z J I D
0 0 0 - - 1 1 0
0 0 1 0 - 1 1 0
0 0 1 1 0 1 1 0

S N B R Z J I D
0 0 0 1 - 0 - 1
0 0 1 0 - 0 - 1
0 0 1 1 0 0 - 1

Fig. 3.7 OBDDs representing the composition of each visibility constraint in Fig. 3.5 with the negated disjunction of the confidentiality constraints in Fig. 3.4, and their one-paths

To satisfy Condition 1 (confidentiality) and Condition 2 (visibility) in Definition 3.7, a set of truth assignments must include, for each $v \in \mathcal{V}$, at least a complete truth assignment implicitly represented by a (partial) truth assignment corresponding to a one-path in $\mathscr{P}_v$. However, not all the sets of truth assignments that include at least one complete truth assignment implicitly represented by a (partial) truth assignment in $\mathscr{P}_v$, for each $v \in \mathcal{V}$, are correct, since they may violate Condition 3 in Definition 3.7 (unlinkability). In the following, we discuss how to combine truth assignments in $\mathscr{P}_{v_1}, \ldots, \mathscr{P}_{v_k}$ to compute a correct set of truth assignments.

3.3.3 Comparison of Assignments

Goal of our approach is to compute a correct set of truth assignments that solves either the minimal or the locally minimal fragmentation problem. To this purpose, we first introduce the concepts of *linkable* and *mergeable* truth assignments.

Definition 3.9 (Linkable Truth Assignments). Given two assignments I_i and I_j over Boolean variables $\mathscr{B}$, we say that I_i and I_j are *linkable*, denoted $I_i \leftrightarrow I_j$, iff $\exists a \in \mathscr{B} : I_i(a) = I_j(a) = 1$.

According to Definition 3.9, two assignments are linkable iff there is a Boolean variable in $\mathscr{B}$ such that the truth value of the variable is set to 1 by the two given assignments, that is, the fragments corresponding to them have an attribute in common. For instance, assignments $[S = 0, N = 0, B = 1, R = 0, Z = 1, J = 0, I = -, D = -]$ and $[S = 0, N = 0, B = 1, R = 0, Z = -, J = 0, I = -, D = 1]$ are linkable since they both assign 1 to variable Birth. In the following, we will use the term *disjoint*, and notation $I_i \not\leftrightarrow I_j$, to refer to two truth assignments I_i and I_j that are not linkable. For instance, assignments $[S = 0, N = 0, B = 0, R = -, Z = -, J = 1, I = 1, D = 0]$ and $[S = 0, N = 1, B = 0, R = -, Z = -, J = -, I = 0, D = 0]$ are disjoint. Note that variables with value 0 and - do not have any impact on the linkability of two truth assignments.

Definition 3.10 (Mergeable Truth Assignments). Given two assignments I_i and I_j over Boolean variables $\mathscr{B}$, we say that I_i and I_j are *mergeable*, denoted $I_i \rightleftharpoons I_j$, iff $\nexists a$ s.t. $I_i(a) = 1$ and $I_j(a) = 0$, or viceversa.

According to Definition 3.10, two truth assignments are mergeable iff the truth value of each variable a in $\mathscr{B}$ in the two assignments is not in contrast, where being in contrast for variable a means that a is assigned 1 by one assignment and is assigned 0 by the other one. For instance, the two assignments $[S = 0, N = 0, B = 1, R = 0, Z = 1, J = 0, I = -, D = -]$ and $[S = 0, N = 0, B = 1, R = 0, Z = -, J = 0, I = -, D = 1]$ are mergeable. While these two assignments are also linkable, linkability and mergeability are two independent properties and none of them implies the other. For instance, assignments $[S = 0, N = 0, B = 1, R = 0, Z = 1, J = 0, I = -, D = -]$ and $[S = 0, N = 0, B = 1, R = 0, Z = -, J = 1, I = 1, D = 0]$ are linkable (Birth is set to 1 by both assignments) but not mergeable (there is a conflict on variable Job), while $[S = 0, N = 0, B = 1, R = 0, Z = 1, J = -, I = -, D = -]$ and $[S = 0, N = 0, B = -, R = 0, Z = -, J = 1, I = 1, D = 0]$ are mergeable but not linkable.

It is interesting to note that the sets of complete truth assignments implicitly represented by mergeable partial truth assignments are overlapping (i.e., they have assignments in common), and that a complete truth assignment cannot be represented by two different partial truth assignments with variables in contrast. This is equivalent to say that two partial truth assignments are mergeable only if they represent at least a common complete truth assignment, as formally observed in the following.

Fig. 3.8 Assignment
merging operator

$\odot$	0	1	-
0	0	n.a.	0
1	n.a.	1	1
-	0	1	-

Observation 3 *Given a set $\mathscr{B} = \{a_1, \ldots, a_n\}$ of Boolean variables and two truth assignments I_i and I_j over $\mathscr{B}$:*

$$I_i \rightleftharpoons I_j \iff \exists I_k \text{ s.t. } \forall a \in \mathscr{B}, \ I_k(a) = I_i(a) \text{ or } I_i(a) = \text{-},$$
$$\text{and } I_k(a) = I_j(a) \text{ or } I_j(a) = \text{-}.$$

For instance, consider mergeable truth assignments [$S = 0, N = 0, B = 1, R = 0$, $Z = 1, J = 0, I = \text{-}, D = \text{-}$] and [$S = 0, N = 0, B = 1, R = 0, Z = \text{-}, J = 0, I = \text{-}, D = 1$]. They both implicitly represent the following two complete truth assignments: [$S = 0, N = 0, B = 1, R = 0, Z = 1, J = 0, I = 0, D = 1$] and [$S = 0, N = 0, B = 1, R = 0, Z = 1, J = 0, I = 1, D = 1$].

Mergeable (partial) assignments can be composed (merged) according to operator $\odot$ in Fig. 3.8. Merging truth assignments I_i and I_j results in a new truth assignment I_{ij}, where the truth value of a variable coincides with its truth value in the assignment in which it does not appear as a don't care variable. If a variable appears as a don't care variable in both I_i and I_j, then its value in the new assignment remains don't care. The result of the composition of I_i with I_j represents in a compact form all the complete truth assignments implicitly represented by both I_i and I_j. Note that if I_i and I_j are two (partial) truth assignments in the set $\mathscr{P}_{v_i}$ and $\mathscr{P}_{v_j}$, respectively, then $I_{ij}=I_i \odot I_j$ represents a set of complete truth assignments that satisfies all the confidentiality constraints and both v_i and v_j. For instance, with reference to the example in Fig. 3.7, [$S = 0, N = 0, B = 1, R = 0, Z = 1, J = 0, I = \text{-}, D = \text{-}$] is a one-path in $\mathscr{P}_{v_1}$ and [$S = 0, N = 0, B = 1, R = 0, Z = \text{-}, J = 0, I = \text{-}, D = 1$] is a one-path in $\mathscr{P}_{v_3}$. These two assignments are mergeable and the result of their merging computed through operator $\odot$ is [$S = 0, N = 0, B = 1, R = 0, Z = 1, J = 0, I = \text{-}, D = 1$], which implicitly represents two complete truth assignments (differing for the value of I) that satisfy both v_1 and v_3 and that do not violate any confidentiality constraint. Also, we note that no pair of one-paths in $\mathscr{P}_v$ is mergeable since they are two distinct one-paths of the same OBDD, and therefore differ by at least one edge, meaning that they are in conflict on at least one variable.

3.4 Graph Modeling of the Minimal Fragmentation Problem

To compute a correct set $\mathscr{I}$ of truth assignments (i.e., $\forall v_i \in \mathscr{V}$, $\mathscr{I}$ includes at least one complete truth assignment implicitly represented by a one-path in $\mathscr{P}_{v_i}$, and each pair of truth assignments in $\mathscr{I}$ is disjoint), we propose to model the one-paths of $\mathscr{P}_{v_i}$, for each $v_i \in \mathscr{V}$, and their relationships described in Sect. 3.3.3 through a *fragmentation graph*. We then translate the problem of computing a minimal set of truth assignments into the equivalent problem of computing a *maximum weighted clique* of the fragmentation graph.

A fragmentation graph is an undirected graph that implicitly represents all the truth assignments that may belong to a correct set of truth assignments as they satisfy all the confidentiality constraints and an arbitrary subset of visibility constraints. Edges in a fragmentation graph connect truth assignments that could appear together in a correct set of truth assignments. The fragmentation graph has therefore a node for each partial truth assignment in the set $\mathscr{P}^{\odot}$ obtained from the closure of $\mathscr{P}$ under operator $\odot$, where $\mathscr{P} = \mathscr{P}_{v_1} \cup \ldots \cup \mathscr{P}_{v_k}$ is the set of one-paths extracted from the OBDDs representing $v_i \wedge \neg(c_1 \vee \ldots \vee c_m)$, $i = 1, \ldots, k$ (see Sect. 3.3). Note that each truth assignment in $\mathscr{P}_{v_i}$ is explicitly associated with visibility constraint v_i. The rationale is that the truth assignments in $\mathscr{P}_{v_i}$ satisfy at least v_i, while not violating the confidentiality constraints. Set $\mathscr{P}^{\odot}$ includes both the truth assignments in $\mathscr{P}$ and the truth assignments resulting from the merging of any subset of mergeable one-paths in $\mathscr{P}$. The merging of two (partial) truth assignments I_i and I_j generates a (partial) truth assignment I_{ij} that is associated with a set of visibility constraints computed as the set-theoretic union of those associated with I_i and I_j. We have therefore the guarantee that $\mathscr{P}^{\odot}$ contains all the (partial) truth assignments that represent fragments satisfying all the confidentiality constraints and a subset of the visibility constraints. Each node in the fragmentation graph is modeled as a pair $\langle I,V \rangle$, where I is a truth assignment in $\mathscr{P}^{\odot}$ and V is the set of the visibility constraints associated with I. Note that a complete truth assignment that satisfies a set $\{v_i, \ldots, v_j\} \subseteq \mathscr{V}$ of visibility constraints is represented by $2^n - 1$ nodes in the fragmentation graph, with $n = |\{v_i, \ldots, v_j\}|$, one for each subset of $\{v_i, \ldots, v_j\}$. Clearly, the set of nodes in the graph implicitly representing I may also represent other (different) truth assignments. The edges of the fragmentation graph connect nodes that represent disjoint truth assignments associated with non-overlapping sets of visibility constraints. Note that we add these edges because if there exist two nodes n_i and n_j representing two disjoint partial truth assignments with overlapping sets of visibility constraints, by construction, $\mathscr{P}^{\odot}$ must include also a node n_k that represents a partial truth assignment that is mergeable with the truth assignment represented by n_i (n_j, respectively) and is associated with a set of visibility constraints non-overlapping with the set of visibility constraints associated with n_j (n_i, respectively). The fragmentation graph therefore has an edge connecting node n_k with node n_j, thus making the edge between nodes n_i and n_j redundant. A fragmentation graph is formally defined as follows.

Definition 3.11 (Fragmentation Graph). Given a set $\mathscr{B} = \{a_1, \ldots, a_n\}$ of Boolean variables, a set $\mathscr{C} = \{c_1, \ldots, c_m\}$ of confidentiality constraints over $\mathscr{B}$, a set $\mathscr{V} = \{v_1, \ldots, v_k\}$ of visibility constraints over $\mathscr{B}$, and a set $\mathscr{P} = \mathscr{P}_{v_1} \cup \ldots \cup \mathscr{P}_{v_k}$ of one-paths in $O_1, \ldots, O_k$, a *fragmentation graph* is an undirected graph $G_F(N_F, E_F)$ where:

- $N_F = \{\langle I,V \rangle \colon I \in \mathscr{P}^{\odot} \wedge V \subseteq \mathscr{V} \wedge \forall v \in V, I(v)=1\}$, with $\mathscr{P}^{\odot}$ the closure of $\mathscr{P}$ under $\odot$;
- $E_F = \{(n_i, n_j) \colon n_i, n_j \in N_F \wedge n_i.I \not\approx n_j.I \wedge n_i.V \cap n_j.V = \emptyset\}$, with $n_i.I$ the truth assignment represented by node n_i, and $n_i.V$ the set of visibility constraints associated with $n_i.I$.

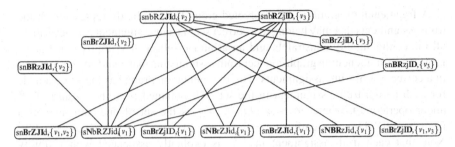

Fig. 3.9 Fragmentation graph representing the one-paths extracted from the OBDDs in Fig. 3.7 and their closure under operator ⊙

Note that nodes with sets of visibility constraints that have at least one visibility constraint in common are not connected by an edge in G_F since, in a correct set of truth assignments, it is sufficient that each visibility constraint is satisfied by one assignment. In fact, the release of multiple assignments satisfying the same visibility constraint may imply the release of unnecessary fragments, that is, of a fragmentation which is not minimal. Figure 3.9 illustrates the fragmentation graph resulting from the ⊙-closure on $\mathscr{P}_{v_1}$, $\mathscr{P}_{v_2}$, $\mathscr{P}_{v_3}$ in Fig. 3.7. In this figure and in the following, for readability purposes, we denote truth assignments by reporting attribute initials with a different notation, depending on the truth value assigned to the corresponding variable. More precisely, variables set to 1 are represented in uppercase and boldface (e.g., **A**), variables set to 0 are represented in lowercase (e.g., a), and variables set to - are represented in uppercase (e.g., A).

We note that a clique in G_F that includes, for each $v \in \mathscr{V}$, at least a node n such that $v \in n.V$ (i.e., $n.I$ is associated with v and satisfies it), represents a correct set $\mathscr{I}$ of truth assignments (Definition 3.7). In fact, by definition of fragmentation graph, the nodes in the clique represent a set of disjoint (and possibly partial) truth assignments (Condition 3) such that each of them satisfies all the confidentiality constraints (Condition 1). Also, each visibility constraint $v \in \mathscr{V}$ is satisfied by at least one of the truth assignments in the clique, the one represented by node n with $v \in n.V$ (Condition 2). Analogously, each correct set $\mathscr{I}$ of truth assignments is implicitly represented by a clique in G_F, and the same clique may represent more than one correct set of truth assignments. A correct set $\mathscr{I}$ of truth assignments is composed of complete truth assignments only, while the nodes in the fragmentation graph may represent partial truth assignments. Given a clique in the fragmentation graph, don't care variables in the truth assignments represented by the nodes in the clique must be set to either 0 or 1 to obtain one of the correct sets of truth assignments represented by the clique, with the restriction that no variable can assume value 1 in more than one fragment. Hence, we conveniently set all the don't care variables to 0. For instance, nodes ⟨snBrZjID,$\{v_1,v_3\}$⟩ and ⟨snbRZJId,$\{v_2\}$⟩ form a clique for the fragmentation graph in Fig. 3.9 such that the corresponding assignments satisfy all the confidentiality and visibility constraints in Fig. 3.3. This clique corresponds to the set of truth assignments $\mathscr{I} = \{[S=0, N=0, B=1, R=0, Z=1, J=0, I=0, D=1], [S=0, N=0, B=0, R=0, Z=0, J=1, I=1, D=0]\}$. We note

that the clique also implicitly represents $\mathscr{I} = \{[S = 0, N = 0, B = 1, R = 0, Z = 1,$
$J = 0, I = 0, D = 1], [S = 0, N = 0, B = 0, R = 1, Z = 0, J = 1, I = 1, D = 0]\}$.

The problem of computing a correct set $\mathscr{I}$ of truth assignments can now be reformulated as the problem of computing a clique C of the fragmentation graph G_F such that $\bigcup_{n \in C} n.V = \mathscr{V}$. We are interested in computing a *minimal set of truth assignments* (Problem 3.3), which corresponds to a clique of the fragmentation graph that satisfies all the confidentiality and visibility constraints while *minimizing the number of nodes* composing it. The problem of computing a minimal set of truth assignments (Problem 3.3), or equivalently the problem of computing a minimal fragmentation (Problem 3.1), is then translated into the problem of computing a maximum weighted clique for the fragmentation graph, where a weight function w assigns a weight to the nodes of the graph so to model our minimization requirement. The maximum weighted clique problem has been widely studied in the literature and is formulated as follows [87, 88].

Problem 3.5 (Maximum Weighted Clique). Given a weighted undirected graph $G(N, E, w)$, with $w : N \rightarrow \mathbb{R}^+$, determine a subset $C \subseteq N$ of nodes in N such that:

1. $\forall n_i, n_j \in C, (n_i, n_j) \in E$ (C is a *clique*);
2. $\nexists C' \subseteq N$ such that: (1) C' is a clique, and (2) $\sum_{n \in C'} w(n) > \sum_{n \in C} w(n)$ (C has *maximum weight*).

To reformulate the minimal set of truth assignments problem into the maximum weighted clique problem, we define the weight function w in a way that satisfies the following three properties, which guarantee the equivalence between a maximum weighted clique in G_F (if it exists) and a minimal set of truth assignments.

1. *Monotonicity of w with respect to the number of visibility constraints*: given two cliques, the one associated with a higher number of visibility constraints has higher weight.
2. *Anti-monotonicity of w with respect to the number of nodes*: given two cliques associated with the same number of visibility constraints, the one composed of fewer nodes has higher weight.
3. *Equivalence of solutions*: cliques associated with the same number of visibility constraints and composed of the same number of nodes have the same weight.

A weight function that satisfies all the properties above is $w : N_F \rightarrow \mathbb{N}^+$ with $w(n) = (|\mathscr{V}| \cdot |n.V|) - 1$, where $|\mathscr{V}|$ is the number of visibility constraints, n is a node in N_F, and $|n.V|$ is the number of visibility constraints associated with n. The weight of a set $N_F' \subseteq N_F$ of nodes is the sum of the weights of the nodes composing it, that is, $w(N_F') = \sum_{n \in N_F'} w(n)$. We first prove that our weight function satisfies the properties above, and then we show that such properties guarantee the equivalence between the minimum set of truth assignments problem and the maximum weighted clique problem.

Property 3.1 (Weight Function). Given a fragmentation graph $G_F(N_F, E_F)$, a weight function $w : N_F \rightarrow \mathbb{N}^+$ with $w(n) = (|\mathcal{V}| \cdot |n.V|) - 1$, and two cliques of G_F, $C_i = \{n_{i_1}, \ldots, n_{i_x}\}$ and $C_j = \{n_{j_1}, \ldots, n_{j_y}\}$, the following conditions hold:

1. $\sum_{k=1}^{x} |n_{i_k}.V| > \sum_{k=1}^{y} |n_{j_k}.V| \implies w(C_i) > w(C_j)$ (monotonicity of w with respect to the number of visibility constraints);
2. $\sum_{k=1}^{x} |n_{i_k}.V| = \sum_{k=1}^{y} |n_{j_k}.V|$ and $x < y \implies w(C_i) > w(C_j)$ (anti-monotonicity of w with respect to the number of nodes);
3. $\sum_{k=1}^{x} |n_{i_k}.V| = \sum_{k=1}^{y} |n_{j_k}.V|$ and $x = y \implies w(C_i) = w(C_j)$ (equivalence of solutions).

Proof. 1. Let us assume, by contradiction, that $w(C_i) \leq w(C_j)$, that is $\sum_{k=1}^{x} w(n_{i_k}) \leq \sum_{k=1}^{y} w(n_{j_k})$. Since $w(n) = (|\mathcal{V}| \cdot |n.V|) - 1$, the above equation can be rewritten as $\sum_{k=1}^{x} (|\mathcal{V}| \cdot |n_{i_k}.V| - 1) \leq \sum_{k=1}^{y} (|\mathcal{V}| \cdot |n_{j_k}.V| - 1)$, which is equivalent to $|\mathcal{V}| \cdot \sum_{k=1}^{x} |n_{i_k}.V| - x \leq |\mathcal{V}| \cdot \sum_{k=1}^{y} |n_{j_k}.V| - y$. This equation can be rewritten as $|\mathcal{V}| \cdot (\sum_{k=1}^{x} |n_{i_k}.V| - \sum_{k=1}^{y} |n_{j_k}.V|) - x + y \leq 0$. Since, by assumption, $\sum_{k=1}^{x} |n_{i_k}.V| > \sum_{k=1}^{y} |n_{j_k}.V|$, we have that $|\mathcal{V}| \cdot (\sum_{k=1}^{x} |n_{i_k}.V| - \sum_{k=1}^{y} |n_{j_k}.V|)$ is greater than $|\mathcal{V}|$. Also, $1 \leq x \leq |\mathcal{V}|$ and $1 \leq y \leq |\mathcal{V}|$. As a consequence, considering the worst case scenario, $\sum_{k=1}^{x} |n_{i_k}.V| - \sum_{k=1}^{y} |n_{j_k}.V| = 1$, $x = |\mathcal{V}|$, and $y = 1$, the equation becomes $|\mathcal{V}| - |\mathcal{V}| + 1 \leq 0$, which is a contradiction proving the monotonicity of w with respect to the number of visibility constraints.

2. Let us now assume, by contradiction, that $w(C_i) \leq w(C_j)$, that is $|\mathcal{V}| \cdot \sum_{k=1}^{x} |n_{i_k}.V| - x \leq |\mathcal{V}| \cdot \sum_{k=1}^{y} |n_{j_k}.V| - y$. Since by assumption $\sum_{k=1}^{x} |n_{i_k}.V| = \sum_{k=1}^{y} |n_{j_k}.V|$, the above inequality holds only if $x > y$, which contradicts our hypothesis and proves the anti-monotonicity of w with respect to the number of nodes.

3. Let us now assume, by contradiction, that $w(C_i) \neq w(C_j)$, that is $|\mathcal{V}| \cdot \sum_{k=1}^{x} |n_{i_k}.V| - x \neq |\mathcal{V}| \cdot \sum_{k=1}^{y} |n_{j_k}.V| - y$. Since by assumption $\sum_{k=1}^{x} |n_{i_k}.V| = \sum_{k=1}^{y} |n_{j_k}.V|$, the above inequality holds only if $x \neq y$, which contradicts our hypothesis and proves the equivalence of solutions. $\square$

To illustrate Property 3.1, consider the fragmentation graph in Fig. 3.9, and the cliques: $C_1 = \{\langle \text{snBrZjID}, \{v_1, v_3\}\rangle, \langle \text{snbRZJId}, \{v_2\}\rangle\}$, $C_2 = \{\langle \text{sNbRZJid}, \{v_1\}\rangle, \langle \text{snbRZJId}, \{v_2\}\rangle\}$, $C_3 = \{\langle \text{sNbRZJid}, \{v_1\}\rangle, \langle \text{snbRZJId}, \{v_2\}\rangle, \langle \text{snbRZjID}, \{v_3\}\rangle\}$, and $C_4 = \{\langle \text{snBrZJId}, \{v_1, v_2\}\rangle, \langle \text{snbRZjID}, \{v_3\}\rangle\}$, with weight $w(C_1) = 7$, $w(C_2) = 4$, $w(C_3) = 6$, and $w(C_4) = 7$, respectively. According to the monotonicity of the weight function with respect to the number of visibility constraints, $w(C_1) = 7 > w(C_2) = 4$ since the nodes in C_1 are associated with three visibility constraints, while the nodes in C_2 are associated with two constraints only. According to the anti-monotonicity of the weight function with respect to the number of nodes, $w(C_1) = 7 > w(C_3) = 6$ although C_1 (composed of two nodes) and C_3 (composed of three nodes) are associated with all the visibility constraints in Fig. 3.3. According to the equivalence of solutions, $w(C_1) = w(C_4) = 7$ since the nodes in C_1 and in C_4 are associated with all the visibility constraints, and C_1 and C_4 are composed of two nodes.

Given a fragmentation graph G_F, a clique C of G_F represents a correct set of truth assignments iff C is associated with all the visibility constraints in $\mathcal{V}$. It is interesting to note that, according to the definition of weight function w of the fragmentation graph G_F as $w(n)=(|\mathcal{V}| \cdot |n.V|) - 1$, C is associated with (and then satisfy) all the visibility constraints only if the weight of C is higher than or equal to $|\mathcal{V}| \cdot (|\mathcal{V}| - 1)$. Formally, this property can be formulated as follow.

Property 3.2. Given a fragmentation graph $G_F(N_F, E_F)$, a weight function w : $N_F \rightarrow \mathbb{N}^+$, with $w(n) = (|\mathcal{V}| \cdot |n.V|) - 1$, and a clique C of G_F:

$$\forall v \in \mathcal{V}, \exists n \in C \text{ s.t. } v \in n.V \iff w(C) \geq |\mathcal{V}| \cdot (|\mathcal{V}| - 1).$$

Proof. The weight of a clique $C=\{n_1,\ldots,n_i\}$ is computed as: $\sum_{j=1}^{i}(|\mathcal{V}| \cdot |n_j.V| - 1)$ $= |\mathcal{V}| \cdot \sum_{j=1}^{i} |n_j.V| - i$. Since, by hypothesis, C includes a node associated with v for each visibility constraint $v \in \mathcal{V}$ then $\sum_{j=1}^{i} |n_j.V| = |\mathcal{V}|$ and therefore $w(C) = |\mathcal{V}| \cdot |\mathcal{V}| - i$. In the worst case, each node in the clique is associated with one visibility constraint and the clique is then composed of $|\mathcal{V}|$ nodes. The weight of the clique is then $w(C) = |\mathcal{V}| \cdot |\mathcal{V}| - |\mathcal{V}| = |\mathcal{V}| \cdot (|\mathcal{V}| - 1)$. Therefore, by Property 3.1, all cliques of G_F associated with less than $|\mathcal{V}|$ visibility constraints have weight lower than $|\mathcal{V}| \cdot (|\mathcal{V}| - 1)$.   □

Property 3.2 guarantees that it is sufficient to check if the weight of the maximum weighted clique of G_F is higher than or equal to $|\mathcal{V}| \cdot (|\mathcal{V}| - 1)$ to determine whether a correct set of truth assignments exists for the considered instance of the problem. To illustrate, consider the fragmentation graph in Fig. 3.9. Clique C_1 = {$\langle$sNbRZJid,$\{v_1\}\rangle$, $\langle$snbRZJId,$\{v_2\}\rangle$} is associated with two out of the three visibility constraints in $\mathcal{V}$, and has weight $2+2=4$, which is lower than $3 \cdot (3-1) = 6$. Clique C_2 = {$\langle$sNbRZJid,$\{v_1\}\rangle$, $\langle$snbRZJId,$\{v_2\}\rangle$, $\langle$snbRZjID,$\{v_3\}\rangle$} is associated with all the visibility constraints, and has weight $2 + 2 + 2 = 6$.

We now formally prove that Properties 3.1 and 3.2 discussed above guarantee that the problem of computing a minimal set of truth assignments (Problem 3.3) is equivalent to the problem of computing a maximum weighted clique of a fragmentation graph with weight at least $|\mathcal{V}| \cdot (|\mathcal{V}| - 1)$.

Theorem 3.1 (Problem Equivalence). *The minimal set of truth assignments problem (Problem 3.3) is equivalent to the problem of determining a maximum weighted clique of weight at least $|\mathcal{V}| \cdot (|\mathcal{V}| - 1)$ of the fragmentation graph $G_F(N_F, E_F)$ (Definition 3.11), with weight function $w : N_F \rightarrow \mathbb{N}^+$ s.t. $w(n)=(|\mathcal{V}| \cdot |n.V|) - 1$.*

Proof. The proof of this theorem immediately follows from Properties 3.1 and 3.2. Indeed, the maximum weighted clique $C = \{n_1,\ldots,n_i\}$ of the fragmentation graph G_F satisfies the maximum number of visibility constraints, according to the monotonicity of w with respect to the number of visibility constraints associated with the nodes in C. If there are different cliques in G_F associated with the same number of visibility constraints, C is the one composed of the minimum number of nodes, according to the anti-monotonicity of w with respect to the number of nodes. Let us now suppose that the set of nodes composing the clique C having maximum weight is associated with all the visibility constraints. Property 3.2 guarantees that $w(C)$ is, in the worst case, equal to $|\mathcal{V}| \cdot (|\mathcal{V}| - 1)$.   □

Since the minimal set of truth assignments problem and the minimal fragmentation problem are equivalent, the minimal fragmentation problem is also equivalent to the maximum weighted clique problem on the fragmentation graph with the weight function defined above.

In the following section, we will present an algorithm for computing a minimal set of truth assignments, exploiting the equivalence proved by Theorem 3.1. In Sect. 3.6, we will introduce a heuristic algorithm for computing a locally minimal set of truth assignments.

3.5   Computing a Minimal Set of Truth Assignments

The algorithm we propose for computing a minimal set of truth assignments (see Fig. 3.10) takes as input a set $\mathcal{B} = \{a_1, \ldots, a_n\}$ of Boolean variables (representing the attributes in R), a set $\mathcal{C} = \{c_1, \ldots, c_m\}$ of confidentiality constraints, a set $\mathcal{V} = \{v_1, \ldots, v_k\}$ of visibility constraints, and executes the following three steps: (1) it computes the set of one-paths of the OBDDs representing Boolean formulas $v_i \wedge \neg(c_1 \vee \ldots \vee c_m)$, $i = 1, \ldots, k$; (2) it builds the fragmentation graph; (3) it determines a maximum weighted clique of the fragmentation graph, and checks if the clique represents a correct set of truth assignments. In the following, we describe these steps more in details.

Step 1: Compute One-Paths For each visibility constraint $v_i \in \mathcal{V}$, the algorithm defines the OBDD O_i representing Boolean formula $v_i \wedge \neg(c_1 \vee \ldots \vee c_m)$. Then, it extracts from O_i the set $\mathcal{P}_{v_i}$ of one-paths (lines 1–4), $i = 1, \ldots, k$. If, for a given O_i, the set $\mathcal{P}_{v_i}$ is empty, v_i cannot be satisfied without violating the confidentiality constraints and therefore the algorithm terminates, returning an empty set of truth assignments (line 5).

Step 2: Build the Fragmentation Graph The algorithm first builds an undirected weighted graph $G(N, M \cup D, w)$ such that for each truth assignment I in $\mathcal{P}_{v_i}$, $i = 1, \ldots, k$, there is a node $n \in N$, with $n.I = I$, $n.V = \{v_i\}$, and $n.weight = (|\mathcal{V}| \cdot |n.V|) - 1$ (lines 10–14). Then, for each pair of nodes n_i and n_j in N, the algorithm inserts edge (n_i, n_j) in M if n_i and n_j represent a pair of mergeable truth assignments that are associated with non-overlapping sets of visibility constraints. This edge indicates that the one-paths represented by n_i and n_j can be merged, thus obtaining a truth assignment associated with both the visibility constraints in $n_i.V$ and in $n_j.V$ (lines 20–22). Edge (n_i, n_j) is inserted in D if n_i and n_j represent two disjoint truth assignments associated with non-overlapping sets of visibility constraints. In this case, edge (n_i, n_j) indicates that the one-paths represented by n_i and n_j can belong to the same correct set of truth assignments, and that these one-paths guarantee the satisfaction of different subsets of visibility

---

INPUT: $\mathscr{B} = \{a_1,\ldots,a_n\}$, $\mathscr{C} = \{c_1,\ldots,c_m\}$, $\mathscr{V} = \{v_1,\ldots,v_k\}$ /* variables and constraints */
OUTPUT: $\mathscr{I}_{sol} = \{I_1,\ldots,I_l\}$ /* minimal set of truth assignments */
MAIN

```
1:   /* Step 1: extract the one-paths from the OBDDs representing constraints */
2:   for each vᵢ∈𝒱 do
3:       let Oᵢ be the OBDD representing vᵢ∧¬(c₁∨…∨cₘ)
4:       let 𝒫ᵥᵢ be the set of one-paths of Oᵢ
5:       if 𝒫ᵥᵢ=∅ then return(∅) /* no solution exists */
6:   /* Step 2: build the fragmentation graph G */
7:   N := ∅ /* set of nodes in G */
8:   M := ∅ /* set of edges connecting nodes representing mergeable truth assignments */
9:   D := ∅ /* set of edges connecting nodes representing disjoint truth assignments */
10:  for each v∈𝒱 do /* insert nodes in G */
11:      for each I∈𝒫ᵥ do
12:          n := ⟨I,{v}⟩
13:          N := N ∪ {n}
14:          n.weight := (|𝒱| · |n.V|) − 1
15:  N' := N
16:  for each nᵢ∈N do /* insert edges in G */
17:      N' := N' − {nᵢ}
18:      satisfied := nᵢ.V
19:      for each nⱼ∈N' do
20:          if nᵢ.I⇌nⱼ.I ∧ nᵢ.V∩nⱼ.V=∅ then /* the nodes represent mergeable truth assignments */
21:              M := M ∪ {(nᵢ,nⱼ)}
22:              satisfied := satisfied ∪ nⱼ.V
23:          if nᵢ.I⇸nⱼ.I ∧ nᵢ.V∩nⱼ.V=∅ then /* the nodes represent disjoint truth assignments */
24:              D := D ∪ {(nᵢ,nⱼ)}
25:              satisfied := satisfied ∪ nⱼ.V
26:      if satisfied≠𝒱 then /* remove nᵢ from G, since it cannot be part of any solution */
27:          M := M − {(nᵢ,nⱼ): nⱼ∈N}
28:          D := D − {(nᵢ,nⱼ): nⱼ∈N}
29:          N := N − {nᵢ}
30:  while M≠∅ do /* close the one-paths in N w.r.t. ⊙ operator */
31:      M' := M
32:      M := ∅
33:      while M'≠∅ do
34:          let (nᵢ,nⱼ) be an edge in M' /* choose a mergeable edge */
35:          M' := M' − {(nᵢ,nⱼ)}
36:          nᵢⱼ := ⟨nᵢ.I⊙nⱼ.I, nᵢ.V∪nⱼ.V⟩ /* compute the merged node */
37:          nᵢⱼ.weight := |𝒱| · |vᵢⱼ.V| − 1 /* weight of the new node */
38:          if nᵢⱼ.V=𝒱 then /* nᵢⱼ is a clique of size 1 */
39:              𝒮_{sol} := {nᵢⱼ.I}
40:              assign 0 to don't care variables in nᵢⱼ.I
41:              return(𝒮_{sol})
42:          N := N ∪ {nᵢⱼ} /* insert the node in the fragmentation graph */
43:          for each nₖ∈{n∈N:(n,nᵢ)∈M ∨ (n,nⱼ)∈M} do
44:              if nᵢⱼ.I⇌nₖ.I ∧ nᵢⱼ.V∩nₖ.V=∅ then M := M ∪ {(nᵢⱼ,nₖ)}
45:          for each nₖ∈{n∈N:(n,nᵢ)∈D ∨ (n,nⱼ)∈D} do
46:              if nᵢⱼ.I⇸nₖ.I ∧ nᵢⱼ.V∩nₖ.V=∅ then D := D ∪ {(nᵢⱼ,nₖ)}
47:      for each nᵢ∈N do
48:          if ⋃n.V: n∈{n∈N:(n,nᵢ)∈M∪D} ≠𝒱 then /* remove nᵢ if it cannot be part of a solution */
49:              M := M − {(nᵢ,nⱼ): nⱼ∈N}
50:              D := D − {(nᵢ,nⱼ): nⱼ∈N}
51:              N := N − {nᵢ}
52:  /* Step 3: find the maximum weighted clique */
53:  C := FindMaxWeightClique(G)
54:  if ∑_{n∈C}w(n)<|𝒱| · (|𝒱|−1) then return(∅) /* no solution exists */
55:  𝒮_{sol} := ∅
56:  for each n∈C do
57:      I := n.I
58:      assign 0 to don't care variables in I
59:      𝒮_{sol} := 𝒮_{sol} ∪ {I}
60:  return(𝒮_{sol})
```

Fig. 3.10 Algorithm that computes a minimal set of truth assignments

constraints (lines 23–25). Note however that, as already discussed in Sect. 3.11, the truth assignments associated with n_i and n_j may also satisfy additional (possibly overlapping) visibility constraints that are not explicitly associated with them. If n_i and the nodes to which it is connected do not satisfy all the visibility constraints in $\mathscr{V}$, n_i cannot belong to any maximum weighted clique representing a correct set of truth assignments. In fact, a clique is a solution of the fragmentation problem only when, for each visibility constraint v in $\mathscr{V}$, there is a node in the clique such that v is associated with such a node. For this reason, the algorithm removes n_i from G (lines 26–29).

The algorithm then transforms the graph G representing the one-paths in $\mathscr{P} = \mathscr{P}_{v_1} \cup \ldots \cup \mathscr{P}_{v_k}$ into a fragmentation graph by computing the closure of $\mathscr{P}$ (i.e., the nodes in N) under merging operator $\odot$. To this end, the algorithm creates a copy M' of the set M of edges and initializes M to the empty set (lines 31–32). Then, the algorithm iteratively extracts an edge (n_i, n_j) from M', and determines a new node n_{ij} such that $n_{ij}.I = n_i.I \odot n_j.I$ and $n_{ij}.V = n_i.V \cup n_j.V$ (lines 34–36). The weight $n_{ij}.weight$ is set to $|\mathscr{V}| \cdot |n_{ij}.V| - 1$ (see Sect. 3.4), thus reflecting the number of visibility constraints associated with the node (line 37). Before inserting n_{ij} in G, the algorithm checks if n_{ij} satisfies all the visibility constraints (line 38). If this is the case, n_{ij} represents a maximum weighted clique for G. $\mathscr{I}_{sol}$ is then set to $n_{ij}.I$, don't care variables are set to 0, and the algorithm terminates returning $\mathscr{I}_{sol}$ (lines 39–41). Otherwise, node n_{ij} is inserted in G, and the algorithm checks if nodes adjacent either to n_i or to n_j are also adjacent (with a mergeable or disjoint edge) to n_{ij}, thus possibly inserting in M or in D the corresponding edges (lines 42–46). Note that the algorithm needs only to check n_{ij} against the nodes in N that are mergeable/disjoint with $n_i.I$ or $n_j.I$, since satisfying any of these conditions is a precondition for being mergeable/disjoint with $n_{ij}.I$. When the set M' of edges is empty, the algorithm checks whether there are nodes in N that can be removed from G since they cannot belong to any maximum weighted clique (lines 47–51). The algorithm then iteratively repeats the process of removing edges from M (i.e., it creates a copy M' of M and inserts new nodes and edges in N, M, and D, respectively) until the set M of edges is empty, that is, no edge is inserted in M during the process of merging nodes connected through the edges in M' (i.e., until G is a fragmentation graph).

Step 3: Compute a Maximum Weighted Clique The algorithm exploits a known algorithm [87] to compute a maximum weighted clique of the fragmentation graph (line 53). Function **FindMaxWeightedClique** takes the fragmentation graph as input and returns a maximum weighted clique. If the weight of the clique is lower than $|\mathscr{V}| \cdot (|\mathscr{V}| - 1)$, the considered instance of the problem does not admit a correct set of truth assignments (line 54). Otherwise, if $w(C)$ is at least $|\mathscr{V}| \cdot (|\mathscr{V}| - 1)$, the one-paths represented by the nodes in C are inserted in $\mathscr{I}_{sol}$, don't care variables are set to 0 (lines 56–59), and $\mathscr{I}_{sol}$ is returned (line 60).

Example 3.1. Consider relation PATIENTS and the confidentiality and visibility constraints over it in Fig. 3.1. The execution of the algorithm in Fig. 3.10 proceeds as follows.

1) *Compute one-paths.* The algorithm builds O_1, O_2, and O_3 in Fig. 3.7, representing formula $v_i \wedge \neg(c_1 \vee \ldots \vee c_5)$, $i = 1, 2, 3$, and extracts their one-paths, which are listed in Fig. 3.7.

2) *Build the fragmentation graph.* The algorithm inserts in G a node for every one-path in $\mathscr{P}_{v_1}$, $\mathscr{P}_{v_2}$, and $\mathscr{P}_{v_3}$ (see Fig. 3.11a). Figure 3.11b shows the graph obtained connecting the nodes in Fig. 3.11a that represent mergeable truth assignments (dotted edges) and disjoint truth assignments (continuous edges). Nodes $\langle s\mathbf{NBR}z\mathrm{Jid}, \{v_1\}\rangle$ and $\langle sn\mathbf{BR}z\mathbf{JId}, \{v_2\}\rangle$ in Fig. 3.11a do not appear in the graph in Fig. 3.11b since they neither are associated with v_3 nor could be connected with a node that is associated with v_3, and therefore cannot be part of a clique. The algorithm then computes the closure of the nodes in G. It first merges nodes $\langle sn\mathbf{BrZ}\mathrm{JId}, \{v_1\}\rangle$ and $\langle sn\mathbf{BrZ}\mathrm{JId}, \{v_2\}\rangle$, inserts the resulting node $\langle sn\mathbf{BrZ}\mathrm{JId}, \{v_1,v_2\}\rangle$ in N, and checks if it can be connected by an edge in D with node $\langle snb\mathbf{RZ}j\mathbf{ID}, \{v_3\}\rangle$ and/or with node $\langle s\mathbf{N}b\mathbf{RZ}j\mathrm{id}, \{v_1\}\rangle$ (the nodes adjacent to the merged nodes). Since $\langle sn\mathbf{BrZ}\mathrm{JId}, \{v_1,v_2\}\rangle$ and $\langle snb\mathbf{RZ}j\mathbf{ID}, \{v_3\}\rangle$ represent disjoint assignments and are associated with non-overlapping sets of visibility constraints, the algorithm inserts edge $(\langle sn\mathbf{BrZ}\mathrm{JId}, \{v_1,v_2\}\rangle, \langle snb\mathbf{RZ}j\mathbf{ID}, \{v_3\}\rangle)$ in D, while it does not insert the edge connecting $\langle sn\mathbf{BrZ}\mathrm{JId}, \{v_1,v_2\}\rangle$ with $\langle s\mathbf{N}b\mathbf{RZ}j\mathrm{id}, \{v_1\}\rangle$ since v_1 is associated with both nodes. The resulting graph is illustrated in Fig. 3.11c, where the new node is doubly circled. Nodes $\langle sn\mathbf{BrZ}j\mathbf{ID}, \{v_1\}\rangle$ and $\langle sn\mathbf{BrZ}j\mathbf{ID}, \{v_3\}\rangle$ are then merged. The algorithm then inserts the resulting node $\langle sn\mathbf{BrZ}j\mathbf{ID}, \{v_1,v_3\}\rangle$ in N, and edge $(\langle sn\mathbf{BrZ}j\mathbf{ID}, \{v_1,v_3\}\rangle, \langle snb\mathbf{RZ}\mathbf{JId}, \{v_2\}\rangle)$ in D. Figure 3.11d illustrates the resulting graph, where the new node is doubly circled. Since there are no more mergeable edges in M, the algorithm checks whether there are nodes in N that can possibly be removed from G. Node $\langle sn\mathbf{BrZ}\mathrm{JId}, \{v_1\}\rangle$ is only connected with a node associated with v_3 and has no connections with nodes associated with v_2, and therefore it is removed from G. Figure 3.11d illustrates the resulting fragmentation graph.

3) *Compute a maximum weighted clique.* Once the fragmentation graph has been built, the algorithm calls function **FindMaxWeightClique** that returns one of the two maximum weighted cliques in G, $C = \{\langle sn\mathbf{BrZ}j\mathbf{ID}, \{v_1,v_3\}\rangle, \langle snb\mathbf{RZ}\mathbf{JId}, \{v_2\}\rangle\}$. The weight of this clique is $w(C) = 7$ and is higher than threshold $|\mathscr{V}| \cdot (|\mathscr{V}| - 1) = 6$. Therefore, C represents a solution to the minimal set of truth assignments problem. The algorithm extracts from C the corresponding set of truth assignments, and the don't care variables are set to 0, thus obtaining $\mathscr{I}_{sol} = \{[\text{S}=0, \text{N}=0, \text{B}=1, \text{R}=0, \text{Z}=1, \text{J}=0, \text{I}=0, \text{D}=1], [\text{S}=0, \text{N}=0, \text{B}=0, \text{R}=0, \text{Z}=0, \text{J}=1, \text{I}=1, \text{D}=0]\}$ that is finally returned. We note that this set of truth assignments corresponds to the minimal fragmentation $\mathscr{F} = \{\{\texttt{Birth},\texttt{ZIP},\texttt{Disease}\}, \{\texttt{Job},\texttt{InsRate}\}\}$ in Fig. 3.2.

The correctness and complexity of the algorithm in Fig. 3.10 are stated by the following theorems.

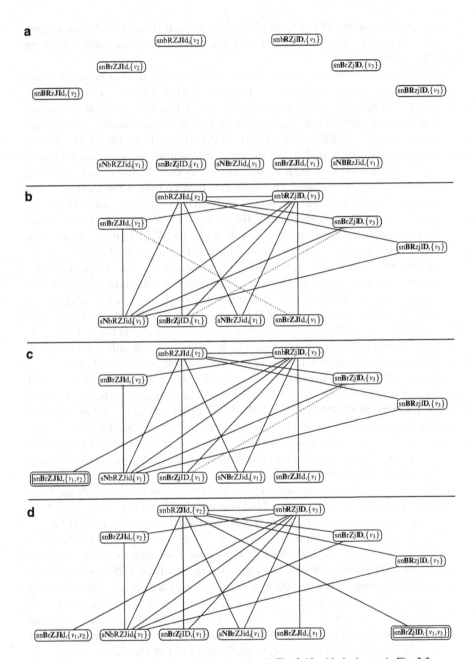

Fig. 3.11 Example of the execution of the algorithm in Fig. 3.10 with the inputs in Fig. 3.3

Theorem 3.2 (Correctness of the Exact Algorithm). *Given a set $\mathscr{B}$ of Boolean variables, a set $\mathscr{C}$ of confidentiality constraints over $\mathscr{B}$, and a set $\mathscr{V}$ of visibility constraints over $\mathscr{B}$, the algorithm in Fig. 3.10 terminates and computes (if it exists) a minimal set of truth assignments.*

Proof. To prove the correctness of the algorithm in Fig. 3.10, we have to show that (1) it terminates; (2) it computes a correct set of truth assignments; (3) if there exists a correct set $\mathscr{I}$ of truth assignments with respect to $\mathscr{C}$ and $\mathscr{V}$, the algorithm finds it; and (4) it computes a minimal set of truth assignments.

Termination Since the number of confidentiality and visibility constraints is finite, the **for each** loop in Step 1 terminates. The first two **for each** loops in Step 2 (line 10 and line 16, respectively) terminate since for each $v \in \mathscr{V}$ the set $\mathscr{P}_v$ of one-paths is finite, and N includes at most one node for each one-path in $\mathscr{P}_{v_1} \cup \ldots \cup \mathscr{P}_{v_k}$. The **while** loop in Step 2 (line 30) terminates since the number of nodes that it inserts in N is finite. In fact, let n_{ij} be a node obtained through the combination of n_i and n_j, which are nodes connected by a mergeable edge: (1) n_{ij} is inserted in N only if N does not include a node n associated with a truth assignment and a set of visibility constraints equal to those of node n_{ij} (N is a set); (2) n_{ij} is adjacent to neither n_i nor n_j; and (3) edge $(n_i, n_j) \in M$ is removed from M when node n_{ij} is inserted in N. Therefore, at each iteration of the **while** loop, at most one node is inserted in N, an edge is removed from M, and a limited number of edges is inserted in M. Since the number of Boolean variables in $\mathscr{B}$ and of visibility constraints in $\mathscr{V}$ is finite, the number of possible nodes generated by merging nodes in N is finite. As a consequence, the **while** loop terminates. Function **FindMaxWeightClique** in Step 3 (line 53) terminates since it exploits a classical algorithm for finding a maximum weight clique. The last **for each** loop in Step 3 (line 56) terminates since C is a subset of N, which is a finite set of nodes.

Correctness of the Set of Truth Assignments $\mathscr{I}_{sol}$ is correct iff it satisfies the conditions in Definition 3.7.

1. $\forall c \in \mathscr{C}, \forall I \in \mathscr{I}_{sol} \colon I(c) = 0$ (confidentiality). In the last **for each** loop of Step 3 (line 56), the algorithm extracts $\mathscr{I}_{sol}$ from the clique C computed by function **FindMaxWeightClique** (the don't care variables in the truth assignments represented by the nodes in C are set to 0). Since function **FindMaxWeightClique** does not modify the truth assignments represented by the nodes in the graph received as input, $\mathscr{I}_{sol}$ does not violate confidentiality constraints iff the nodes in the fragmentation graph resulting from Step 2 represent truth assignments that do not violate confidentiality constraints. Each node in G either represents a truth assignment $I \in \mathscr{P}_{v_i}$ or a truth assignment resulting from the composition of a subset of one-paths in $\mathscr{P}_{v_1} \cup \ldots \cup \mathscr{P}_{v_k}$ under operator $\odot$. In the first case, I represents a one-path in the OBDD modeling Boolean formula $v \wedge \neg(c_1 \vee \ldots \vee c_m)$, $v \in \mathscr{V}$, and therefore it satisfies all the confidentiality constraints. In the second case, I represents in a compact way the complete truth assignments implicitly represented by the composed assignments. Since the assignments composed to generate I satisfy all the confidentiality constraints, also I satisfies all of them.

2. $\forall v \in \mathcal{V}$, $\exists I \in \mathcal{I}_{sol}$: $I(v) = 1$ (visibility). In Step 3, the algorithm checks if the clique C computed by function **FindMaxWeightClique** has weight at least $|\mathcal{V}| \cdot (|\mathcal{V}| - 1)$, which is equivalent to check if $\forall v \in \mathcal{V}$, $\exists n \in C$ such that $v \in n.V$ as proved by Property 3.2. If the weight of the clique C is greater than or equal to $|\mathcal{V}| \cdot (|\mathcal{V}| - 1)$, the algorithm computes a solution $\mathcal{I}_{sol}$ obtained by setting to 0 all the don't care variables in the truth assignments represented by the nodes in C. Therefore $\mathcal{I}_{sol}$ satisfies all the visibility constraints.

3. $\forall I_i, I_j \in \mathcal{I}_{sol}, i \neq j$, $\forall a \in \mathcal{B}$ s.t. $I_i(a) = 1$: $I_j(a) = 0$ (unlinkability). In the last **for each** loop of Step 3 (line 56), the algorithm extracts $\mathcal{I}_{sol}$ from the clique C computed by function **FindMaxWeightClique** by setting to 0 all the don't care variables in the truth assignments represented by the nodes in the clique. Since function **FindMaxWeightClique** does not modify the graph received as input, $\mathcal{I}_{sol}$ satisfies unlinkability iff C is a clique and G includes only edges connecting nodes representing unlinkable truth assignments. Since the **while** loop in Step 2 of the algorithm (line 30) removes all the edges in M connecting nodes representing mergeable truth assignments, the graph G given as input to the **FindMaxWeightClique** function includes only edges in D, which connect nodes representing disjoint truth assignments. Any pair of nodes in C is then connected by an edge in D (i.e., nodes in C represent unlinkable assignments).

Completeness Suppose by contradiction that there exists a correct set $\mathcal{I}$ of truth assignments and that our algorithm returns an empty solution. The algorithm returns an empty solution only if **FindMaxWeightClique** returns a clique for which at least one visibility constraint in $\mathcal{V}$ remains unsatisfied (line 54). Since function **FindMaxWeightClique** implements a known algorithm for the maximum weighted clique problem and according to Theorem 3.1, the function returns a clique that does not satisfy all the visibility constraints only if a clique representing a correct set of truth assignments does not exists in G. However, since we assume that $\mathcal{I}$ is a correct set of truth assignments, $\mathcal{I}$ has to be represented by a clique in G.

Suppose now by contradiction that $\mathcal{I}$ is not represented by a clique in G. Each $I \in \mathcal{I}$ satisfies all the confidentiality constraints and at least one visibility constraint (otherwise I could be removed from $\mathcal{I}$ preserving its correctness). Let $v_{i_1}, .., v_{i_k}, \in \mathcal{V}$ be the visibility constraints satisfied by I. By construction of the OBDDs $O_{i_1}, \dots, O_{i_k}$, $\mathcal{P}_{i_1}, \dots, \mathcal{P}_{i_k}$ must contain at least one one-path $I_{i_1}, \dots, I_{i_k}$ that implicitly represents I. Since, by Observation 3, truth assignments are mergeable only if they represent at least a common complete truth assignment, $I_{i_1}, \dots, I_{i_k}$ are mergeable (they all implicitly represent I). For each $I \in \mathcal{I}$ and for each subset $V \subseteq \{v_{i_1}, .., v_{i_k}\}$ of visibility constraints satisfied by I, the fragmentation graph computed by our algorithm will then include a node n implicitly representing I, with $n.V = V$. Since $\mathcal{I}$ is a correct set of truth assignments, there is at least a complete truth assignment $I \in \mathcal{I}$ that satisfies v for each $v \in \mathcal{V}$. Therefore, $\mathcal{V}$ can be partitioned in non-empty and non-overlapping subsets $V_i, i = 1, \dots, |\mathcal{I}|$, such that each $I_i \in \mathcal{I}$ is associated with V_i and V_i includes only visibility constraints satisfied by I_i. As a consequence, there exists a set N of nodes in G with a node n_i for each $I_i \in \mathcal{I}$ such that n_i implicitly represents I_i and n_i is associated with the set V_i of visibility constraints. For each pair $I_i,I_j \in \mathscr{I}$, I_i and I_j are neither mergeable nor in conflict. As a consequence, nodes n_i and n_j in N implicitly representing I_i and I_j, respectively, are not in conflict (i.e., they do not associate conflicting values to the same variable) and are then connected by an edge in D. Therefore, N is a clique for G that implicitly represents $\mathscr{I}$, thus contradicting the initial hypothesis.

Minimality Suppose by contradiction that the algorithm computes a correct set $\mathscr{I}$ of k truth assignments and that there exists a correct set $\mathscr{I}'$ of $k' < k$ truth assignments. We prove that, if $\mathscr{I}'$ exists, the set $\mathscr{I}$ of truth assignments computed by our algorithm includes k' truth assignments. In the last **for each** loop of Step 3 (line 56), the algorithm extracts $\mathscr{I}$ from the clique C of maximum weight in G computed by function **FindMaxWeightClique** by setting to 0 all the don't care variables in the truth assignments represented by the nodes in the clique. According to the anti-monotonicity of the weight function w with respect to the number of nodes (Property 3.1), C is the clique satisfying all the visibility constraints composed of the minimum number k of nodes. Since function **FindMaxWeightClique** implements a known algorithm for the maximum weighted clique problem, there cannot exist a clique C' of G satisfying all the visibility constraints and composed of $k' < k$ nodes. In other words, there cannot exist a correct set $\mathscr{I}'$ of $k' < k$ truth assignments, where for each $I \in \mathscr{I}'$ there exists a node n in G such that $n.I$ implicitly represents I. However, since we assume that $\mathscr{I}$ is a correct set of truth assignments, $\mathscr{I}'$ has to be represented by a clique in G.

Suppose now by contradiction that $\mathscr{I}'$ is not represented by a clique in G. Let I be a complete truth assignment in $\mathscr{I}'$. Since $\mathscr{I}'$ is correct, I satisfies all the confidentiality constraints. Moreover, I is associated with (and then satisfies) at least one visibility constraint, otherwise I could be removed from $\mathscr{I}'$ preserving its correctness, thus contradicting the hypothesis of minimality of $\mathscr{I}'$. Let $v_{i_1},\ldots,v_{i_k}, \in \mathscr{V}$ be the visibility constraints associated with I. By construction of the OBDDs $O_{i_1},\ldots,O_{i_k}, \mathscr{P}_{i_1},\ldots,\mathscr{P}_{i_k}$ must contain at least one one-path $I_{i_1},\ldots,I_{i_k}$ that implicitly represents I. Since, by Observation 3, truth assignments are mergeable only if they represent at least a common complete truth assignment, $I_{i_1},\ldots,I_{i_k}$ are mergeable (they all implicitly represent I). The truth assignment I' obtained as $I_{i_1} \odot \ldots \odot I_{i_k}$ implicitly represents I. As a consequence, the fragmentation graph computed by our algorithm will include a node n with $n.I = I'$ and $n.V = \{v_{i_1},\ldots,v_{i_k}\}$ that implicitly represents I. This is true for each complete truth assignment $I \in \mathscr{I}'$. Therefore, G includes a clique that implicitly represents $\mathscr{I}'$ and composed of k' nodes. As a consequence, the clique computed by our algorithm implicitly represents $\mathscr{I}'$. This contradicts the original hypothesis that our algorithm computes a set of truth assignments that is not minimal. $\square$

Theorem 3.3 (Complexity of the Exact Algorithm). *Given a set $\mathscr{B}$ of Boolean variables, a set $\mathscr{C}$ of confidentiality constraints over $\mathscr{B}$, and a set $\mathscr{V}$ of visibility constraints over $\mathscr{B}$, the complexity of the algorithm in Fig. 3.10 is $O(2^{\prod_{v \in \mathscr{V}} |\mathscr{P}_v| \cdot |\mathscr{B}|} + (|\mathscr{V}| + |\mathscr{C}|)2^{|\mathscr{B}|})$ in time, where $\mathscr{P}_v$ is the set of one-paths of the OBDD representing $v \wedge \neg(c_1 \vee \ldots \vee c_m)$.*

Proof. The construction of the OBDDs in Step 1 can be, in the worst case, exponential in the number of variables in the formula they represent, that is, $O(2^{|\mathcal{B}|})$. Therefore, the construction of the OBDDs representing the confidentiality constraints in $\mathcal{C}$, the visibility constraints in $\mathcal{V}$, and their combination has computational complexity $O((|\mathcal{V}|+|\mathcal{C}|)2^{|\mathcal{B}|})$. The construction of the fragmentation graph in Step 2 requires to compute the closure of the set $\mathcal{P}_{v_1} \cup \ldots \cup \mathcal{P}_{v_k}$ under operator $\odot$ since nodes in G represent, in the worst case, all the truth assignments in $\mathcal{P}^{\odot}$. To this purpose, the algorithm inserts edges in M and in D, connecting pairs of nodes representing mergeable or disjoint truth assignments, respectively, that are associated with non-overlapping sets of visibility constraints. The cost of inserting edges in G is then $O(\prod_{v\in\mathcal{V}}|\mathcal{P}_v| \cdot |\mathcal{B}|)$ since the cost of evaluating if two truth assignments are mergeable or disjoint is linear in the number of Boolean variables composing the truth assignments. Since for each edge in M the algorithm inserts a node in G, which can only be connected to the nodes adjacent to the incident nodes of the removed edge, the overall cost of building G is $O(\prod_{v\in\mathcal{V}}|\mathcal{P}_v| \cdot |\mathcal{B}|)$. Also, G includes at most $O(\prod_{v\in\mathcal{V}}|\mathcal{P}_v|)$ nodes. Function **FindMaxWeightClique** has exponential cost in the number of nodes of the input graph (i.e., $O(2^{\prod_{v\in\mathcal{V}}|\mathcal{P}_v|\cdot|\mathcal{B}|})$) since the maximum weighted clique problem is NP-hard. The last **for each** loop in Step 3 (line 56) has computational complexity $O(|C| \cdot |\mathcal{B}|)$, since it scans all the nodes in C to set to 0 the don't care variables in the truth assignments they represent. The cost of this loop is however dominated by the cost of the previous steps of the algorithm. The computational complexity of the algorithm is therefore $O(2^{\prod_{v\in\mathcal{V}}|\mathcal{P}_v|\cdot|\mathcal{B}|} + (|\mathcal{V}| + |\mathcal{C}|)2^{|\mathcal{B}|})$.   □

The computational cost of the algorithm is obtained as the sum of the cost of building the OBDDs, which is $O((|\mathcal{V}| + |\mathcal{C}|)2^{|\mathcal{B}|})$, and of the cost of determining $\mathcal{I}_{sol}$ by building the fragmentation graph and searching for its maximum weighted clique, which is $O(2^{\prod_{v\in\mathcal{V}}|\mathcal{P}_v|\cdot|\mathcal{B}|})$. We note that the computational cost of the construction of the OBDDs is exponential in the worst case, but in the majority of real-world applications OBDD-based approaches are computationally efficient [19, 68].

3.6   Computing a Locally Minimal Set of Truth Assignments

Since the problem of computing a minimal set of truth assignments is NP-hard, the computational complexity of any algorithm that finds a solution to the problem is exponential in the size of the input. In this section, we therefore propose a heuristic algorithm that computes a locally minimal set of truth assignments (Problem 3.4) with a limited computational effort. The algorithm exploits Theorem 3.1 to take advantage of the graph modeling of the problem but does not explicitly create the fragmentation graph. The idea consists in using the relationships between the one-paths extracted from the OBDDs representing confidentiality and visibility constraints to iteratively build a clique. The algorithm does not compute the closure of the one-paths in $\mathcal{P}_{v_1} \cup \ldots \cup \mathcal{P}_{v_k}$ under operator $\odot$, but composes them when necessary. It then starts from an empty clique C and, at each iteration, tries to insert in C a node n (possibly composing it with nodes in C) that is associated with a visibility constraint that is not associated with any node already in C. The algorithm terminates when it finds a clique C of weight at least $|\mathcal{V}| \cdot (|\mathcal{V}| - 1)$.

Figure 3.12 illustrates the pseudocode of the algorithm that takes as input a set $\mathcal{B} = \{a_1, \ldots, a_n\}$ of Boolean variables (representing the attributes in R), a set $\mathcal{C} = \{c_1, \ldots, c_m\}$ of confidentiality constraints, and a set $\mathcal{V} = \{v_1, \ldots, v_k\}$ of visibility constraints and computes, if it exists, a locally minimal set of truth assignments. The algorithm executes four steps: (1) it extracts the set of one-paths from the OBDDs representing Boolean formulas $v_i \wedge \neg(c_1 \vee \ldots \vee c_m)$, $i = 1, \ldots, k$; (2) it creates a node for each of these one-paths; (3) it iteratively builds a clique of the fragmentation graph; (4) it combines the one-paths represented by the nodes in the clique, if this combination does not violate confidentiality constraints, to minimize the number of assignments in the computed set. In the following, we describe these steps more in details.

Step 1: Compute One-Paths Like for the exact algorithm (Sect. 3.5, step 1), for each $v_i \in \mathcal{V}$ the algorithm extracts from the OBDD O_i representing Boolean formula $v_i \wedge \neg(c_1 \vee \ldots \vee c_m)$ the set $\mathcal{P}_{v_i}$ of one-paths (lines 2–4). If, for a given O_i, the set $\mathcal{P}_{v_i}$ is empty, the algorithm terminates and returns an empty solution (line 5).

Step 2: Generate Nodes Representing One-Paths The algorithm inserts a node $n = \langle I, \{v\} \rangle$ in graph G for each one-path $I \in \mathcal{P}_{v_1} \cup \ldots \cup \mathcal{P}_{v_k}$. Unlike the exact algorithm, it does not explicitly insert the edges in G connecting pairs of nodes that represent mergeable and disjoint truth assignments. In contrast, it implicitly considers these relationships in the building process of a clique. The algorithm then partitions nodes in G according to the visibility constraint associated with them, and orders the obtained sets of nodes N_i, $i = 1, \ldots, |\mathcal{V}|$, by increasing cardinality (lines 10–13). The reason for this ordering is to consider first the visibility constraints that can be satisfied by a smaller set of truth assignments (represented by a smaller set of nodes in the graph). Nodes in N_i, $i = 1, \ldots, |\mathcal{V}|$, are ordered by decreasing number of don't care variables in the truth assignments they represent (lines 14–15). The intuition is that nodes representing truth assignments with a higher number of don't care variables implicitly represent a larger set of complete truth assignments (where don't care variables can be set to either 0 or 1) and therefore they impose less constraints on subsequent choices of the nodes that can be inserted in a clique with them. Indeed, as already noted in Sect. 3.3.3, don't care variables do not affect the linkability or the mergeability of truth assignments.

Step 3: Build a Clique for the Fragmentation Graph The algorithm iteratively builds a clique by calling recursive function **DefineClique** (line 17). Function **DefineClique** receives as input a clique C of the fragmentation graph and an integer number i, $1 \le i \le k$, indicating that C either includes a node in N_j, $j = 1, \ldots, (i - 1)$, or a node resulting from the combination of a node in N_j with another node in N_l, with $l < j$ (i.e., C includes a node n such that $v \in n.V$,

---

INPUT: $\mathscr{B} = \{a_1,\ldots,a_n\}$, $\mathscr{C} = \{c_1,\ldots,c_m\}$, $\mathscr{V} = \{v_1,\ldots,v_k\}$ /* variables and constraints */
OUTPUT: $\mathscr{I}_{sol} = \{I_1,\ldots,I_l\}$ /* locally minimal set of truth assignments */

MAIN

1: /* **Step 1:** extract the one-paths from the OBDDs representing constraints */
2: **for each** $v_i \in \mathscr{V}$ **do**
3:     let O_i be the OBDD representing $v_i \wedge \neg(c_1 \vee \ldots \vee c_m)$
4:     let $\mathscr{P}_{v_i}$ be the set of one-paths of O_i
5:     **if** $\mathscr{P}_{v_i} = \emptyset$ **then return**($\emptyset$) /* no solution exists */
6: /* **Step 2:** generate nodes representing the one-paths in O_i, $i = 1,\ldots,k$ */
7: $N := \emptyset$
8: **for each** $v \in \mathscr{V}$ **do** /* define a node for each one-path */
9:     **for each** $I \in \mathscr{P}_v$ **do**
10:         $n := \langle I,\{v\}\rangle$
11:         $N := N \cup \{n\}$
12: /* partition N depending on the visibility constraint that each node satisfies */
13: let $N_i = \{n \in N : n.V = v\}$, for all $v \in \mathscr{V}$, with $|N_i| > |N_j|$ iff $i > j$
14: **for each** $v \in \mathscr{V}$ **do**
15:     order nodes in N_i by decreasing number of don't care variables in $n.I$
16: /* **Step 3:** build a clique for the fragmentation graph */
17: $C := \textbf{DefineClique}(\emptyset,1)$
18: /* **Step 4:** minimize the number of truth assignments in $\mathscr{I}_{sol}$ */
19: $\mathscr{I}_{sol} := \emptyset$
20: **for each** $n \in C$ **do** assign 0 to don't care variables in $n.I$
21: **while** $C \neq \emptyset$ **do**
22:     $n_i := \textbf{ExtractNode}(C)$
23:     $I_i := n_i.I$
24:     **for each** $n_j \in C$ **do**
25:         $I_j := n_j.I$
26:         **if** $I_i \vee I_j$ satisfies $\neg(c_1 \vee \ldots \vee c_m)$ **then**
27:             $I_i := I_i \vee I_j$
28:             $C := C - \{n_j\}$
29:     $\mathscr{I}_{sol} := \mathscr{I}_{sol} \cup \{I_i\}$
30: **return**($\mathscr{I}_{sol}$)

DEFINE_CLIQUE(C,i)

31: **for** $j := 1,\ldots,|N_i|$ **do**
32:     $satisfied := \text{TRUE}$ /* true if C includes a node that belongs to N_i */
33:     $LinkableNodes := \{n \in C : n.I \leftrightarrow n_j.I\}$ /* nodes in C representing truth assignments linkable to $n_j.I$ */
34:     $C' := C \setminus LinkableNodes$ /* remove from C the nodes that represent truth assignments linkable to $n_j.I$ */
35:     $n := n_j$
36:     **while** $satisfied$ AND $LinkableNodes \neq \emptyset$ **do**
37:         $n_l := \textbf{ExtractNode}(LinkableNodes)$ /* extract a node representing a truth assignment linkable to $n_j.I$ */
38:         **if** $n_l.I \rightleftharpoons n.I$ **then** $n := \langle n_l.I \odot n.I, n_l.V \cup n.V \rangle$ /* merge the two nodes */
39:         **else** $satisfied := \text{FALSE}$ /* $n.I$ is linkable but not mergeable with $n_l.I$, then $C' \cup \{n\}$ cannot be a clique */
40:     **if** $satisfied$ **then**
41:         $C' := C' \cup \{n\}$
42:         **if** $i = |\mathscr{V}|$ **then return**(C') /* C' represents a clique with weight at least $|\mathscr{V}| \cdot (|\mathscr{V}| - 1)$ */
43:         $C' := \textbf{DefineClique}(C',i+1)$ /* recursive call */
44:         **if** $C' \neq \emptyset$ **then return**(C') /* C' represents a clique with weight at least $|\mathscr{V}| \cdot (|\mathscr{V}| - 1)$ */
45: **return**($\emptyset$)

Fig. 3.12 Algorithm that computes a locally minimal set of truth assignments

for each visibility constraint v associated with the nodes in $N_1, \ldots, N_j$). For each node n_j in N_i, function **DefineClique** verifies whether n_j can be inserted in C, that is, if: (1) for each node n in C, $n.I$ and $n_j.I$ are disjoint; or (2) $n_j.I$ is mergeable with a subset of the truth assignments represented by the nodes in C and the resulting truth assignment is disjoint from all the other truth assignments represented by nodes in C. To efficiently check if n_j satisfies one of the conditions above, the function first identifies the set *LinkableNodes* of nodes in C representing truth assignments linkable with $n_j.I$ (line 33). For each n_l in *LinkableNodes*, if $n_l.I$ is mergeable with $n.I$ (with n initialized to n_j), $n.I$ is set to $n.I \odot n_l.I$, and $n.V$ is set to $n.V \cup n_l.V$ (lines 37–39). If $n_l.I$ is linkable but not mergeable with $n.I$, n cannot be part of clique C since $n_l.I$ and $n.I$ are not disjoint (line 39). We note that nodes in C representing truth assignments that are mergeable and disjoint to $n_j.I$ are not combined in a unique node. In fact, by composing a pair of disjoint truth assignments, the algorithm would discard, without evaluation, all the correct solutions where the two truth assignments are represented by distinct nodes. If all the nodes in *LinkableNodes* can be combined with n_j (i.e., the one-paths they represent are all mergeable), the algorithm then determines a new clique C' obtained by removing *LinkableNodes* from C and inserting n in C' (lines 40–41). If $i = |\mathcal{V}|$, C' satisfies all the visibility constraints, has a weight at least equal to $|\mathcal{V}| \cdot (|\mathcal{V}| - 1)$, and is returned (line 42). Otherwise, function **DefineClique** is recursively called with C' and $i + 1$ as input (line 43). If the clique resulting from this recursive call is not empty, it represents a correct set of truth assignments and is therefore returned (line 44). If no node in N_i can be inserted in C, an empty clique is returned and the algorithm looks for a different clique of the fragmentation graph.

Step 4: Minimize the Number of Assignments The clique C computed by function **DefineClique** may represent a correct set of truth assignments that is not locally minimal. In fact, it may include one-paths that can be combined without violating confidentiality constraints. Every pair of nodes in C is then checked and their truth assignments are ORed whenever they can be combined without violating confidentiality constraints (i.e., the algorithm performs the union of the corresponding fragments). To this purpose, the algorithm first assigns value 0 to don't care variables in the truth assignments represented by the nodes in C (line 20). Then, it iteratively extracts a node n_i from C, assigns $n_i.I$ to I_i and, for each n_j in C, it checks if I_i can be composed with one-path I_j, with $I_j = n_j.I$ without violating confidentiality constraints (lines 21–28). If this is the case, I_i is set to $I_i \vee I_j$, and n_j is removed from C. When the algorithm has checked if I_i can be combined with all the one-paths represented by nodes in C, it inserts I_i in $\mathcal{I}_{sol}$ (line 29). It is important to note that the algorithm does not check if I_i can be combined with the truth assignments already in $\mathcal{I}_{sol}$. In fact, all the truth assignments in $\mathcal{I}_{sol}$ have already been checked against all the assignments in C, and therefore also against I_i. Finally, the algorithm returns $\mathcal{I}_{sol}$ (line 30).

Example 3.2. Consider relation PATIENTS and the confidentiality and visibility constraints over it in Fig. 3.1. The execution of the algorithm in Fig. 3.12 proceeds as follows.

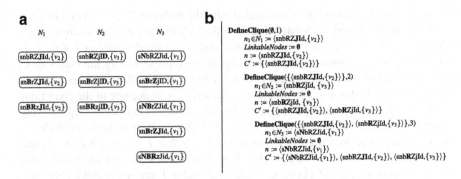

Fig. 3.13 Example of the execution of the algorithm in Fig. 3.12 with the inputs in Fig. 3.3

1) *Compute one-paths.* The algorithm first builds O_1, O_2, and O_3 in Fig. 3.7, representing $v_i \wedge \neg(c_1 \vee \dots \vee c_5)$, $i = 1, 2, 3$, and extracts their one-paths, which are listed in Fig. 3.7.

2) *Generate nodes representing one-paths.* The algorithm creates a node for each one-path in $\mathscr{P}_{v_1}$, $\mathscr{P}_{v_2}$, and $\mathscr{P}_{v_3}$, obtaining the set N of nodes illustrated in Fig. 3.13a. The algorithm partitions N in three sets N_1, N_2, and N_3 depending on the visibility constraint associated with each node in N, and orders these sets by increasing cardinality (i.e., $|N_1| \leq |N_2| \leq |N_3|$). N_1 includes the nodes associated with v_2, N_2 includes the nodes associated with v_3, and N_3 includes the nodes associated with v_1. The nodes in N_1, N_2, and N_3 are then ordered by decreasing number of don't care variables, as illustrated in Fig. 3.13a.

3–4) *Build a clique for the fragmentation graph and minimize the number of assignments.* Figure 3.13b illustrates the recursive calls to function **DefineClique** showing for each execution: the value of input parameters C and i; the candidate node n_j in N_i to insert in C; its relationships with nodes already in C; and the computed clique C'. The clique finally returned by the function includes three nodes: $C = \{\langle \text{sNbRZJid}, \{v_1\}\rangle, \langle \text{snbRZJId}, \{v_2\}\rangle, \langle \text{snbRZjId}, \{v_3\}\rangle\}$, which cannot be further combined without violating confidentiality constraints. The corresponding set of truth assignments is $\mathscr{I}_{sol} = \{[\text{S}=0, \text{N}=1, \text{B}=0, \text{R}=0, \text{z}=0, \text{J}=0, \text{I}=0, \text{D}=0], [\text{S}=0, \text{N}=0, \text{B}=0, \text{R}=0, \text{z}=0, \text{J}=1, \text{I}=1, \text{D}=0], [\text{S}=0, \text{N}=0, \text{B}=0, \text{R}=1, \text{z}=0, \text{J}=0, \text{I}=0, \text{D}=1]\}$, which corresponds to locally minimal fragmentation $\mathscr{F} = \{\{\text{Name}\}, \{\text{Job}, \text{InsRate}\}, \{\text{Race}, \text{Disease}\}\}$. We note that this fragmentation is not minimal, since there exists at least a correct fragmentation composed of two fragments (Example 3.1).

The correctness and complexity of the algorithm in Fig. 3.12 are stated by the following theorems.

Theorem 3.4 (Correctness of the Heuristic Algorithm). *Given a set $\mathscr{B}$ of Boolean variables, a set $\mathscr{C}$ of confidentiality constraints over $\mathscr{B}$, and a set $\mathscr{V}$*

of visibility constraints over $\mathcal{B}$, the algorithm in Fig. 3.12 terminates and computes (if it exists) a locally minimal set of truth assignments.

Proof. To prove the correctness of the algorithm in Fig. 3.12, we need to prove that: (1) it terminates; (2) it computes a correct set of truth assignments; (3) if there exists a correct set $\mathcal{I}$ of truth assignments with respect to $\mathcal{C}$ and $\mathcal{V}$, the algorithm finds it; and (4) it computes a locally minimal set of truth assignments.

Termination Since the number of confidentiality constraints, the number of visibility constraints, and the number of one-paths in $\mathcal{P}_v$, with $v \in \mathcal{V}$, is finite, the three **for each** loops in Step 1 (line 2) and in Step 2 (line 8 and line 14, respectively) terminate. The recursive call to function **DefineClique** in Step 3 (line17) terminates when variable i is greater than or equal to $|\mathcal{V}|$. We note that at each recursive call of function **DefineClique**, at most one node is inserted in C. Therefore, if function **DefineClique** terminates, C is a finite set. Function **DefineClique** terminates because: (1) the sets N_i, $i = 1, \ldots, |\mathcal{V}|$, of nodes are finite ($\forall v_i \in \mathcal{V}$, $\mathcal{P}_{v_i}$ is a finite set of one-paths); (2) *LinkableNodes* is a subset of $\mathcal{I}_{sol}$; and (3) variable i increases by one at each recursive call. The **for** loop and the **while** loop in function **DefineClique** (line 31 and line 36, respectively) terminate since the clique C received as input includes at most i nodes and is therefore finite.

Correctness of the Set of Truth Assignments $\mathcal{I}_{sol}$ is correct iff it satisfies the conditions in Definition 3.7.

1. $\forall c \in \mathcal{C}$, $\forall I \in \mathcal{I}_{sol}$: $I(c) = 0$ (confidentiality). The **while** loop in Step 4 (line 21) computes $\mathcal{I}_{sol}$ (starting from the one-paths represented by nodes in C) by trying to compose sets of truth assignments represented by nodes in C through $\vee$ operator and explicitly checking if the result of the composition violates confidentiality constraints. Since truth assignments are composed only if their composition does not violate the confidentiality constraints, $\mathcal{I}_{sol}$ satisfies all the confidentiality constraints iff the truth assignments represented by nodes in the clique C computed by function **DefineClique** do not violate the confidentiality constraints. Function **DefineClique** inserts a node n in C if n either belongs to N_i (i.e., it represents a one-path in $\mathcal{P}_{v_k}$) or has been obtained by composing a set of nodes in $N_1, \ldots, N_k$ (i.e., it represents the composition of a subset of one-paths in $\mathcal{P}_{v_x}, \ldots, \mathcal{P}_{v_y}$ under operator $\odot$). Since $\mathcal{P}_v$ represents the one-paths in the OBDD modeling Boolean formula $v \wedge \neg(c_1 \vee \ldots \vee c_m)$, $v \in \mathcal{V}$, all the truth assignments in $\mathcal{P}_v$ satisfy confidentiality constraints. Also, since the truth assignment resulting from the composition of I_i and I_j under $\odot$ represents, in a compact way, the set of complete truth assignments implicitly represented by both I_i and I_j, also $I_i \odot I_j$ does not violate confidentiality constraints. As a consequence, each node $n \in C$ represents a truth assignment that satisfies all the confidentiality constraints.
2. $\forall v \in \mathcal{V}$, $\exists I \in \mathcal{I}_{sol}$: $I(v) = 1$ (visibility). Recalling that in Step 4 all the don't care variables in truth assignments represented by nodes in C are set to 0 (line 20), and that the algorithm computes $\mathcal{I}_{sol}$ by trying to compose the truth assignments represented by nodes in C without violating confidentiality constraints (**for each** loop in line 24), $\mathcal{I}_{sol}$ satisfies the visibility constraints if,

at the end of function **DefineClique**, $\forall v \in \mathcal{V}$, $\exists\, n \in C$ such that $v \in n.V$. Function **DefineClique** is recursively called for $i = 1, \ldots, |\mathcal{V}|$ and, at each recursive call, it inserts in C a node $n_j \in N_i$ that represents a truth assignment I in $\mathcal{P}_v$. In fact, node n_j is either inserted as a new node in C, or composed with a node n already in C. As already noted, the node resulting from the composition of n_j with n is associated with (and then satisfies) both the visibility constraints in $n.V$ and in $n_j.V$. Therefore, at the end of the i-th recursive call, C is associated with (and then satisfies) all the visibility constraints v such that $v \in n.V$ and n is a node in N_j, with $j \leq i$. We can conclude that, at the end of the $|\mathcal{V}|$-th recursive call, C includes, for each $v \in \mathcal{V}$, at least a node n with $v \in n.V$.

3. $\forall I_i, I_j \in \mathcal{I}_{sol}, i \neq j, \forall a \in \mathcal{B}$ s.t. $I_i(a) = 1$: $I_j(a) = 0$ (unlinkability). Since Step 4 sets to 0 all the don't care variables in the truth assignments represented by nodes in C, $\mathcal{I}_{sol}$ satisfies unlinkability iff the truth assignments represented by the nodes in C computed by function **DefineClique** are disjoint. Function **DefineClique** tries to insert, at each iteration of the **for** loop (line 31), a node n_j in C. The function does not insert $n_j \in N_i$ in C if there exists at least a node in C that represents a truth assignment *linkable but not mergeable* with $n_j.I$, and composes $n_j.I$ with all the linkable and mergeable truth assignments represented by a node already in C. All nodes in C therefore represent disjoint truth assignments.

Completeness Completeness is guaranteed if recursive function **DefineClique** computes, if it exists, a clique C of the fragmentation graph that satisfies all the visibility constraints in $\mathcal{V}$. Function **DefineClique** is recursively called for $i = 1, \ldots, |\mathcal{V}|$ and, at each recursive call, it inserts in C a node n_j in N_i, which represents a truth assignment in $\mathcal{P}_v$ (i.e., a truth assignment associated with and then satisfying visibility constraint v). If there is no clique in G including C together with a node in N_i, the function uses a back-track strategy and tries to insert in C a different node from N_{i-1}. Note that two nodes are combined (operator $\odot$) by function **DefineClique** iff they represent linkable truth assignments (i.e., they represent fragments with a common attribute). Indeed, a correct set of truth assignments cannot contain two linkable truth assignments (Condition 3 in Definition 3.7). Therefore, the composition performed in this phase is mandatory for finding a correct set of truth assignments. Nodes representing non linkable but mergeable truth assignments are not combined in this phase (they will be combined by Step 4 to guarantee local minimality). Recursive function **DefineClique** tries all the possible subsets of nodes in G including a node for each set $N_i, i = 1, \ldots, k$, using the back-track strategy. Thus, if there exist a clique for G, it will be found by the recursive call.

Local Minimality $\mathcal{I}_{sol}$ is locally minimal iff no pair of truth assignments in $\mathcal{I}_{sol}$ can be composed through the $\vee$ operator without violating confidentiality constraints. $\mathcal{I}_{sol}$ is computed by the **while** loop in Step 4 (line 21), where the algorithm tries to iteratively combine ($\vee$) the truth assignments represented by nodes in C, after all don't care variables have been set to 0. Such a combination is performed only if the disjunction of the confidentiality constraints is not violated.

As a consequence, no pair of truth assignments in $\mathscr{I}_{sol}$ are combined through the $\vee$ operator without violating the confidentiality constraints. $\qquad\square$

Theorem 3.5 (Complexity of the Heuristic Algorithm). *Given a set $\mathscr{B}$ of Boolean variables, a set $\mathscr{C}$ of confidentiality constraints over $\mathscr{B}$, and a set $\mathscr{V}$ of visibility constraints over $\mathscr{B}$, the complexity of the algorithm in Fig. 3.12 is $O(\prod_{v\in\mathscr{V}}|\mathscr{P}_v|\cdot|\mathscr{B}| + (|\mathscr{V}| + |\mathscr{C}|)2^{|\mathscr{B}|})$ in time, where $\mathscr{P}_v$ is the set of one-paths of the OBDD representing $v\wedge\neg(c_1\vee\ldots\vee c_m)$.*

Proof. The construction of the OBDDs in Step 1 can be, in the worst case, exponential in the number of variables in the formula they represent, that is, $O(2^{|\mathscr{B}|})$. Therefore, the construction of the OBDDs representing the confidentiality constraints in $\mathscr{C}$ and the visibility constraints in $\mathscr{V}$, and their combination have computational complexity $O((|\mathscr{V}| + |\mathscr{C}|)2^{|\mathscr{B}|})$. The cost of building a node n for each one-path in $\mathscr{P}_{v_1}\cup\ldots\cup\mathscr{P}_{v_k}$ is linear in the number of one-paths. The cost of partitioning the resulting set of nodes in sets of nodes that are associated with the same visibility constraint and of ordering these sets by their cardinality is $O(\sum_{v\in\mathscr{V}}|\mathscr{P}_v| + |\mathscr{V}|\log|\mathscr{V}|)$. The cost of further ordering the nodes in each set N_i by decreasing number of don't care variables in the one-path they represent is $O(\sum_{v\in\mathscr{V}}(|\mathscr{B}||\mathscr{P}_v| + |\mathscr{P}_v|\log|\mathscr{P}_v|))$, since each set N_i includes $|\mathscr{P}_v|$ nodes (one for each one-path) and each one-path in $\mathscr{P}_v$ has $|\mathscr{B}|$ variables. The overall cost of Step 2 is then $O(|\mathscr{V}|\log|\mathscr{V}| + |\mathscr{P}_v|\sum_{v\in\mathscr{V}}(1 + |\mathscr{B}| + \log|\mathscr{P}_v|))$. Recursive function **DefineClique** is invoked by the algorithm in Fig. 3.12 at most $\prod_{v\in\mathscr{V}}|\mathscr{P}_v|$ times, since it needs to evaluate any possible combination of nodes (truth assignments), including a node from each N_i (a truth assignment from each $\mathscr{P}_v$, $v\in\mathscr{V}$). The comparison between two truth assignments $n_i.I$ and $n_j.I$ represented by two nodes in G has computational complexity $O(|\mathscr{B}|)$, since each Boolean variable in $\mathscr{B}$ must be checked. In the worst case, each node in N_i (truth assignment in $\mathscr{P}_v$) is compared with all the nodes in N_j (truth assignments in all the other sets of one-paths), $i \neq j$. The first **for each** loop in Step 4 has computational complexity $O(|C|\cdot|\mathscr{B}|)$, since it scans all the truth assignments represented by nodes in C to set to 0 all the don't care variables. The **while** loop in Step 4 has instead computational complexity $O(|C|^2\cdot|\mathscr{B}|)$, since it compares each pair of truth assignments represented by nodes in C. The computational complexity of the algorithm is therefore $O(\prod_{v\in\mathscr{V}}|\mathscr{P}_v|\cdot|\mathscr{B}| + (|\mathscr{V}| + |\mathscr{C}|)2^{|\mathscr{B}|})$, since the costs of Step 2 and of Step 4 are dominated by the costs of Step 1 and of Step 3. $\qquad\square$

We note that the computational cost of the algorithm includes, like the exact algorithm, the (exponential) cost of building the OBDDs. Indeed, both the algorithms first transform the input of the fragmentation problem into a set of one-paths, which represents the input to the problem of computing a (maximum weighted) clique of the fragmentation graph. The advantage of our heuristic over the exact algorithm illustrated in Sect. 3.5 is related to the search of the clique, which is exponential in the number of one-paths in the exact approach, and polynomial in the number of one-paths in the heuristic approach.

3.7 Experimental Results

The exact and heuristic algorithms presented in Sects. 3.5 and 3.6, respectively, have been implemented as C programs to experimentally assess their behavior in terms of execution time and quality of the solution. To efficiently manage OBDDs we used the CUDD libraries [99], and to compute the maximum weighted clique of our fragmentation graph we used the implementation of the algorithm described in [87]. The experiments have been carried out on a laptop equipped with Intel 2 Duo 2GHz processor, 4 GB RAM, running Windows 7, 32 bit version.

As formally proved by Theorems 3.3 and 3.5, the computational complexity of both the exact and heuristic algorithms depends on the number of one-paths extracted from the OBDDs representing the constraints. As a consequence, we compared the execution time and the quality of the solution computed by the two algorithms varying the number of one-paths in the range between 10 and 30,000. The configurations considered in our experiments have been obtained starting from a relation schema composed of a number of attributes varying from 10 to 40. For each configuration, we randomly generated sets of confidentiality and visibility constraints. The number of confidentiality and visibility constraints varies from 5 to 25 and from 2 to 10, respectively. Each confidentiality and visibility constraint includes a number of attributes that varies from 2 to 8 and from 2 to 4, respectively. In line with real world scenarios, constraints include a limited number of attributes. Also, the number of visibility constraints is lower than the number of confidentiality constraints, since this choice reflects most real world scenarios, where the need for privacy imposes more constraints than the need for data release.

Our experimental results evaluate three aspects: (1) the number of one-paths extracted from the OBDDs representing the constraints; (2) the execution time of the exact and heuristic algorithms; and (3) the quality of the solution, in terms of number of fragments, computed by the exact and the heuristic algorithms.

Number of One-Paths One of the main advantages of OBDDs is that the number of their one-paths is not related to the complexity of the Boolean formulas they represent. Complex Boolean formulas expressed on a high number of variables may therefore be characterized by an extremely low number of one-paths. We then experimentally measure the number of one-paths of configurations with a growing number of attributes and of confidentiality and visibility constraints. Figure 3.14 illustrates the number of one-paths characterizing configurations with a number of attributes varying from 10 to 40 (the scale of the y-axis is logarithmic). The results illustrated in the graph have been computed as the average of the number of one-paths obtained with 30 simulations for each configuration, where the number of constraints in each configuration varies as explained above. Note that the overall number of simulations is more than 30 since we discarded the best and worst cases, and those configurations characterized by visibility constraints that are in contrast with confidentiality constraints (i.e., configurations that do not admit a solution). As expected, the average number of one-paths grows more than linearly with the number of attributes. It is however interesting to note that the number of one-paths

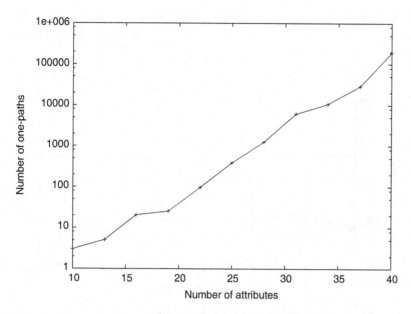

Fig. 3.14 Average number of one-paths varying the number of attributes

remains considerably lower than $2^{|\mathscr{B}|}$ in all the considered configurations. This is consistent with real world scenarios, where confidentiality constraints (visibility constraints, respectively) involve a limited number of attributes.

Execution Time As expected from the analysis of the computational complexity of our algorithms (see Theorems 3.3 and 3.5), the heuristic algorithm outperforms the exact algorithm. Indeed, consistently with the fact that the minimal fragmentation problem is NP-hard, the exact approach requires exponential time in the number of one-paths, that is, of nodes in the fragmentation graph, which is even higher than the number of one-paths extracted from OBDDs. We run the exact algorithm only for configurations with at most 1,000 one-paths, since this configuration is characterized by a fragmentation graph including more than 6,000 nodes and more than 190,000 edges. To further confirm the exponential growth of the computational time required by the exact algorithm, we compute the fragmentation graph also for larger configurations (up to 5,000 one-paths, for which the computation of the fragmentation graph takes more than 806.99 s). Figure 3.15 compares the execution time of our heuristic and exact algorithms (for configurations with up to 1,000 one-paths), varying the number of one-paths represented by the OBDDs (the scale of both the x-axis and the y-axis is logarithmic). The figure also reports the time required for computing the fragmentation graph for configurations including between 1,000 and 5,000 one-paths, and the execution time of the heuristic algorithm for configurations including between 5,000 and 30,000 one-paths, highlighting the benefit of the heuristic approach that does not explicitly build the fragmentation graph.

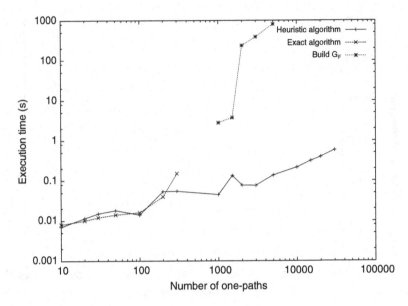

Fig. 3.15 Execution time of the exact and heuristic algorithms

To better understand the impact of building the OBDDs modeling the constraints and extracting their one-paths, we measure the execution time required by this step, which is common to the exact and heuristic algorithms. It is interesting to note that the impact of this step on the overall execution time of both our algorithms is negligible. In fact, it remains under 454 milliseconds in all the considered configurations.

Quality of the Solution Figure 3.16 reports the comparison between the number of fragments obtained by the execution of the exact and the heuristic algorithms (the scale of the x-axis is logarithmic). The comparison shows that, in the majority of the configurations where the comparison was possible (i.e., for configurations with less than 1,000 one-paths), our heuristic algorithm computes a locally minimal fragmentation that is also minimal since the fragmentations computed by the two algorithms have the same number of fragments. Figure 3.16 reports the number of fragments in the locally minimal fragmentations computed by the heuristic algorithm also for configurations with a number of one-paths between 1,000 and 5,000. It is interesting to note that also for these configurations, characterized by a considerable number of attributes and of confidentiality and visibility constraints, the number of fragments in the locally minimal fragmentation remains limited (in our experiments, it varies between 1 and 3 fragments). We can then conclude that our heuristic algorithm is efficient, computes a solution close to optimum, and can therefore be conveniently adopted in many scenarios.

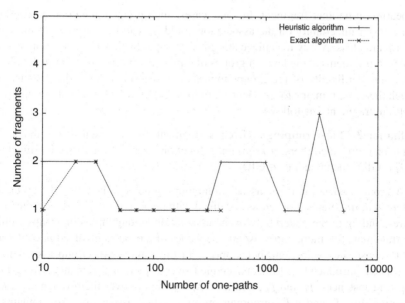

Fig. 3.16 Number of fragments of the solution computed by the exact and heuristic algorithms

3.8 Enhancing Fragmentation with Privacy-Preserving Associations

In the following sections we will discuss how minimal a fragmentation, possibly computed with the algorithms we have proposed so far, can be complemented with *loose associations* to enrich the utility of the released fragments. Loose associations have been proposed in [38] for fragmentations composed of a single pair of fragments only. In the remainder of the chapter, we first illustrate how the publication of multiple loose associations between pairs of fragments of a generic fragmentation can potentially expose sensitive associations, and then describe an approach for supporting the more general case of publishing a loose association among an arbitrary set $\{F_1, \dots, F_n\}$ of fragments.

3.8.1 Rationale

Fragmentation completely breaks the associations among attributes appearing in different fragments. In fact, since attributes are assumed to be independent,[1] any tuple appearing in a fragment could have, as its corresponding part, any other tuple

---

[1]We maintain such an assumption of the original proposal to avoid complicating the treatment with aspects not related to loose associations. Dependencies among attributes can be taken into

appearing in another fragment. In some cases, such protection can be an overkill and a lower uncertainty on the association could instead be preferred, to mitigate information loss. A way to achieve this consists in publishing an association among tuples in fragments at the level of groups of tuples (in contrast to individual tuples), where the cardinality of the groups impacts the uncertainty over the association, which therefore remains *loose*. Hence, group associations are based on grouping of tuples in fragments, as follows.

Definition 3.12 (k-Grouping). Given a fragment F_i, its instance f_i, and a set GID_i of group identifiers, a *k-grouping* function over f_i is a surjective function $\mathcal{G}_i{:}f_i \rightarrow \mathsf{GID}_i$ such that $\forall g_i \in \mathsf{GID}_i :\mid \mathcal{G}_i^{-1}(g_i) \mid \geq k$.

A group association is the association among groups, induced by the grouping enforced in fragments. Looseness is defined with respect to a degree k of protection corresponding to the uncertainty of the association among tuples in groups within the fragments (or, more correctly, among values of attributes involved in confidentiality constraints whose attributes appear in the fragments). Group associations have been introduced in [38] and defined over a pair of fragments. Given two fragment instances, f_l and f_m, and a (k_l,k_m)-grouping over them (meaning a k_l-grouping over f_l and a k_m-grouping over f_m) group association A_{lm} contains a pair $(\mathcal{G}_l(t[F_l]),\mathcal{G}_m(t[F_m]))$, for each tuple $t \in r$. For instance, consider Fig. 3.17c, illustrating a fragmentation composed of two fragments of the relation in Fig. 3.17a satisfying the constraints in Fig. 3.17b. Figure 3.18a illustrates a (2,2)-grouping over fragments f_l and f_m in Fig. 3.17c, and the induced group association over them. The group association, graphically represented by the edges among the rectangles corresponding to groups of tuples in Fig. 3.18a, is released as a table containing the pairs of group identifiers in A_{lm} and by complementing fragments with a column reporting the identifier of the group to which each tuple belongs (Fig. 3.18b). In the following, for simplicity, given a tuple t in the original relation, we denote with l (m, respectively) tuple $t[F_l]$ ($t[F_m]$, respectively) in fragment f_l (f_m, respectively).

The degree of looseness guaranteed by a group association depends not only on the uncertainty given by the cardinality of the groups, but also on the uncertainty given by the association among attribute values for those attributes appearing together in a confidentiality constraint c that is covered by the fragments (i.e., $c \subseteq F_l \cup F_m$). For instance, a looseness of $k = 4$ for the association in Fig. 3.18 ensures that for each value of $t[F_l \cap c]$ there are at least $k = 4$ different values for $t[F_m \cap c]$, for each confidentiality constraint c covered by F_l and F_m. If well defined (i.e., the groupings satisfy the properties given in [38]), a (k_l,k_m)-grouping ensures the association among the fragments to be k-loose with $k = k_l \cdot k_m$, where k is the degree of protection granted to the sensitive associations.

Note that the release of a group association between F_l and F_m may only put at risk constraints whose attributes are all contained in the fragments (i.e., all

consideration by extending the requirement of unlinkability among fragments to include the consideration of such dependencies (for more details, see [43]).

a   MEDICALDATA

	Name	YoB	Edu	ZIP	Job	MarStatus	Disease	Race	InsCompany	Salary	InsAmount
t_1	Alice	1974	B.Sc	90015	Assistant	Married	Flu	Black	BestCompany	1000	150
t_2	Bob	1965	MBA	90038	Manager	Widow	Diabetis	White	BestCompany	5000	70
t_3	Carol	1976	Ph.D	90001	Manager	Married	Calculi	Black	MyCompany	2000	100
t_4	David	1972	M.Sc	90087	Doctor	Divorced	Asthma	Asian	HerCompany	4000	150
t_5	Greg	1975	M.Sc	90025	Doctor	Single	Flu	Indian	MyCompany	1000	70
t_6	Hal	1970	Th.D	90007	Clerk	Single	Calculi	Indian	BestCompany	2000	120
t_7	Eric	1960	Primary	90025	Chef	Divorced	Diabetis	White	YourCompany	4000	110
t_8	Fred	1974	Ed.D	90060	Teacher	Widow	Asthma	Asian	YourCompany	5000	60

b $\mathscr{C}$

$c_1=\{\texttt{YoB, Edu}\}$
$c_2=\{\texttt{ZIP, Job}\}$
$c_3=\{\texttt{Name, Disease}\}$
$c_4=\{\texttt{YoB, ZIP, Disease}\}$
$c_5=\{\texttt{YoB, ZIP, MarStatus}\}$

c

	F_l	
	Name	YoB
l_1	Alice	1974
l_2	Bob	1965
l_3	Carol	1976
l_4	David	1972
l_5	Greg	1975
l_6	Hal	1970
l_7	Eric	1960
l_8	Fred	1974

F_m		
Edu	ZIP	
B.Sc	90015	m_1
MBA	90038	m_2
Ph.D	90001	m_3
M.Sc	90087	m_4
M.Sc	90025	m_5
Th.D	90007	m_6
Primary	90025	m_7
Ed.D	90060	m_8

Fig. 3.17 An example of relation (**a**), a set $\mathscr{C}$ of confidentiality constraints over it (**b**), and a fragmentation that satisfies the confidentiality constraints in $\mathscr{C}$ (**c**)

confidentiality constraints c such that $c \subseteq F_l \cup F_m$). For instance, the association in Fig. 3.18 may put at risk only the sensitive association modeled by confidentiality constraint $c_1=\{\texttt{YoB, Edu}\}$, and satisfies k-looseness for $k = 4$ (and therefore any lower k). In fact, any value of YoB is associated with at least (exactly, in this case) four different values of Edu and viceversa.

3.8.2 Exposure Risk

The proposal in [38] supports group associations between pairs of fragments. Given a generic fragmentation $\mathscr{F}$ composed of an arbitrary number of fragments, different group associations can be published on different fragments pairs. A simple example shows how such a publication, while guaranteeing protection of the specific associations released in loose form, can however expose other sensitive associations.

Consider the example in Fig. 3.19, where relation MEDICALDATA in Fig. 3.17a has been split into three fragments $F_l=\{\texttt{Name, YoB}\}$, $F_m=\{\texttt{Edu, ZIP}\}$, and $F_r=\{\texttt{Job, MarStatus, Disease}\}$. The (2-2)-grouping over F_l and F_m, and the (2-2)-grouping over F_m and F_r induce two 4-loose group associations: A_{lm} between F_l and F_m, and A_{mr} between F_m and F_r, respectively. The looseness of A_{lm} guarantees protection with respect to constraint $c_1=\{\texttt{YoB, Edu}\}$, covered by F_l and F_m, ensuring that for each value of YoB in F_l the group association provides at least four possible values of Edu in F_m (and viceversa). The looseness of A_{mr}

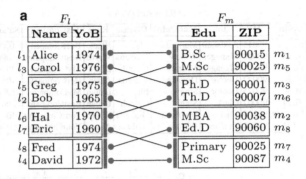

Fig. 3.18 Graphical representation (**a**) and corresponding relations (**b**) of a 4-loose association between fragments F_l and F_m in Fig. 3.17c

guarantees protection with respect to constraint $c_2=\{\texttt{ZIP},\texttt{Job}\}$, covered by F_m and F_r, ensuring that for each value of $\texttt{ZIP}$ in F_m the group association provides at least four possible values of $\texttt{Job}$ in F_r (and viceversa). This independent definition of the two associations does not take into consideration constraints expressing sensitive associations among attributes that are not covered by the pairs of fragments on which a group association is specified (c_3, c_4, and c_5 in our example), which can then be exposed. Consider, for example, constraint $c_3=\{\texttt{Name},\ \texttt{Disease}\}$. Alice (tuple l_1 in f_l) is mapped to group ny1 which is associated by A_{lm} with groups ez11 and ez12, that is, tuples m_1, m_3, m_5, and m_6 in f_m. These tuples are also grouped as ez22 and ez21, associated by A_{mr} with groups jmd1 and jmd2, that is, tuples r_1, r_3, r_5, and r_6 in f_r. Hence, by combining the information of the two associations, we know that l_1 in f_l is associated with one of these four tuples in f_r. While an uncertainty of four is guaranteed with respect to the association among tuples, such an uncertainty is not guaranteed at the level of values, which could then expose sensitive associations. In particular, since the disease in both r_1 and r_5 is Flu and the disease in both r_3 and r_6 is Calculi, there are only two possible diseases associated with Alice, each of which has 50 % probability of being the real one.

This simple example shows how group associations between pairs of fragments, while guaranteeing protection of the associations between the attributes in each

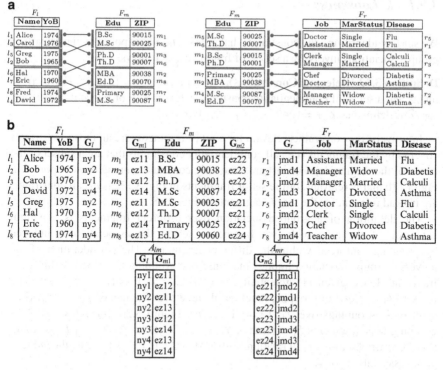

Fig. 3.19 Graphical representation (**a**) and corresponding relations (**b**) of a 4-loose association A_{lm} between F_l and F_m, and a 4-loose association A_{mr} between F_m and F_r, with F_l, F_m, and F_r three fragments of relation MEDICALDATA in Fig. 3.17a

pair of fragments, could indirectly expose other associations, which are not being released in loose form. To counteract this problem, group associations should be specified in a concerted form. In the next section, we extend and redefine group associations and the related properties to guarantee a given looseness degree to be enforced over an arbitrary number of associations and fragments.

3.9 Loose Associations

Our approach to ensure that the publication of different associations does not cause improper leakage is based on the definition of a single loose association encompassing all the fragments on which the data owner wishes to specify associations so to take into account *all* the confidentiality constraints. Any projection over this "universal" group association will then produce different group associations, over any arbitrary number of fragments, which are not exposed to linking attacks such as the one illustrated in the previous section.

3.9.1 k-Looseness

We start by identifying the constraints that are potentially exposed by the release of group associations involving a set $\mathscr{T}$ of fragments, as follows.

Definition 3.13 (Relevant Constraints). Given a set $\mathscr{T} = \{F_1, \ldots, F_n\}$ of fragments and a set $\mathscr{C}$ of confidentiality constraints, the set $\mathscr{C}_{\mathscr{T}}$ of *relevant constraints* for $\mathscr{T}$ is defined as $\mathscr{C}_{\mathscr{T}} = \{c \in \mathscr{C} : c \subseteq F_1 \cup \ldots \cup F_n\}$.

Intuitively, the constraints relevant for a set of fragments are all those constraints covered by the fragments (i.e., all confidentiality constraints that are a subset of the union of the fragments). For instance, the only constraint among those reported in Fig. 3.17b that is relevant for the set of fragments in Fig. 3.17c is c_1; all constraints are instead relevant for the set of fragments in Fig. 3.18.

The definition of a group association over different fragments is a natural extension of the case with two fragments, where the association is induced by groupings enforced within the different fragments. The consideration of the universal group association implies that only one grouping is applied within each fragment. Hence, given a fragmentation $\mathscr{F} = \{F_1, \ldots, F_n\}$, a $(k_1, \ldots, k_n)$-grouping is a set $\{\mathscr{G}_1, \ldots, \mathscr{G}_n\}$ of grouping functions defined over fragments $\{f_1, \ldots, f_n\}$ (i.e., a set of k_i-groupings over f_i, $i = 1, \ldots, n$). Figure 3.20 illustrates a (2,2,2)-grouping over fragments $F_l = \{\texttt{Name}, \texttt{YoB}\}$, $F_m = \{\texttt{Edu}, \texttt{ZIP}\}$ and $F_r = \{\texttt{Job}, \texttt{MarStatus}, \texttt{Disease}\}$ of relation MEDICALDATA in Fig. 3.17a, and the induced group association A_{lmr}.

Like for the case of two fragments, a group association permits to establishing relationships among the tuples in the different fragments, while maintaining the uncertainty on which tuple in each fragment is actually associated with each tuple in another fragment. Such an uncertainty is given by the cardinality of the groupings. The reconstruction made available by a group association, and obtained as the joins of the fragments in $\mathscr{F}$ and A, generates in fact all possible combinations among the tuples of associated groups. Let us denote with $\mathscr{F} \bowtie A$ such a join. Guaranteeing k-looseness for the sensitive associations represented by relevant constraints requires ensuring that the reconstruction of tuples, made possible by the association among groups, is such that: for each constraint c relevant for $\mathscr{F}$ and for each fragment F, there are at least k tuples t^a in $\mathscr{F} \bowtie A$ such that, if $t_1^a[F \cap c] = \ldots = t_k^a[F \cap c]$, then $t_1^a[c \setminus F] \neq \ldots \neq t_k^a[c \setminus F]$. The k-looseness requirement must then take into consideration not only the number of tuples in other fragments with which a tuple can be associated but also the diversity of their values for the attributes involved in confidentiality constraints. In fact, different tuples that have the same values for these attributes do not provide the diversity needed to ensure k-looseness. We then start by identifying these tuples, as follows.

Definition 3.14 (Alike). Given a fragmentation $\mathscr{F} = \{F_1, \ldots, F_n\}$ with its instance $\{f_1, \ldots, f_n\}$, and the set $\mathscr{C}_{\mathscr{F}}$ of confidentiality constraints relevant for $\mathscr{F}$, tuples $t_i, t_j \in f_z$, $z = 1, \ldots, n$, are said to be *alike* with respect to a constraint $c \in \mathscr{C}_{\mathscr{F}}$, denoted $t_i \simeq_c t_j$ iff $c \cap F_z \neq \emptyset$ and $t_i[c \cap F_z] = t_j[c \cap F_z]$. Two tuples are said to be

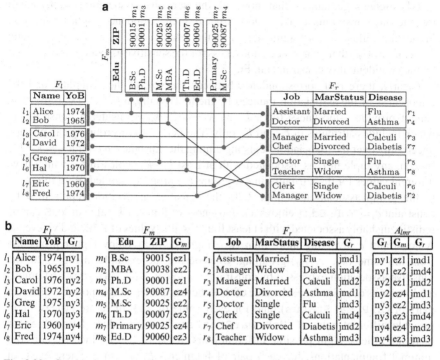

Fig. 3.20 Graphical representation (**a**) and corresponding relations (**b**) of a 4-loose association among three fragments F_l, F_m, and F_r of relation MEDICALDATA in Fig. 3.17a

alike with respect to a set $\mathscr{C}_{\mathscr{F}}$ of relevant constraints, denoted $t_i \simeq_{\mathscr{C}_{\mathscr{F}}} t_j$, if they are alike with respect to at least one constraint $c \in \mathscr{C}_{\mathscr{F}}$.

According to this definition, given a fragmentation $\mathscr{F}$, two tuples in a fragment instance f_i of fragment $F_i \in \mathscr{F}$ are alike if they have the same values for the attributes in at least one constraint relevant for $\mathscr{F}$. For instance, with reference to the fragments in Fig. 3.20, $r_4 \simeq_{c_3} r_8$ since $r_4[\text{Disease}] = r_8[\text{Disease}] = \text{Asthma}$. Since we are interested in evaluating the alike relationship with respect to the set $\mathscr{C}_{\mathscr{F}}$ of relevant constraints, in the following we omit the subscript of the alike relationship whenever clear from the context (i.e., we write $t_i \simeq t_j$ instead of $t_i \simeq_{\mathscr{C}_{\mathscr{F}}} t_j$).

We can now define k-looseness of a group association among arbitrary sets of fragments, as follows.

Definition 3.15 (k-Looseness). Given a fragmentation $\mathscr{F} = \{F_1, \ldots, F_n\}$ with its instance $\{f_1, \ldots, f_n\}$, the set $\mathscr{C}_{\mathscr{F}}$ of confidentiality constraints relevant for $\mathscr{F}$, and a group association A over $\{f_1, \ldots, f_n\}$, A is said to be k-*loose* with respect to $\mathscr{C}_{\mathscr{F}}$ iff $\forall c \in \mathscr{C}_{\mathscr{F}}$, let $\mathscr{F}_c = \{F \in \mathscr{F} : F \cap c \neq \emptyset\}$, $\forall F_i \in \mathscr{F}_c$ and $\forall g_i \in \text{GID}_i$ let $T = \bigcup_{t^a \in A} \{\mathscr{G}_j^{-1}(t^a[\text{G}_j]) \times \ldots \times \mathscr{G}_l^{-1}(t^a[\text{G}_l]) : t^a[\text{G}_i] = g_i\}$ with $\{F_j, \ldots, F_l\} = \mathscr{F}_c \setminus \{F_i\}$ $\implies |T| \geq k$ and $\forall t_x, t_y \in T$, $x \neq y$, $t_x \not\simeq_c t_y$.

k-Looseness guarantees that none of the sensitive associations represented by relevant constraints can be reconstructed with confidence higher than $1/k$. Figure 3.20 illustrates a fragmentation of the relation in Fig. 3.17a and a group association A_{lmr} that guarantees 4-looseness for the sensitive associations expressed by the confidentiality constraints in Fig. 3.17b.

Clearly, there is a correspondence between the size of the groupings and the k-looseness of the association induced by them. Trivially, a $(k_1, \ldots, k_n)$-grouping cannot provide k-looseness for a $k > k_1 \cdot \ldots \cdot k_n$. Consider a constraint c, which includes attributes in F_i and F_j only. The $(k_1, \ldots, k_n)$-grouping can provide uncertainty over the associations existing among the attributes in c for a $k \leq k_i \cdot k_j$. Indeed, any tuple in f_i is associated with at least $k_i \cdot k_j$ tuples in f_j, which have different values for the attributes in c if groups are properly defined. With reference to the group association in Fig. 3.20, the sensitive association represented by constraint $c_1=\{\texttt{YoB}, \texttt{Edu}\}$ enjoys a k-looseness of four: each value of $\texttt{YoB}$ can be indistinguishably associated with at least four possible values of $\texttt{Edu}$, and viceversa. A constraint c involving more than two fragments may enjoy higher protection from the same $(k_1, \ldots, k_n)$-grouping. Considering the example in Fig. 3.20, the sensitive association expressed by constraint $c_5=\{\texttt{YoB}, \texttt{ZIP}, \texttt{MarStatus}\}$ enjoys a k-looseness of eight: for each value of $\texttt{YoB}$ there are at least eight possible different pairs of $(\texttt{ZIP}, \texttt{MarStatus})$, and for each value of $\texttt{ZIP}$ there are at least eight possible different pairs of $(\texttt{YoB}, \texttt{MarStatus})$, for each value of $\texttt{MarStatus}$ there are at least eight possible different pairs of $(\texttt{YoB}, \texttt{ZIP})$. Since we consider minimal fragmentations, for each pair of fragments F_i, F_j in $\mathscr{F}$ there exists at least a confidentiality constraint c relevant for F_i and F_j only (i.e., $\forall \{F_i, F_j\} \in \mathscr{F}$, $i \neq j$, $\exists c \in \mathscr{C}$ s.t. $c \subseteq F_i \cup F_j$, Theorem A.2 in [38]), which enjoys a k-looseness of $k_i \cdot k_j$. Hence, a $(k_1, \ldots, k_n)$-grouping can ensure k-looseness with $k \leq min\{k_i \cdot k_j : i, j = 1, \ldots, n, i \neq j\}$ for the constraints in $\mathscr{C}_{\mathscr{F}}$. Whether the $(k_1, \ldots, k_n)$-grouping provides k-looseness for lower values of k depends on how the groups are defined. In the following, we introduce three heterogeneity properties of grouping (revising and extending those provided in [38]) whose satisfaction ensures k-looseness for $k = min\{k_i \cdot k_j : i, j = 1, \ldots, n, i \neq j\}$.

3.9.2 Heterogeneity Properties

The heterogeneity properties ensure diversity of the induced associations, which are defined as sensitive by confidentiality constraints. They operate at three different levels: groupings, group associations, and value associations.

The first property we introduce is *group heterogeneity*, which ensures diversity within each group by imposing that groups in a fragment do not include tuples with the same values for the attributes in relevant constraints. In this way, the minimum size k_i of the groups in fragment F_i, $i = 1, \ldots, n$, reflects the minimum number of different values in the group for each subset of attributes that appear together in a relevant constraint.

Property 3.3 (Group Heterogeneity). Given a fragmentation $\mathscr{F}=\{F_1,\ldots,F_n\}$ with its instance $\{f_1,\ldots,f_n\}$, and the set $\mathscr{C}_{\mathscr{F}}$ of confidentiality constraints relevant for $\mathscr{F}$, grouping functions $\mathscr{G}_i$ over f_i, $i = 1,\ldots,n$, satisfy *group heterogeneity* iff $\forall t_z, t_w \in f_i$ with $t_z \simeq t_w \implies \mathscr{G}_i(t_z) \neq \mathscr{G}_i(t_w)$.

This property is a straightforward extension of the one operating on two fragments, as its enforcement is local to each individual fragment to take into account all constraints relevant for $\mathscr{F}$ (not only those relevant for a pair). For instance, in Fig. 3.20 the grouping functions of the three fragments satisfy group heterogeneity for $\mathscr{C}_{\mathscr{F}}=\{c_1,\ldots,c_5\}$ while the grouping function of fragment F_r in Fig. 3.21a violates it with respect to confidentiality constraint $c_4=\{\text{YoB, ZIP, Disease}\}$. In fact, fragment F_r includes a group with tuples with the same value for attribute $c_4 \cap F_r = \text{Disease}$ (i.e., Diabetes).

The second property we introduce is *association heterogeneity*, which imposes diversity in the group association. For a group association A between two fragments, this property requires that A does not include duplicate tuples, that is, at most one association can exist between each pair of groups of the two fragments. By considering the more general case of a group association among an arbitrary number of fragments, this property requires that for each constraint c in $\mathscr{C}_{\mathscr{F}}$, each group in a fragment f_i such that $F_i \cap c \neq \emptyset$ appears at least k tuples in A that differ *at least* in the group of one of the fragments f_j storing attributes in c (i.e., $c \cap F_j \neq \emptyset$). In other words, the association heterogeneity property implies that A cannot have two tuples with the same group identifier for all attributes G_{i_j}, $j = 1,\ldots,l$ corresponding to fragments storing attributes that appear in a constraint. Since we consider minimal fragmentations, there exists at least one relevant constraint for each pair of fragments in $\mathscr{F}$. Therefore, a group association A satisfies the association heterogeneity property if it does not have two tuples with the same group identifier for any pair of group attributes $\text{G}_i, \text{G}_j, i, j = 1,\ldots,n$, and $i \neq j$.

Property 3.4 (Association Heterogeneity). A group association A satisfies *association heterogeneity* iff $\forall (g_{i_1},\ldots,g_{i_n}), (g_{j_1},\ldots,g_{j_n}) \in A$ such that $g_{i_z} = g_{j_z} \implies g_{i_w} \neq g_{j_w}, w = 1,\ldots,n$ and $w \neq z$.

Figure 3.20 illustrates a group association that satisfies the association heterogeneity property, while the group association in Fig. 3.21b violates it since a group of fragment f_l is associated twice with a group in fragment f_r.

The third property we introduce is *deep heterogeneity*, which captures the need of guaranteeing diversity in the associations of values behind the groups. Considering a pair of fragments f_i and f_j, deep heterogeneity requires that a group in f_i be associated with groups in f_j that do not include duplicated values for the attributes in a constraint $c \subseteq F_i \cup F_j$ (i.e., tuples are not alike with respect to c). In fact, if the groups in f_j with which a group in f_i is associated contain alike tuples with respect to c, the $k_i \cdot k_j$ corresponding tuples do not contain $k_i \cdot k_j$ different values for the attributes in c, meaning that the group association offers less protection than expected. For instance, groups jmd1 and jmd3 in Fig. 3.20 have the same values for attribute Disease (i.e., Flu and Asthma). Therefore, a group in f_l

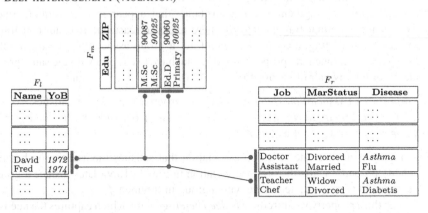

Fig. 3.21 Examples of violations of heterogeneity properties with respect to constraint c_4={YoB, ZIP, Disease}

cannot be associated with both jmd1 and jmd3 because of constraint c_3={Name, Disease} (otherwise, the association between F_l and F_r would be 2-loose instead of 4-loose). Considering the more general case of a group association among an arbitrary number of fragments, and a constraint c composed of attributes stored in fragments $\{F_1, \ldots, F_n\}$, deep heterogeneity requires a group f_i $(i = 1, \ldots, n)$ be associated with groups in $\{f_1, \ldots, f_n\} \setminus \{f_i\}$ that do not permit to reconstruct (via the loose join $\mathscr{F} \bowtie A$) possible semi-tuples that have the same values for all the attributes in c. Note that deep heterogeneity does not require diversity over *all* the fragments storing the attributes composing a constraint, since this condition would be more restrictive than necessary to guarantee k-looseness. In fact, it is sufficient, for each tuple in a fragment f_i, to break the association with *one* of the fragments f_j $(j = 1, \ldots, n, i \neq j)$ storing the attributes in c. For instance, with reference to the example in Fig. 3.20, it is sufficient that each group in f_l be associated with groups of non alike tuples either in f_m or in f_r to guarantee a 4-looseness for the sensitive association modeled by c_5. The deep heterogeneity property is formally defined as follows.

Property 3.5 (Deep Heterogeneity). Given a fragmentation $\mathscr{F} = \{F_1, \ldots, F_n\}$ with its instance $\{f_1, \ldots, f_n\}$, and the set $\mathscr{C}_\mathscr{F}$ of constraints relevant for $\mathscr{F}$, a group association A over $\mathscr{F}$ satisfies *deep heterogeneity* iff $\forall c \in \mathscr{C}_\mathscr{F}$; $\forall F_z \in \mathscr{F}, F_z \cap c \neq \emptyset$; $\forall (g_{i_1}, g_{i_2} \ldots g_{i_n}), (g_{j_1}, g_{j_2} \ldots g_{j_n}) \in A$ the following condition is satisfied:
$$g_{i_z} = g_{j_z} \implies \bigvee_{l=1,\ldots,n, \, l \neq z} \nexists t_x, t_y : t_x \in \mathscr{G}_l^{-1}(g_{i_l}), t_y \in \mathscr{G}_l^{-1}(g_{j_l}), t_x \simeq_c t_y.$$

Given a constraint c whose attributes appear in fragments $\{F_{i_1}, \ldots, F_{i_j}\}$, deep heterogeneity is satisfied with respect to c if no two tuples t, t' in A that have the same group g_y in f_{i_y} are associated with groups that include alike tuples with respect to c for all the fragments f_{i_x}, $x = 1, \ldots, j$ and $x \neq y$. This property must be true for all the groups in each fragment. This guarantees that, for each constraint, no sensitive association can be reconstructed with confidence higher than $1/k$. An example of group association that satisfies deep heterogeneity is illustrated in Fig. 3.20. Note that deep heterogeneity is satisfied even though the two tuples in group ny2 for f_l are associated with groups jmd1 and jmd2 in f_r, which include tuples $r_1 \simeq_{c_5} r_3$ and $r_4 \simeq_{c_5} r_7$. In fact, constraint c_5 is not covered by F_l and F_r but by the three fragments all together, and heterogeneity of the associations in which r_1 and r_3 (r_4 and r_7, respectively) are involved is provided by the tuples in f_m. Figure 3.21c illustrates an example of violation of the deep heterogeneity property with respect to confidentiality constraint $c_4 = \{$YoB, ZIP, Disease$\}$. In fact, the groups in F_m and F_r with which a group in F_l is associated include tuples that are alike with respect to confidentiality constraint c_4 (i.e., two tuples in F_m have the same value for attribute ZIP and two tuples in F_r have the same value for attribute Disease), clearly reducing the protection offered by the association. In fact, the tuples that can be reconstructed by joining these two groups in f_m and f_r include occurrences of the same values for the attributes in c_4 (i.e., ZIP=90025 and Disease=Asthma). Hence, the association YoB=1972, ZIP=90025, and Disease=Asthma holds with probability higher than $1/k$.

If the three properties above are satisfied by a $(k_1, \ldots, k_n)$-grouping and its induced group association, then the group association is k-loose for any $k \leq min\{k_i \cdot k_j : i, j = 1, \ldots, n, i \neq j\}$, as stated by the following theorem.

Theorem 3.6. *Given a fragmentation* $\mathscr{F} = \{F_1, \ldots, F_n\}$ *with its instance* $\{f_1, \ldots, f_n\}$, *the set* $\mathscr{C}_{\mathscr{F}}$ *of constraints relevant for* $\mathscr{F}$, *and a* $(k_1, \ldots, k_n)$-*grouping that satisfies Properties 3.3, 3.4, and 3.5, the group association A induced by the* $(k_1, \ldots, k_n)$-*grouping is k-loose with respect to* $\mathscr{C}_{\mathscr{F}}$ *(Definition 3.15) for each* $k \leq \min\{k_i \cdot k_j : i, j = 1, \ldots, n, i \neq j\}$.

Proof. To assess the protection offered by the release of a $(k_1, \ldots, k_n)$-grouping that satisfies Properties 3.3, 3.4, and 3.5, we first analyze the protection provided to the sensitive association represented by an arbitrary confidentiality constraint c in $\mathscr{C}_{\mathscr{F}}$.

By Definition 3.12, each group $g_a \in \mathsf{GID}_i$ contains at least k_i tuples, $\forall F_i \in \mathscr{F}$. Each group $g_a \in \mathsf{GID}_i$ appears in at least k_i tuples in A, each associating g_a to a different group g_b in GID_j, for each fragment F_j in $\mathscr{F}$ by Property 3.4. Hence, each $g_a \in \mathsf{GID}_i$ is associated with at least k_i different groups in GID_j, $\forall F_j \in \mathscr{F} : F_j \cap c \neq \emptyset, i \neq j$. Each tuple t^a in A having $t^a[\mathsf{G}_i] = g_a$ has at least $\prod_j k_j$ (with $F_j \in \mathscr{F}$: $F_j \cap c \neq \emptyset, i \neq j$) occurrences in the join $\mathscr{F} \bowtie A$. Let us denote with $groups\_a_i$ the tuples in $\mathscr{F} \bowtie A$ of the occurrences of a tuple t_i^a in A. Tuples in $groups\_a_i$ are not alike w.r.t. c. In fact, by Properties 3.3, each group in GID_j is composed of at least k_j tuples that are not alike with respect to c, $\forall F_j \in \mathscr{F}$ such that $F_j \cap c \neq \emptyset$. By Property 3.5, for each pair of tuples t_x^a, t_y^a in A with $t_x^a[\mathsf{G}_i] = t_y^a[\mathsf{G}_i] = g_a$, the tuples in $groups\_a_x \cup groups\_a_y$ are not alike with respect to c. Hence, $\mathscr{F} \bowtie A$ has at least $k_i \cdot \prod_j k_j$ tuples, all with $t^a[\mathsf{G}_i] = g_a$, that are note alike with respect to c.

Then, a $(k_1, \ldots, k_n)$-grouping satisfying Properties 3.3, 3.4, and 3.5 induces a group association that is k-loose with respect to c for each $k \leq \prod k_i$, $\forall F_j \in \mathscr{F}$ such that $F_j \cap c \neq \emptyset$.

Since we consider minimal fragmentations only, for each pair of fragments F_i, F_j in $\mathscr{F}$ there exists at least a confidentiality constraint c that is relevant for F_i and F_j only. Hence, the $(k_1, \ldots, k_n)$-grouping satisfying Properties 3.3, 3.4, and 3.5 induces a group association that is k-loose with $k = k_i \cdot k_j$ between F_i and F_j (i.e., it guarantees a protection degree $k_i \cdot k_j$ to the constraints relevant for F_i and F_j).

We can then conclude that the $(k_1, \ldots, k_n)$-grouping satisfying Properties 3.3, 3.4, and 3.5 induces a group association that is k-loose with respect to $\mathscr{C}_{\mathscr{F}}$ for each $k \leq \min\{k_i \cdot k_j : i, j = 1, \ldots, n, i \neq j\}$. □

We note that the protection degree that a $(k_1, \ldots, k_n)$-grouping that satisfies Properties 3.3, 3.4, and 3.5 offer may be different (but not less than k) for each confidentiality constraint c in $\mathscr{C}_{\mathscr{F}}$. Indeed, the protection degree for a constraint c is $\min\{k_i \cdot k_j : F_i, F_j \in \mathscr{F} \wedge F_i \cap c \neq \emptyset \wedge F_j \cap c \neq \emptyset\}$.

3.9.3 Some Observations on k-Looseness

The consideration of all the constraints relevant for the fragments involved in a group association guarantees that no sensitive association can be reconstructed with a probability greater than $1/k$. For instance, confidentiality constraint $c_3 = \{\texttt{Name},$

Disease} is properly protected, for a looseness of 4, by the group association in
Fig. 3.20 while, as already illustrated in Sect. 3.8.2, the two group associations in
Fig. 3.19 grant only a 2-looseness protection to it.

Given a k-loose association A among a set $\mathcal{F}$ of fragments, the release of
this loose association is equivalent to the release of $2^n - n$, with $n = |\mathcal{F}|$, k-
loose associations (one for each subset of fragments in $\mathcal{F}$). Indeed, the projection
over a subset of attributes in A represents a k-loose association for the fragments
corresponding to the projected group attributes. This is formally captured by the
following observation.

Observation 4 *Given a fragmentation $\mathcal{F} = \{F_1, \ldots, F_n\}$, a subset $\{F_i, \ldots, F_j\}$
of $\mathcal{F}$, and a k-loose association $A(G_1, \ldots, G_n)$ over $\mathcal{F}$, group association
$A'(G_i, \ldots, G_j)$ is a k-loose association over $\{F_i, \ldots, F_j\}$.*

For instance, with respect to the 4-loose association in Fig. 3.20, the projection
of A over attributes G_l, G_m is a 4-loose association between F_l and F_m.

Since a k-loose association defined over a set $\mathcal{F}$ of fragments guarantees that
sensitive associations represented by constraints in $\mathcal{C}_{\mathcal{F}}$ be properly protected, the
release of multiple loose associations among arbitrary (and possibly overlapping)
subsets of fragments in $\mathcal{F}$ provides the data owner with the same protection guarantee. The data owner can therefore decide to release either one loose association
A encompassing all the associations among the fragments in $\mathcal{F}$, or a subset of
loose associations defined among arbitrary subsets of fragments in $\mathcal{F}$ by projecting
the corresponding attributes from A. This is formally captured by the following
observation.

Observation 5 *Given a fragmentation $\mathcal{F} = \{F_1, \ldots, F_n\}$ and a k-loose association
$A(G_1, \ldots, G_n)$ over it, the release of an arbitrary set of k-loose associations
$\{A_1(G_h, \ldots, G_i), \ldots, A_m(G_j, \ldots, G_k)\}$, with $\{G_h, \ldots, G_k\} \subseteq \{G_1, \ldots, G_n\}$, provides
at least the same protection guarantees as the release of A.*

For instance, the data owner can decide to release the group associations obtained
projecting $\langle G_l, G_m \rangle$ and $\langle G_m, G_r \rangle$ from the group association in Fig. 3.20. This
solution does not suffer from the privacy breach illustrated in Sect. 3.8.2, while
providing associations between groups of the same size (i.e., the same utility for
data recipients).

According to the two observations above, the data owner can release more than
one group association among arbitrary subsets of fragments in $\mathcal{F}$ without causing
any privacy breaches. Note however that if the group associations of interest operate
on disjoint subsets of fragments (i.e., no fragment is involved in more than one
group association), they can be defined independently from each other without risks
of unintended disclosure of sensitive associations. This is formally captured by the
following observation.

Observation 6 *Given a fragmentation $\mathcal{F}$, and a set $\{F_1, \ldots, F_n\}$ of subsets of
fragments in $\mathcal{F}$, the release of n loose associations A_i, $i = 1, \ldots, n$ does not
expose any sensitive association if $F_i \cap F_j = \emptyset$, $i, j = 1, \ldots, n$, with $i \neq j$.*

3.10   Queries and Data Utility with Loose Associations

The reason for publishing group associations among fragments, representing vertical views over the original data, is to provide some (not precise) information on the associations among the tuples in the fragments while ensuring not to expose the sensitive associations defined among their attributes (for which the degree of uncertainty k should be maintained). Group associations then increase the utility of the data released for queries involving different fragments. However, given a set of fragments, different group associations might be defined satisfying a given degree k of looseness to be provided. There are two different issues that have to be properly addressed in the construction of group associations: one is how to select the size k_i of the grouping of each fragment f_i such that the product of any two k_i is equal to or greater than k; and one is how to group tuples within the fragments so to maximize utility.

With respect to the first issue of sizing the groups, there are different possible values of the different k_i which can satisfy the degree k of protection. For instance, for a group association between two fragments, we can use $(k,1)$, $(\lceil \sqrt{k} \rceil, \lfloor \sqrt{k} \rfloor)$, and $(1,k)$. In the case of multiple fragments, the best utility can be achieved by distributing as much evenly as possible the sizing of the groups, hence imposing on each group a size close to $\sqrt{k}$. An uneven distribution would in fact result in an over-protection of the group associations over some of the fragments (a value of looseness much higher than the required k for constraints covered by a subset of the fragments in $\mathscr{F}$). Experiments show that this would lead to a significant reduction in the precision of the queries. For instance, a looseness of 12 over three fragments could be achieved with a $(3,4,4)$-grouping; a solution creating a $(1,12,12)$-grouping would indeed provide the required protection overall but would probably provide little utility for the association between the second and third fragments (whose association would in fact be 144-loose for the constraints that are relevant for the second and third fragment only).

With respect to the issue of grouping within a fragment, we first note that queries that involve a single fragment (i.e., all the attributes in the query belong to the same fragment) are not affected by fragmentation as they can be answered exactly by querying the fragment. For instance, with respect to the fragments in Fig. 3.22, query q ="SELECT AVG(Salary) FROM MEDICALDATA GROUP BY Job" involves attributes that belong to the fragment F_r only. Hence, the execution of the query over fragment F_r returns exactly the same result as its execution over the original relation MEDICALDATA in Fig. 3.17a. We therefore focus our discussion on queries that involve two or more fragments, on which group associations are to be defined, with the goal of determining how to group the tuples in fragments so that the induced group associations maximize query utility. In particular, we consider aggregate queries of the form "SELECT Att, AGG$_i(a_i)$, . . . ,AGG$_j(a_j)$ FROM R GROUP BY Att", where AGG$_i$, . . . ,AGG$_j$ are aggregation functions (e.g., COUNT, AVG, MIN, MAX functions), and a_i, . . . , a_j as well as set Att (this latter optional in the SELECT clause) are attributes that appear in fragments. For instance, with

		F_m					F_r				
	Edu	ZIP	Race	InsCompany			Job	MarStatus	Disease	Salary	InsAmount	
m_5	M.Sc	90025	Indian	MyCompany	●	●	Doctor	Single	Flu	1000	70	r_5
m_6	Th.D	90007	Indian	BestCompany	●	●	Assistant	Married	Flu	1000	150	r_1
m_1	B.Sc	90015	Black	BestCompany	●	●	Clerk	Single	Calculi	2000	120	r_6
m_3	Ph.D	90001	Black	MyCompany	●	●	Manager	Married	Calculi	2000	100	r_3
m_7	Primary	90025	White	YourCompany	●	●	Chef	Divorced	Diabetis	4000	110	r_7
m_2	MBA	90038	White	BestCompany	●	●	Doctor	Divorced	Asthma	4000	150	r_4
m_4	M.Sc	90087	Asian	HerCompany	●	●	Manager	Widow	Diabetis	5000	70	r_2
m_8	Ed.D	90060	Asian	YourCompany	●	●	Teacher	Widow	Asthma	5000	60	r_8

Fig. 3.22   An example of group association between two fragments F_m and F_r of Fig. 3.17a where tuples are grouped taking into account the similarity of the values of attributes Race and Salary

reference to Fig. 3.22, query q="SELECT AVG(Salary) FROM MEDICALDATA GROUP BY Race" aims at computing the average salary grouped by the race of patients. We measure utility of a group association as the average improvement over the accuracy of the results (i.e., with less error) with respect to the results obtained in absence of group association. Intuitively, utility is obtained as 1 minus the ratio of the average difference with respect to the real values in presence of group associations, and the average difference with respect to the real values in absence of group associations.

The execution of queries over group associations brings in, together with the real tuples on which the query should be executed, all the tuples together with them in their groups and the uncertainty – by definition – of which sub-tuples in a fragment are associated with which sub-tuples in other fragments. Our observation is therefore that groups within fragments should be formed so to contain as much as possible tuples that are similar for the attributes involved in the queries (have close values for continuous attributes). The intuition behind this is that, although the query is evaluated on a possibly larger number of tuples included in the returned groups, such tuples – assuming similar values – maintain the query result within a reasonable error, thus providing utility of the response. The more the attributes involved in the query on which such an observation has been taken into account in the grouping, the better the utility provided by the group associations for the query. In fact, similarity of values within groups (even when ensuring diversity of the values) might provide limited uncertainty of values within a group. We therefore expect that not all the attributes involved in confidentiality constraints should be taken into account in this process.

Let us see now an example of queries over our fragmentation involving attributes such that none, some, or all of them have been subject to the observation above in the grouping (i.e., groups include similar values for none of, some of, or all the attributes in the query). Consider the fragments and group association in Fig. 3.22, computed over relation MEDICALDATA in Fig. 3.17a, where the group association has been produced grouping tuples with similar Race values for fragment f_m and similar Salary values for fragment f_r. We can then see the following three different cases.

- *A query q_{ns} involves none of the attributes whose similarity has been considered in the grouping.* An example of such a query on the group association in Fig. 3.22

is q_{ns} = "SELECT Edu,AVG(InsAmount) FROM MEDICALDATA GROUP BY Edu", requiring the average insurance amount for the different education levels recorded. In this case, the utility of the association typically remains limited. We note however that the utility for this kind of queries has always been positive in our experimental analysis, reaching values close to 40 % for some queries.

- A query q_{as} involves also (but not only) attributes whose similarity has been considered in the grouping. An example of such a query on the group association in Fig. 3.22 is q_{as} = "SELECT InsCompany,AVG(Salary) FROM MEDICAL-DATA GROUP BY InsCompany," requiring, for each insurance company, the average salary of insurance holders. Enjoying the fact that the additional tuples involved in the computation will typically have salary close to the values of real tuples, this query provides quite appreciable utility with respect to the real result. As we will discuss in Sect. 3.12, utility for queries of this type has typically shown values close to 80 % in our experimental evaluation.
- A query q_{os} involves only attributes whose similarity has been considered in the grouping. An example of such a query on the group association in Fig. 3.22 is q_{os} = "SELECT Race, AVG(Salary) FROM MEDICALDATA GROUP BY Race" requiring the average salary of patients grouped by race. This query can benefit from the fact that similarity has been considered for both the attributes involved, which ensures that the additional tuples, brought-in in the evaluation because of the looseness of the association, have values of the involved attributes close to the ones on which the computation would have been executed if the query was performed on the original relation. As we will discuss in Sect. 3.12, the utility for this kind of queries is very high, and has typically shown values near 100 % in our experimental evaluation.

Figure 3.23 shows the results of the queries above when executed over the group association in Fig. 3.22 or over the original relation in Fig. 3.17a.

3.11 Computing a k-Loose Association

The heuristic algorithm for computing a k-loose association that aims for greater utility in query evaluation is illustrated in Fig. 3.24. The algorithm takes as input a relation r defined over relation schema $R(a_1, \ldots, a_m)$, a fragmentation $\mathcal{F} = \{F_1, \ldots, F_n\}$ and its instance $\{f_1, \ldots, f_n\}$, a set $\mathcal{C}_{\mathcal{F}}$ of confidentiality constraints relevant for $\mathcal{F}$, privacy parameters $k_1, \ldots, k_n$, and a set $\mathcal{A}$ of attributes often involved in the expected queries. The algorithm returns a k-loose group association (with $k = min\{k_i \cdot k_j : i, j = 1, \ldots, n, i \neq j\}$), and the corresponding grouping functions $\mathcal{G}_1, \ldots, \mathcal{G}_n$. Intuitively, the algorithm first assigns tuples to groups so that each group in a fragment contains tuples with similar values for attributes in $\mathcal{A}$, without considering heterogeneity properties. Our solution to compute such an optimal grouping is based on the observation that similarity can be conveniently translated into an ordering of values within the attribute domains. Maximum

a

q_{ns}			q_{as}			q_{os}	
Edu	AVG(**InsAmount**)		**InsCompany**	AVG(**Salary**)		**Race**	AVG(**Salary**)
B.Sc	110		BestCompany	2500		Asian	4500
Ed.D	97.5		HerCompany	4500		Black	1500
MBA	97.5		MyCompany	1500		Indian	1500
M.Sc	104		YourCompany	4500		White	4500
Ph.D	110						
Primary	97.5						
Th.D	110						

Execution over the group association in Figure 3.22

b

q_{ns}			q_{as}			q_{os}	
Edu	AVG(**InsAmount**)		**InsCompany**	AVG(**Salary**)		**Race**	AVG(**Salary**)
B.Sc	150		BestCompany	2666		Asian	4500
Ed.D	60		HerCompany	4000		Black	1500
MBA	70		MyCompany	1500		Indian	1500
M.Sc	110		YourCompany	4500		White	4500
Ph.D	100						
Primary	110						
Th.D	120						

Execution over the original relation in Figure 3.17(a)

c

q_{ns}			q_{as}			q_{os}	
Edu	AVG(**InsAmount**)		**InsCompany**	AVG(**Salary**)		**Race**	AVG(**Salary**)
B.Sc	104		BestCompany	3000		Asian	3000
Ed.D	104		HerCompany	3000		Black	3000
MBA	104		MyCompany	3000		Indian	3000
M.Sc	104		YourCompany	3000		White	3000
Ph.D	104						
Primary	104						
Th.D	104						

Execution over the fragments in Figure 3.22 without group association

Fig. 3.23 Results of sample queries on a group association (**a**), on the original relation (**b**), and on fragments without group association (**c**) for queries involving attributes none (q_{ns}), some (q_{as}), or all (q_{os}) of which have been considered for similarity in the grouping

similarity can in fact be guaranteed by keeping in the same groups elements that are contiguous in the ordered sequence of attribute values. The algorithm first orders tuples in fragments based on their values for attributes in $\mathscr{A}$, and then partitions the tuples in groups of size k. In this way, each group will contain k tuples that, thanks to the ordering, have similar values for attributes in $\mathscr{A}$. Clearly, different ordering criteria can be applied to different attributes, to properly model the similarity requirement. As an example, for numerical values, we adopt the traditional $\geq$ order relationship. The groupings obtained by ordering the tuples according to $\mathscr{A}$ are optimal with respect to similarity (and hence utility of query responses), but they do not provide any guarantee with respect to the confidentiality of sensitive associations. For each fragment, the algorithm then tries to assign the tuples to the group closest to the optimal group so that also the heterogeneity properties are

---

INPUT
r: relation defined over relation schema $R(a_1, \ldots, a_m)$
$\mathscr{F}$: fragmentation composed of fragments $\{F_1, \ldots, F_n\}$
$\{f_1, \ldots, f_n\}$: instances of fragments $\{F_1, \ldots, F_n\}$
$\mathscr{C}_{\mathscr{F}}$: set of confidentiality constraints relevant for $\mathscr{F}$
$k_1, \ldots, k_n$: privacy parameters for $\{F_1, \ldots, F_n\}$
$\mathscr{A}$: set of attributes to be considered for similarity

OUTPUT
A: k-loose association with $k = min\{k_i \cdot k_j : i, j = 1, \ldots, n, i \neq j\}$
$\mathscr{G}_1, \ldots, \mathscr{G}_n$: grouping function for $\{F_1, \ldots, F_n\}$

MAIN
1:   *To Place* := r /* tuples that need to be allocated to groups */
2:   $A := \emptyset$
3:   /* **Step 1**: pre-calculate groups to which sub-tuples in fragments should be allocated */
4:   **for** $i = |\mathscr{F}| \ldots 1$ **do**
5:     order r by $\mathscr{A} \cap F_i$ /* order tuples according to the attributes in $\mathscr{A}$ in fragment F_i */
6:     *current* := 0 /* current group identifier */
7:     $j := 0$ /* number of tuples in $g^i_{current}$ */
8:     **for each** $t \in r$ **do** /* pre-allocate each semi-tuple to a group */
9:       *OptimalGrouping*$[t][F_i] := g^i_{current}$ /* optimal assignment for t in F_i */
10:       $j := j + 1$
11:       **if** $j = k_i$ **then** /* create a new group */
12:         *current* := *current* + 1
13:         $j := 0$
14:   /* **Step 2**: allocate tuples to groups without generating over-quota groups */
15:   **for each** $t \in$ *To Place* **do** /* allocate t to a group in each fragment; define related tuple ta in A */
16:     $ta :=$ **Find Assignment**$(t,$ NULL, 1, FALSE, *OptimalGrouping*$)$
17:     **if** $ta \neq$ NULL **then** /* t has been assigned to a group in each fragment */
18:       $A := A \cup \{ta\}$
19:       *To Place* := *To Place* $\setminus \{t\}$
20:   /* **Step 3**: allocate non-assigned tuples, possibly generating over-quota groups */
21:   **for each** $t \in$ *To Place* **do**
22:     $ta :=$ **Find Assignment**$(t,$ NULL, 1, TRUE, *OptimalGrouping*$)$
23:     **if** $ta \neq$ NULL **then** /* t has been assigned to a group in each fragment */
24:       $A := A \cup \{ta\}$
25:       *To Place* := *To Place* $\setminus \{t\}$
26:   /* **Step 4**: re-allocate tuples in under-quota groups and delete unassigned tuples */
27:   *To Empty* := $\{g \in$ GID$_i, i = 1, \ldots, m : 0 < |\{ta \in A : ta[i] = g\}| < k_i\}$ /* non-empty under-quota groups */
28:   *To Place* := *To Place* $\cup$ **Re Assign**(*To Empty*)
29:   **for each** $F_i \in \mathscr{F}$ **do** /* remove non-assigned tuples */
30:     **for each** $t \in$ *To Place* **do** $f_i := f_i \setminus \{t[F_i]\}$

Fig. 3.24 Heuristic algorithm that computes a k-loose association

satisfied. In the assignment of tuples to groups, the algorithm follows two main criteria: (1) it favors groups close to the optimal group of each tuple; and (2) it prefers groups of size k_i over larger groups. Our heuristic algorithm implementing this approach is presented in details in the remainder of this section.

The algorithm starts by initializing variable *To_Place*, representing the set of tuples that still need to be allocated to groups, to the tuples in r, and by creating an empty group association A (lines 1–2). The algorithm then operates in four steps as follows.

Step 1: Ordered Grouping For each fragment F_i, the algorithm identifies the optimal grouping, meaning that tuples with similar values for the attributes in $\mathscr{A} \cap F_i$ belong to the same group(s). To this purpose, the algorithm orders the tuples in r according to the attributes in $\mathscr{A} \cap F_i$ (line 5). It then partitions the ordered tuples in sets of k_i contiguous tuples each, and assigns to each partition a different group identifier $g^i_{current}$ (lines 6–13). In this way, contiguous tuples in the ordered relation are ideally assigned to the same group (or to contiguous groups). The result of this step is a matrix *OptimalGrouping* with one row for each tuple t in r, one column for each fragment F in $\mathscr{F}$, and where each cell *OptimalGrouping*$[t][F_i]$ contains the identifier of the optimal group for tuple t in fragment F_i.

Step 2: Under-Quota Grouping The algorithm tries to assign each tuple to the group closest to the optimal one that satisfies all the heterogeneity properties, but without generating *over-quota* groups (i.e., groups in F_i with more than k_i tuples) to maximize utility. In fact, large groups limit the utility that can be obtained in query evaluation. For each tuple t in *To_Place*, the algorithm calls function **Find_Assignment** in Fig. 3.25 (lines 15–16), which allocates tuples to groups according to the heterogeneity properties.

Function **Find_Assignment** receives as input a tuple t, the candidate tuple *assoc_tuple* that represents t in the group association A (which is NULL when t has not been assigned to any group), a fragment identifier i, a Boolean variable *over_quota* (which is TRUE only if over-quota groups are permitted), and the optimal grouping *OptimalGrouping*$[t][F]$ computed in Step 1. This function then tries to assign t to a group in F_i close to the optimal one. Function **Find_Assignment** first checks whether t can be inserted into *OptimalGrouping*$[t][F_i]$, that is, it checks whether the heterogeneity properties are satisfied. If the heterogeneity properties are not satisfied, the function checks the groups of fragment F_i, denoted $g^i_{candidate}$, in increasing order of distance from *OptimalGrouping*$[t][F_i]$ (lines 3–13). In fact, similar values are ideally assigned by Step 1 to groups close to the optimal one. The satisfaction of the heterogeneity properties is verified by calling function **Try_Assignment** in Fig. 3.25 (line 9 and line 13). Function **Try_Assignment** takes as input tuple t, the candidate tuple *assoc_tuple* that represents t in the group association A, the fragment identifier i, and a group identifier g, and returns TRUE if $t[F_i]$ can be assigned to g; FALSE, otherwise. When a correct assignment of t to a group in F_i is found, if F_i is the last fragment in $\mathscr{F}$, function **Find_Assignment** returns tuple *assoc_tuple* representing the computed assignment of t to groups (lines 14–15). Otherwise, function **Find_Assignment** recursively calls itself to assign t to a group in fragment F_{i+1} (line 16). If the recursive call succeeds (i.e., it returns a group association for t), function **Find_Assignment** returns *assoc_tuple*;

FIND ASSIGNMENT(*t*, *assoc tuple*, *i*, *over quota*, *OptimalGrouping*)

1: **if** *over quota* = FALSE **then** *max* := k_i **else** *max* := $2k_i$ /* maximum number of tuples in groups */
2: *allocated* := FALSE /* variable that is TRUE if *t* has been allocated to a group in F_i */
3: g_j^i := *OptimalGrouping*[*t*][F_i] /* optimal allocation for *t* in F_i */
4: *distance* := 0 /* distance from the optimal allocation */
5: *num groups* := $\left\lceil \frac{|r|}{k_i} \right\rceil$ /* number of groups for F_i */
6: **while** *distance* < $\lfloor \frac{1}{2}$*num groups*$\rfloor$ **do**
7:     *candidate* := (*j* + *distance*) mod *num groups* /* candidate allocation */
8:     **if** |{*ta*∈ A : *ta*[*i*]=$g_{candidate}^i$}| < *max* **then** /* the candidate group can allocate other tuples */
9:         *allocated* := **Try Assignment**(*t*, *assoc tuple*, *i*, $g_{candidate}^i$)
10:     **if** *allocated*=FALSE ∧ *distance*≠ 0 **then**
11:         *candidate* := (*j* − *distance*) mod *num groups* /* alternative candidate allocation */
12:         **if** |{*ta*∈ A : *ta*[*i*]=$g_{candidate}^i$}| < *max* **then**
13:             *allocated* := **Try Assignment**(*t*, *assoc tuple*, *i*, $g_{candidate}^i$)
14:     **if** *allocated* = TRUE **then**
15:         **if** *i* = |$\mathscr{F}$| **then** return(*assoc tuple*) /* the tuple has been allocated to a group in each fragment */
16:         *assoc tuple* := **Find Assignment**(*t*, *assoc tuple*, *i*+1, *over quota*, *OptimalGrouping*) /* recursive call for F_{i+1} */
17:         **if** *assoc tuple* ≠ NULL **then** return(*assoc tuple*)
18:     $\mathscr{G}_i(t)$:= NULL /* try a different allocation at higher distance from the optimal one */
19:     *distance* := *distance* + 1
20: **return**(NULL)

TRY ASSIGNMENT(*t*, *assoc tuple*, *i*, *g*)

21: *assoc tuple*[*i*] := *g* /* insert *t* into group *g* for fragment F_i*/
22: $\mathscr{G}_i(t)$:= *g*
23: **if** *g* satisfies Definition 3.3 ∧ /* group heterogeneity */
24:     A∪{*assoc tuple*} satisfies Definition 3.4 ∧ /* association heterogeneity */
25:     A∪{*assoc tuple*} satisfies Definition 3.5 /* deep heterogeneity */ **then**
26:     **return**(TRUE) /* correct assignment */
27: **return**(FALSE)

RE ASSIGN(*To Empty*)

28: *To Remove* := ∅ /* tuples that need to be removed from the fragmentation */
29: **while** *To Empty* ≠ ∅ **do**
30:     g^i := **Extract Group**(*To Empty*)
31:     let *i* be the fragment F_i of g^i
32:     **for each** *ta*∈ A s.t. *ta*[*i*]=g^i **do**
33:         let *t* ∈ *r* be the tuple represented by *ta*
34:         *CandidateGroups* := {*g*∈GID$_i$: |{*ta*∈ A : *ta*[*i*]= *g*}|≥k_i} /* set of over-quota groups of F_i */
35:         *allocated* := FALSE
36:         **while** (*allocated*=FALSE) ∧(*CandidateGroups*≠∅) **do** /* try to re-assign the semi-tuple */
37:             g_j^i := **Extract Group**(*CandidateGroups*) /* candidate group */
38:             *allocated* := **Try Assignment**(*t*, *ta*, *i*, g_j^i)
39:         **if** *allocated* = FALSE **then** /* if the reassignment failed, the tuple must be removed */
40:             *To Remove* := *To Remove* ∪ {*t*}
41:             **for** *l* = 1 ... |$\mathscr{F}$| **do**
42:                 g^l := *ta*[*l*] /* check whether the removal of *t* generates new under-quota groups */
43:                 **if** |{*ta*∈ A : *ta*[*l*]=g^l}|<k_l+1 **then** *To Empty* := *To Empty* ∪ {g^l}
44:                 *ta*[*l*] := NULL
45:                 $\mathscr{G}_i(t)$:= NULL
46: **return**(*To Remove*)

Fig. 3.25 Pseudocode of functions **Find_Assignment**, **Try_Assignment**, and **Re_Assign**

it tries to allocate *t* to a group at higher distance from *OptimalGrouping*[*t*][F_i], otherwise (line 18–19). If *t* cannot be assigned to any group in F_i, the function returns NULL (line 20).

If function **Find_Assignment** returns a tuple *ta*, the algorithm inserts *ta* into the group association *A* and removes *t* from *To_Place* (lines 17–19).

Step 3: Over-Quota Grouping If Step 2 could not allocate all the tuples in r, the algorithm tries to allocate the remaining tuples in To_Place to the existing groups, thus possibly creating over-quota groups. To this purpose, for each tuple t in To_Place, the algorithm calls function **Find_Assignment** with variable $over\_quota$ set to TRUE. The algorithm updates A and To_Place according to the result returned by function **Find_Assignment** (lines 20–25).

Step 4: Re-assignment Once tuples in r (or a subset thereof) have been allocated to groups, the algorithm determines the set To_Empty of groups generated by Steps 2–3 that are under-quota, that is, the groups that do not include the minimum number of tuples necessary to provide privacy guarantees (line 27). The algorithm then calls function **Re_Assign** in Fig. 3.25 (line 28).

Function **Re_Assign** receives as input the set To_Empty of non-empty but under-quota groups, and tries to reallocate their tuples to other groups (lines 30–38). Tuples in under-quota groups that cannot be reallocated will be removed from the fragmentation and are inserted into To_Remove (lines 39–40). When a tuple t is inserted into To_Remove, the corresponding tuple ta in A is removed from the group association and, for each fragment F_l, $\mathscr{G}_l(t)$ is set to NULL (lines 44–45). Due to the removal of t, the group g^l to which t belong in F_l loses a tuple and it might become under-quota with the consequence that it should be removed. If this is the case, g^l is inserted into To_Empty (line 43). Function **Re_Assign** returns the set To_Remove of tuples to be removed from the fragmentation (line 46).

The algorithm then deletes from each fragment both the tuples that have never been assigned to groups and the tuples returned by function **Re_Assign** (lines 29–30).

The utility of the k-loose association computed by this heuristic algorithm as well as its efficiency are evaluated in Sect. 3.12.

3.12 Coverage, Performance, and Utility

We implemented a prototype, written in Python, of the algorithm described in the previous section, and ran several sets of experiments to the aim of evaluating the ability of our approach to compute a k-loose association, while limiting the number of suppressed tuples (i.e., tuples that cannot be included in any group), and of assessing its performance (Sect. 3.12.2). We then analyzed the utility provided in query evaluation (Sect. 3.12.3). We now present the experimental setting (Sect. 3.12.1) and then discuss the experimental results.

3.12.1 Experimental Setting

We considered both synthetic and real-world datasets. Synthetic data allow us to fully control all the parameters used for data generation, such as the variability in the distribution of attributes values, leading to a robust analysis of the behavior of our technique. Real data allow us to assess the applicability of our technique in a concrete setting. Synthetic datasets were generated starting from a relation schema composed of 7 attributes PATIENTS(Name, YoB, Education, ZIP, MarStatus, Disease, Salary), split over two fragments (F_l={Name, MarStatus, Salary} and F_m={YoB, Education, ZIP, Disease}), to satisfy confidentiality constraints c_1={Name, ZIP, MarStatus, Disease} and c_2 = {Name, YoB, Education, MarStatus}. The datasets were randomly generated adopting distinct characterizing parameters for each attribute. A statistical correlation was introduced between Salary and Education; all the other attributes were set using independent distributions. This allowed us to have knowledge of information in the protected data that we were interested in retrieving through the query computing the average Salary of patients with the same Education level.

In our experiments we considered, as a base configuration, a dataset including 10, 000 tuples. We analyzed the behavior of the system varying several parameters. First, we considered the impact of variations of k, considering values ranging between 4 and 20 (k was equal to 12 for experiments that did not change this parameter). Then, we considered changes on a parameter γ that drives the generation of the synthetic dataset, guiding the distribution of the attribute values. Low values of γ produce compact ranges of values for all the attributes and a high probability of similarity among tuples; high values of γ produce values for the attributes covering a wider range, with small similarity among tuples. The interval we considered in the experiments is between 4 and 12 (value 8 was used in experiments that did not consider variations of this parameter). Finally, we considered the impact of the variations of parameters k_l and k_m and, always choosing pairs of values such that $k_l \cdot k_m = k$, we considered several possible pairs (in experiments that did not consider variations of these parameters, we chose the pair k_l and k_r that had $k_l \geq k_m$ and minimum distance between k_l and k_r; e.g., when k= 12, k_l = 4 and k_m= 3). As a real world dataset, we considered the IPUMS dataset [82], which has been widely used in the literature to test anonymization approaches. Among the attributes in the dataset, we considered the projection over attributes {Region, Statefip, Age, Sex, MarSt, Ind, IncWage, IncTot, Educ, Occ, HrsWork, Health}, representing for each citizen: the region where she lives, the state where she lives, her age, her sex, her marital status, the type of industry for which she works, her salary, her annual total income, her education level, her occupation, the number of hours she works per week, and her health status rated on a five point scale. The relation includes 95, 000 tuples with a not null value for the IncWage attribute. When considering the real dataset, we ran experiments over two fragmentations: the first one is composed of two fragments F_l={Region, Statefip, Age, Sex, MarSt, Ind, IncWage, IncTot} and F_m={Educ, Occ, HrsWork, Health} satisfying constraints c_1={Statefip, Ind, Educ, Occ, Health)} and c_2={Age, Sex, MarSt, Educ, Occ, Health}; the second fragmentation has three fragments F_l={Region, Statefip, Ind, IncWage}, F_m={Age, Sex, MarSt, IncTot}, and F_r={Educ, Occ, HrsWork, Health} satisfying constraints c_1={Statefip, Ind, Educ, Occ, Health}, c_2={Age, Sex, MarSt, Educ, Occ, Health}, and c_3={Statefip, Age, Sex, MarSt, Ind}. Experiments have been run on a server

with two Intel(R) Xeon(R) E5504 2.00GHz, 12GB RAM, one 240GB SSD disk, and
Ubuntu 12.04 LTS 64bit operating system. The reported results have been computed
as the average of a minimum of 5 (for the largest configurations) and a maximum of
120 (for more manageable configurations) runs of the same experiment.

3.12.2 Coverage and Performance

We ran a first set of experiments on synthetic data aimed at assessing the coverage
of the solution computed by our algorithm, that is, the number of tuples of the
original relation that could not be published as they could not be allocated to any
group without violating k-looseness. The experiments focused on evaluating how
the number of tuples in the relation (Fig. 3.26a) and the variability in the distribution
of attribute values (Fig. 3.26b) have an impact on the number of tuples that cannot
be released, for different values of k.

Figure 3.26a shows that the algorithm is more likely to suppress tuples when
operating over small datasets, as the number of candidate groups in each fragment
is small. It is then harder to find an assignment for each tuple that satisfies all the
heterogeneity properties. As it can be expected, the percentage of suppressed tuples
grows with k, since it is harder to define larger groups of tuples (especially for small
datasets).

Figure 3.26b illustrates the impact of the variability in attribute value distribution
on the number of suppressed tuples. As visible from the figure, datasets characterized by low variability cause higher suppression. This is due to the fact that it is
hard to assign tuples to groups when there is a higher probability that some of them
have the same values for attributes in relevant confidentiality constraints. Indeed,
two tuples with the same values for attributes in constraints cannot be assigned to
the same group.

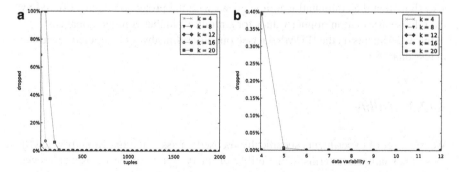

Fig. 3.26 Percentage of tuples in the original relation that are not released, varying the number of
tuples in the relation (**a**) and the variability in the distribution of attribute values (**b**)

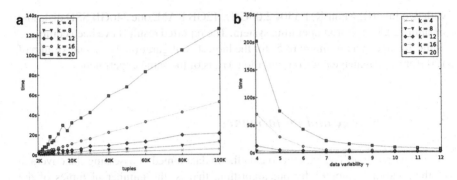

Fig. 3.27 Computational time necessary to determine a k-loose association, varying the number of tuples in the relation (**a**) and the variability in the distribution of attribute values (**b**)

In the experiments performed on the IPUMS dataset, no tuple has been suppressed.

A second set of experiments on synthetic data evaluated the impact of the size of the original relation and of the variability in the distribution of attribute values on the performance of our algorithm.

To prove the scalability of our approach, we ran our algorithm with large instances of the original relation, with a number of tuples varying between 2, 000 and 100, 000. Figure 3.27a, illustrating the time necessary to compute a k-loose association, confirms the scalability of our approach: our prototype is able to find a k-loose association for relations with 100, 000 tuples in less than 1 min for $k=12$ (and we speculate that, according to publicly available Python/C performance ratios [104], an optimized C implementation would take less than 1 s).

Figure 3.27b illustrates the impact of the variability in the distribution of attribute values on the time necessary to compute a k-loose association, considering configurations with 10, 000 tuples. The figure confirms that, as already noted, the lower the variability, the harder the task to find a k-loose association. Both Figs. 3.27a and b also show that the computational time grows with the protection degree offered by the k-loose association: higher values for k require a higher computational cost.

In the experiments on the IPUMS dataset, our algorithm always computed a solution in less than 90 s.

3.12.3   Utility

We ran a set of experiments specifically focused on assessing the gain provided by loose associations, in terms of the utility of query results. We used as a reference the query that identifies the relationship between the Education level of each patient and their Salary (i.e., SELECT AVG(Salary) FROM PATIENTS GROUP BY Education). We then defined a k-loose association that aims at keeping in the same group patients with the same Education level in fragment F_m and with similar Salary in fragment F_l.

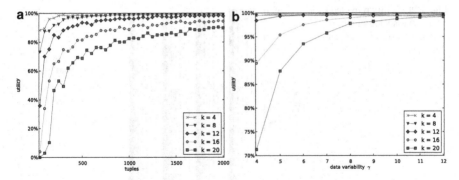

Fig. 3.28 Utility provided by a k-loose association, varying the number of tuples in the relation (**a**) and the variability in the distribution of attribute values (**b**)

Figure 3.28a compares the utility provided by the release of a k-loose association with different values for k, varying the number of tuples in the input dataset. The figure clearly shows that the release of a k-loose association permits to obtain high utility in query evaluation. In most of the considered configurations, utility is nearly 100 %, meaning that the result computed over fragmented data complemented with loose associations is nearly the same obtained on the original relation. This figure also confirms that the quality of the loose association computed by our algorithm improves with the number of tuples in the dataset, as it becomes easier to have tuples with similar values for Education and Salary in the same group.

Figure 3.28b illustrates the impact of the variability in the distribution of attribute values on the obtained utility. Greater values of γ increase the variability and lead to a reduction in the probability for an attribute to present the same values in different tuples. Conflicts arise in a group when tuples present the same values on the attributes involved in a constraint. Then, the probability of conflicts decreases as γ increases. The utility provided by the release of a k-loose association is always high, and increases as the variability in the attribute values increases. Our experiments also clearly show that, in line with the observation that utility and privacy are two contrasting requirements, utility decreases as k increases. It is then expected that improvements in confidentiality guarantees of the solution correspond to worsening in the utility of the released data. It is however worth noticing that, also for the worst case in which $k=20$, if the size of the input dataset is not too limited (i.e., in the order of hundreds of tuples) the measured utility was higher than 80 %, implying a high utility in query evaluation also when adopting privacy parameters higher than the values we expect to be used in real-world scenarios.

We ran a second set of experiments for evaluating the impact of keeping in the same group similar values for an attribute (or a set thereof) of interest for query evaluation (see Sect. 3.10). To this aim, we compared the utility of queries q_{os} (operating on both Education and Salary), q_{as} (operating only on Education or only on Salary), and q_{ns} (operating on neither Education nor Salary). Figure 3.29 compares the utility obtained with 7 different queries

Fig. 3.29 Utility provided by
a k-loose association with
ordering on Education and
Salary

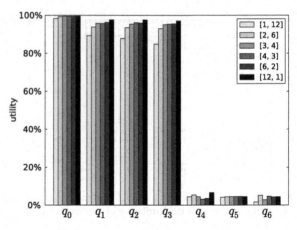

(query q_0 as representative for q_{os}, queries q_1, q_2, q_3 for q_{as}, and queries q_4, q_5, q_6 for q_{ns}) with $k=12$, varying k_l and k_m. Each query is represented by a group of bars, where each bar presents the utility obtained with one of the configurations for parameters k_l and k_m. The results clearly show that the query with highest utility (almost 100 %) is q_0, which benefits on the ordering over both Education and Salary (i.e., query q_{os}). Queries q_2,q_3, and q_4 take advantage only of the ordering over one attribute, which however permits to obtain utility higher than 80 % in all the considered configurations. Our experimental evaluation shows that the release of a loose association provides limited, but not null, utility for queries q_{ns}. We can then conclude that keeping in the same group tuples with similar values permits to achieve better results in the utility of query evaluation.

In the experiments performed on the IPUMS dataset, we first defined a k-loose association between fragments F_l and F_m, and identified two representative sets of queries. The first set of queries operates on the attributes on which fragments of the loose association have been ordered (i.e., q_{os}, represented by query q_0, and q_{as}, represented by queries q_1, q_2, q_3). The second set of queries instead operates only on attributes different from those on which the ordering was performed (i.e., q_{ns}, represented by queries $q_4, \dots, q_{11}$). Figure 3.30a illustrates the utility obtained in executing these two sets of queries over a k-loose association with $k = 12$ and varying the values of k_l and k_m. Each query is represented by a group of bars in the figure. Queries involving at least one of the attributes on which the ordering has been performed (i.e., queries $q_0, \dots, q_3$) showed excellent utility in the result, close to 100 % for all queries. As expected, the utility in executing queries operating on unordered attributes only (i.e., queries $q_4, \dots, q_{11}$) is lower. It is however worth noticing that the results are still appreciable, with most of the queries showing utility between 20 % and 35 %. Compared to the experiments on the synthetic dataset, the queries of type q_{ns} exhibit better utility. In particular, Fig. 3.30a shows that queries q_{as} involving both ordered and unordered attributes exhibit utility values similar to query q_0 that involves ordered attributes only. Our explanation for the higher utility obtained on IPUMS dataset is that real data are more structured and present greater

Fig. 3.30 Utility provided by a k-loose association over two (**a**) and three (**b**) fragments

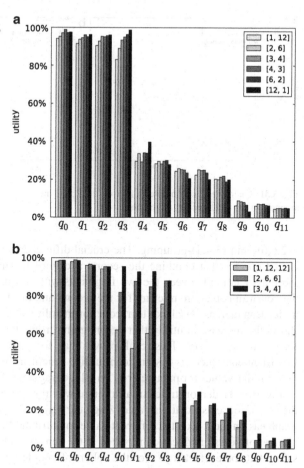

regularity and correlations among attribute values than the randomly generated data in our synthetic dataset, which is characterized by one correlation only (the one between attributes Education and Salary).

Figures 3.29 and 3.30a describe configurations that, keeping k constant, progressively increase the value of parameter k_l (and reduce k_m accordingly). The utility remains relatively stable across all these configurations, even if we can see that, for some queries, the utility decreases as k_l increases, while for a few queries the utility grows with k_l. Overall, we consider as preferable the intermediate solutions, with k_l and k_m near to $\sqrt{k}$, because they are not associated with the lowest levels of utility and because this criterion offers strong benefit when applied to fragmentations with more than two fragments, as observed in the following.

To further evaluate our technique, we performed the same experimental analysis on the fragmentation of IPUMS dataset composed of three (rather than two) fragments. Figure 3.30b reports the utility of queries provided by the release of a k-loose association with $k = 12$, comparing the results obtained with a (1,12,12)-

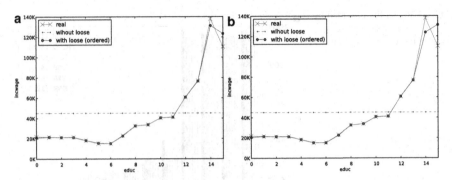

Fig. 3.31 Query results computed ordering on Educ and IncWage on a k-loose association among two (**a**) and three (**b**) fragments

, (2,6,6)- and (3,4,4)-grouping. The crucial difference among these configurations is that queries that combine the second and third fragment will operate on a k-loose association between the two fragments with k equal to 144, 36, and 16 (for the constraints that are relevant for the second and third fragment). As we already noticed, an increase in k leads to a reduction in utility. The graph in Fig. 3.30b clearly shows the increase in utility that occurs going from (1,12,12)- to (3,4,4)-grouping for queries $q_0, \ldots, q_3$. This result proves that, for fragmentations with more than two fragments, there is a significant utility benefit in building loose associations with similar values for parameter k_i on all the fragments.

Figure 3.31 demonstrates in a different way the utility that can be obtained by the use of loose associations, analyzing query q_0 of the previous experiments. The graph has on the x-axis the different values of attribute Educ, which represents the number of years of education reported in the census, and on the y-axis the average salary (attribute IncWage) for the cohort of people with that level of education. In essence, the graphs plot the result of query q_o="SELECT AVG(IncWage) FROM IPUMS_CENSUS GROUP BY Educ". The continuous green line (i.e., the line labeled "real") reports the results obtained on the real data. The dashed blue horizontal line (i.e., the line labeled "without loose") in the middle is the result that we can expect to obtain without loose associations, because IncWage and Educ belong to different fragments and the global average salary will be returned for every education level. The continuous red line (i.e., the line labeled "with loose (ordered)") describes the result obtained with a k-loose associations with $k = 12$. Figure 3.31a shows the results obtained in the configuration with two fragments and assuming a (4,3)-grouping, while Fig. 3.31 illustrates the results obtained in the configuration with three fragments and assuming a (3,4,4)-grouping. In both graphs, the green and red line are overlapping over most of the range, clearly showing the utility that can be obtained by loose associations.

3.13   Chapter Summary

In this chapter, we addressed the problem of fulfilling the needs for protecting sensitive information while guaranteeing visibility requirements in data release. Our solution relies on a graph-based modeling of the fragmentation problem that takes advantage of a novel OBDD-based approach. The fragmentation problem is then reformulated as the computation of a maximum weighted clique over a graph modeling fragments that satisfy confidentiality and visibility constraints. The graph is efficiently computed through OBDDs representing the Boolean formulas corresponding to confidentiality and visibility constraints. We presented both an exact and a heuristic algorithm to solve the fragmentation problem, and experimentally compared their efficiency and the quality of the fragmentations computed by the heuristics. We then presented an approach for enriching the utility of an arbitrary fragmentation through loose associations. We illustrated how the publication of multiple loose associations between pairs of fragments can expose sensitive associations, and presented an approach supporting the definition of a loose association among an arbitrary number of fragments. We described a heuristics for the computation of a loose association, and illustrated the results of an extensive experimental evaluation aimed at analyzing both the efficiency and the effectiveness of the proposed heuristics as well as the utility provided by loose associations in query execution.

Chapter 4
Counteracting Inferences from Sensitive Value Distributions

At a first sight, excluding sensitive data from the release (i.e., releasing only a collection of non sensitive data), might seem a safe approach for protecting data confidentiality. Unfortunately, the possible correlations and dependencies existing among data can introduce inference channels in the data release process, causing sensitive information to be leaked even if such information is not explicitly released. In this chapter, we consider a scenario where data are incrementally released and we address the privacy problem arising when sensitive and non released information depend on (and can therefore be inferred from) non sensitive released data. We propose a model capturing this inference problem, where sensitive information is characterized by peculiar value distributions of non sensitive released data. We then describe how to counteract possible inferences that an observer can draw by applying different statistical metrics on released data. Finally, we perform an experimental evaluation of our solution, showing its efficacy.

4.1 Introduction

The problem of releasing data ensuring privacy to sensitive information is complicated by the fact that the release of a data collection might expose information that is not explicitly included in the release. As a matter of fact, assuming absence of correlations or dependencies among data (as assumed by traditional privacy-preserving techniques) does not fit many real-world scenarios, where data dependencies can be

Part of this chapter is reprinted from Journal of Computer Security, vol. 20, no. 4: M. Bezzi, S. De Capitani di Vimercati, S. Foresti, G. Livraga, P. Samarati, and R. Sassi, "Modeling and Preventing Inferences from Sensitive Value Distributions in Data Release", pp. 393–436 [14], ©2012, with permission from IOS Press.

quite common. Data dependencies can cause inference channels to arise, allowing a recipient to either precisely determine, or reduce the uncertainty about, the values of sensitive, not released, information that is somehow dependent on the released one. This problem has been under the attention of researchers for decades and has been analyzed from different perspectives, resulting in a large body of research that includes: statistical databases and statistical data publications (e.g., [1]); multilevel database systems with the problem of establishing proper classification of data, capturing data relationships and corresponding inference channels (e.g., [35, 66]); ensuring privacy of respondents' identities or of their sensitive information when publishing macro or micro data (e.g., [24, 25]); protection of sensitive data associations due to data mining (e.g., [2]). Several approaches have been proposed addressing all these aspects, and offering solutions to block or limit the exposure of sensitive or private information. However, new scenarios of data release, coupled with the richness of published data and the large number of available data sources, raise novel problems that still need to be addressed.

In this chapter, we address a specific problem related to inferences arising from the dependency of sensitive (not released) information referred to some entities on other properties (released) regarding such entities. In particular, we are concerned with the possible inferences that can be drawn by observing the distribution of values of non sensitive information associated with these entities. As an illustrating example, the age distribution of the soldiers in a military location may permit to infer the nature of the location itself, such as a headquarter (hosting old officials) or a training campus (hosting young privates), which might be considered sensitive. Such a problem of sensitive information derivation becomes more serious as the amount of released data increases, since external observations will tend to be more representative of the real situations and the confidence in the external observations will increase. Although this problem resembles in some aspects the classical problem of controlling horizontal aggregation of data, it differs from it in several assumptions. In particular, we assume a scenario where an external observer could gather the data released to legitimate users and inference is due to peculiar distributions of data values. Also, we are concerned not only with protecting sensitive information associated with specific entities, but also with avoiding possible false positives, where sensitive values may be improperly associated (by the observers) with specific entities.

The contributions of this chapter are multi-fold. First, as mentioned above, we identify and characterize a novel inference problem. We then introduce several metrics to assess the inference exposure due to data release. Our metrics are based on the concepts of *mutual information*, which has been widely used in several security areas ranging from the definition of distinguishers for differential side-channel analysis (e.g., [8, 17, 57, 105]) to data-hiding and watermarking security (e.g., [20]), and of *distance* between the expected and the observed distribution of values of non sensitive information. According to these metrics, we characterize and define a safe release with respect to the considered inference channel. We describe the controls to be enforced in a scenario where tuples are released one at a time, upon request, and we also present an experimental evaluation proving the effectiveness of our solution.

4.1.1 Chapter Outline

The remainder of this chapter is organized as follows. Section 4.2 introduces our reference scenario of inference in data release, raised from a real case study that needed consideration. Section 4.3 formally defines the problem of releasing a dataset without leaking (non released) sensitive information due to the dependency existing between the frequency distribution of some properties of the released dataset and the not released information. Section 4.4 describes two possible strategies that use the mutual information and distance between distributions for counteracting the considered inference problem. Section 4.5 illustrates how the two strategies proposed can be concretely implemented by adopting different metrics that determine when a data release is safe with respect to inference channels that may leak sensitive information. Section 4.6 describes how to control the on-line release of the tuples in a dataset. Section 4.7 discusses the experimental results proving the effectiveness of our solution. Finally, Sect. 4.8 gives our conclusions.

4.2 Reference Scenario and Motivation

We consider a scenario (see Fig. 4.1) where a *data holder* maintains a collection of records stored in a trusted environment. Each record contains different attributes and pertains to a unique data respondent, who is the only authorized party that can require its release. While the records individually taken are not sensitive, their aggregation is considered sensitive since it might enable inferring sensitive information not appearing in the records and not intended for release. We assume

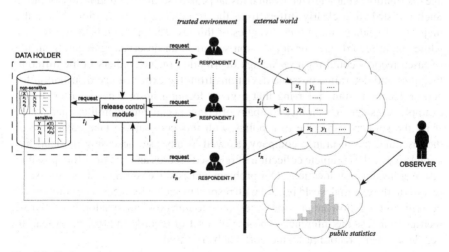

Fig. 4.1 Reference scenario

all requests for records to be genuine and communication to data respondents of responses to their record release requests to be protected. As a consequence, malicious observers are aware neither of the requests submitted by respondents nor of the data holder answers. We also assume that the number of records stored at the data holder site is kept secret. However, once records are released, the data holder has no control on them and therefore *external observers* can potentially gather all the records released. This may happen even with cooperation of respondents, in the case of external servers where released data may be stored.

The data holder must ensure that the collection of records released to the external world be safe with respect to potential inference of sensitive (not released) information that could be possible by aggregating the released records. We consider a specific case of horizontal aggregation and inference channel due to the distribution of values of certain attributes with respect to other attributes. In particular, inference is caused by a distribution of values that deviates from expected distributions, which are considered as typical and are known to the observers. In other worlds, a record is released only if, when combined with records already released, does not cause a deviation of the distribution of the records released from the expected distribution.

In the reminder of this chapter, we refer our examples to a real case scenario characterized as follows. The data holder is a military organization that maintains records on its personnel. Each record refers to a soldier and reports attributes Name, Age, and Location where the soldier is on duty. Some of the military locations are headquarters of the army. The information that a location is a headquarter is considered sensitive and neither appears in the soldiers' records nor it is released in other forms. Soldiers' records can be released upon request of the soldiers. In addition, the age distribution of soldiers is a distribution that can be considered common and widely known to the external world and, in general, typically expected at each location. However, locations where headquarters are based show a different age distribution, characterized by an unusual peak of soldiers of middle age or older. Such a distribution clearly differs from the expected age distribution, where the majority of soldiers are in their twenties or thirties. The problem is therefore that, while single records are considered non sensitive, an observer aggregating all the released records could retrieve the age distribution of the soldiers in the different locations and determine possible deviations from the expected age distribution for certain locations, thus inferring that a given location hosts a headquarter. As an example, consider an insurance company offering special rates to military personnel. If all the soldiers subscribe to a policy with this company to take advantage of the discount, the insurance company (as well as any user accessing its data) has knowledge of the complete collection of released records and can therefore possibly discover headquarter locations. Our problem consists in ensuring that the release of records to the external world be safe with respect to such inferences. The solution we describe in the following provides a response to this problem by adopting different metrics to assess the inference exposure of a set of records and, based on that, to decide whether a record (a set thereof) can be released.

4.3 Data Model and Problem Definition

We provide the notation and formalization of our problem. Our approach is applicable to a generic data model with which the data stored at the data holder site could be organized. For concreteness, we assume data to be maintained as a relational database. Consistently with other proposals (e.g., [94]), we consider the data collection to be a single relation R characterized by a given set A of attributes; each record in the data collection is a tuple t in the relation. Among the attributes contained in the relation, we distinguish a set $Y \subset A$ of attributes whose values represent entities, called *targets*.

Example 4.1. In our running example, relation R is defined on the set $A=\{$Name, Age, Location$\}$ of attributes, with $Y=\{$Location$\}$. We assume that the domain of attribute Location includes values L_1, L_2, L_3, L_4, L_5, representing five different military locations.

While targets, that is, the entities identified by Y (locations in our example), are non sensitive, they are characterized by *sensitive properties*, denoted $s(Y)$, which are not released. In other words, for each $y \in Y$ the associated sensitive information $s(y)$ does not appear in any released record. However, inference on it can be caused by the distribution of the values of a subset of some other attributes $X \subseteq A$ for the specific y. We denote by $P(X)$ the set of *relative frequencies* $p(x)$ of the different values x in the domain of X which appear in relation R. Also, we denote by $P(X|y)$ the relative frequency of each value in the domain of X appearing in relation R and restricted to the tuples for which Y is equal to y. We call this latter the *y-conditioned distribution* of X in R.

Example 4.2. In our running example, $s(Y)$ is the type of location (e.g., headquarter). The sensitive information $s(y)$ of whether a location y is a headquarter (L_2, in our example) can be inferred from the distribution of the age of soldiers given the location. Figure 4.2a shows how tuples stored in relation R are distributed with respect to the values of attributes Age and Location. For instance, of the 10000 tuples, 2029 refer to location L_1, 72 refer to soldiers with age lower than 18. Figure 4.2b reports the corresponding relative frequencies of age distributions. In particular, each column L_i, $i = 1,\dots,5$, reports the L_i-conditioned distribution $P(\text{Age}|L_i)$ (for convenience expressed in percentage). For instance, 3.55 % of the tuples of location L_1 refer to soldiers with age lower than 18. The last column of the table reports the distribution of the age range regardless of the specific location and then corresponds to $P(\text{Age})$ (expressed in percentage). For instance, it states that 2.56 % of the tuples in the relation refer to soldiers with age lower that 18. Figure 4.2c reports the distribution of soldiers in the different locations regardless of their age (again expressed in percentage). For instance, 20.29 % of the 10000 soldiers are based at L_1.

a

Age		L1	L2	L3	L4	L5	Total
		Number of tuples					
<18		72	26	38	47	73	256
18-19		151	53	82	140	223	649
20-24		539	147	449	505	736	2376
25-29		452	114	370	418	613	1967
30-34		335	213	234	318	501	1601
35-39		321	238	277	332	538	1706
40-44		128	219	122	162	220	851
45-49		20	205	50	49	76	400
50-54		9	71	28	34	31	173
≥55		2	13	2	2	2	21
Total		2029	1299	1652	2007	3013	10000

b

Age		L1	L2	L3	L4	L5	P(Age)
		P(Age|L$_i$)					
<18		3.55	2.00	2.31	2.34	2.42	2.56
18-19		7.44	4.08	4.96	6.98	7.40	6.49
20-24		26.56	11.32	27.18	25.16	24.44	23.76
25-29		22.28	8.78	22.40	20.83	20.35	19.67
30-34		16.51	16.40	14.16	15.84	16.63	16.01
35-39		15.82	18.32	16.77	16.54	17.86	17.06
40-44		6.31	16.86	7.38	8.07	7.30	8.51
45-49		0.99	15.78	3.03	2.44	2.52	4.00
50-54		0.44	5.46	1.69	1.69	1.03	1.73
≥55		0.10	1.00	0.12	0.11	0.05	0.21

c

L$_i$	P(L$_i$)
L$_1$	20.29
L$_2$	12.99
L$_3$	16.52
L$_4$	20.07
L$_5$	30.13

Fig. 4.2 Number of tuples in relation R by Age and Location (**a**), L_i-conditioned distributions P(Age| L_i), $i = 1, \ldots, 5$, over relation R (**b**), and location frequencies (**c**)

The existence of a correlation between the distribution of values of attributes X for a given target y and the sensitive information $s(y)$ is captured by the definition of *dependency* as follows.

Definition 4.1 (Dependency). Let R be a relation over attributes A, let X and Y be two disjoint subsets of A, and let $s(Y)$ be a sensitive property of Y. A *dependency*, denoted X⤳Y, represents a relationship existing between the conditional distribution $P(X|y)$ and the value of the sensitive property $s(y)$, for any $y \in Y$.

The existence of a dependency between the y-conditioned distribution of X and the sensitive property $s(y)$ introduces an inference channel, since the visibility on $P(X|y)$ potentially enables an observer to infer the sensitive information $s(y)$ even if not released. For instance, with respect to our running example, Age⤳Location.

Definition 4.1 simply states the existence of a dependency but does not address the issue of possible leakages of sensitive information. In this chapter, we consider the specific case of leakage caused by *peculiar* value distributions that differ from what is considered typical and expected. We then start by characterizing the expected distribution, formally defined as *baseline distribution* as follows.

Definition 4.2 (Baseline Distribution). Let A be a set of attributes, and X be a subset of A. The *baseline distribution* of X, denoted $B(X)$, is the expected distribution of the different values (or range thereof) of X.

The baseline distribution is the distribution publicly released by the data holder and can correspond to the real distribution of the values of attributes X in relation R (i.e., $B(X) = P(X)$) at a given time or can be a "reference" distribution considered typical. We assume the data holder to release truthful information and, therefore, that the baseline distribution resembles the distribution of the values of X in R at a given point in time (note that R may be subject to changes over time, for example, due to the enrollment of new soldiers and the retirement of old soldiers). This being said, in the following, for simplicity, we assume the baseline distribution $B(X)$ to coincide with $P(X)$. When clear from the context, with a slight abuse of notation, we will use $P(X)$ to denote the baseline distribution.

Example 4.3. The baseline distribution $P(\text{Age})$ corresponds to the values (expressed in percentage) in the last column of Fig. 4.2b, which is also graphically reported as a histogram in Fig. 4.3a. Figures 4.3b–f report the histogram representation of the L_i-conditioned distributions for the different locations in R. As clearly visible from the histograms, while locations L_1, L_3, L_4, and L_5 enjoy a value distribution that resembles the expected baseline, location L_2 (the headquarter) shows a considerably different distribution.

Our goal is to avoid the inference of the sensitive information caused by *unusual* distributions of values of X, with respect to specific targets y, in Y that the observer can learn from viewing released tuples (i.e., the y-conditioned distributions

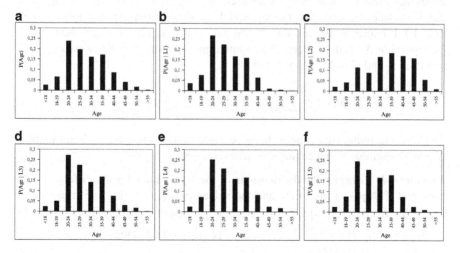

Fig. 4.3 Histogram representation of the baseline distribution (**a**) and of the L_i-conditioned distributions $P(\text{Age}| L_i), i = 1, \dots, 5$, in Fig. 4.2b. (**a**) $P(\text{Age})$, (**b**) $P(\text{Age}|L_1)$, (**c**) $P(\text{Age}|L_2)$, (**d**) $P(\text{Age}|L_3)$, (**e**) $P(\text{Age}|L_4)$, (**f**) $P(\text{Age}|L_5)$

computed over released tuples present some peculiarities that distinguish it from the baseline distribution). To this purpose, in the following sections we illustrate a solution that the data holder can adopt for verifying whether the release of a tuple referred to a target y, together with the previously released tuples, may cause the inference of the sensitive property $s(y)$ and then whether the release of such a tuple can be permitted or should be denied.

4.4 Characterization of the Inference Problem

In our characterization of the problem, X and Y can be intended as two dependent random variables, meaning that there is a correlation between the values of X and Y. Due to this dependency, a potential observer can exploit the distribution of values of X for a given target y (i.e., the y-conditioned distribution) for inferring sensitive property $s(y)$. To counteract this type of inference, we obfuscate the dependency between X and Y in the released dataset, by adopting one of the following two strategies: (1) make X and Y appear as two statistically independent random variables; or (2) minimize the distance between the y-conditioned distribution $P(X|y)$ and the baseline distribution $P(X)$.

Statistical Independence The first strategy ensures that the joint probability $P(X,Y)$ be "similar" to $P(X)P(Y)$. Since when X and Y are two independent variables the joint probability $P(X,Y)$ is equal to $P(X)P(Y)$, this strategy aims at releasing tuples such that the correlation between X and Y is not visible. As a consequence, the knowledge of the distribution of X does not give any information about the sensitive property $s(y)$ for each target y in Y. A classical measure of the dependency between two random variables is the *mutual information*, denoted $I(X,Y)$. It expresses the amount of information that an observer can obtain on Y by observing X, and viceversa. The mutual information $I(X,Y)$ of two random variables X and Y is defined as follows.

$$I(X,Y) = \sum_{x \in X, y \in Y} p(y)p(x|y) \, \log_2 \frac{p(x|y)}{p(x)}$$

The lower the mutual information in the released dataset, the more random variables X and Y resemble statistical independent variables.

Example 4.4. Consider the distributions of the Age values for the different locations and $P(\text{Age})$ in Fig. 4.2b, and the values $p(L_i)$, $i = 1, \dots, 5$, reported in Fig. 4.2c. We have: $I(\text{Age}, \text{Location}) = p(L_1)[p(< 18|L_1) \log_2 \frac{p(<18|L_1)}{p(<18)} + \dots + p(\geq 55|L_1) \log_2 \frac{p(\geq 55|L_1)}{p(\geq 55)}] + \dots + p(L_5)[p(< 18|L_5) \log_2 \frac{p(<18|L_5)}{p(<18)} + \dots + p(\geq 55|L_5) \log_2 \frac{p(\geq 55|L_5)}{p(\geq 55)}] = 0.063285$

Distance Between Distributions The second strategy ensures that when tuples are released, the y-conditioned distribution of all targets y in Y be "similar" to the baseline distribution. Intuitively, this strategy aims at hiding the peculiarities of the distribution of variable X with respect to a specific y so that an observer cannot infer anything about sensitive property $s(y)$. This strategy is then based on the evaluation of the distance between the baseline distribution $P(X)$ and the y-conditioned distribution $P(X|y)$. The distance between two distributions can be computed in different ways. The metrics that will be considered in the following section adopt either the classical notion of *Kullback-Leibler distance* between distributions, denoted Δ, or the *Pearson's cumulative* statistic, denoted F.

The Kullback-Leibler distance nicely fits our scenario since it has a straightforward interpretation in terms of Information Theory. In fact, it represents a possible decomposition of the mutual information [54]. Given two distributions $P(X)$ and $P(X|y)$ their Kullback-Leibler distance is defined as follows.

$$\Delta(X, y) = \sum_{x \in X} p(x|y) \log_2 \frac{p(x|y)}{p(x)}$$

It is easy to see that the mutual information represents the weighted average of the Kullback-Leibler distance for the different targets, where the weight corresponds to the frequency of value y.

Example 4.5. Consider the distributions of Age values for the different locations and the baseline distribution $P(\text{Age})$ in Fig. 4.2b. We have:
$\Delta(\text{Age}, L_1) = p(< 18|L_1) \log_2 \frac{p(<18|L_1)}{p(<18)} + \ldots + p(\geq 55|L_1) \log_2 \frac{p(\geq 55|L_1)}{p(\geq 55)} = 0.047349$.
Similarly, we obtain: $\Delta(\text{Age}, L_2) = 0.358836$, $\Delta(\text{Age}, L_3) = 0.013967$, $\Delta(\text{Age}, L_4) = 0.007375$, and $\Delta(\text{Age}, L_5) = 0.010879$.

The Pearson's cumulative statistic is a well known measure, traditionally used in statistics for evaluating how much two probability distributions are similar. Given two distributions $P(X)$ and $P(X|y)$, their Pearson's cumulative statistic is defined as follows.

$$F(X, y) = \sum_{x \in X} \frac{\left(O_x^y - E_x\right)^2}{E_x}$$

where O_x^y is the frequency of value x for X with respect to y (i.e., the number of tuples in R such that $x = t[X]$ and $y = t[Y]$), and E_x is the expected frequency distribution of the same value x for X according to the baseline distribution $P(X)$.

Example 4.6. Consider the distributions of the Age values for the different locations and the baseline distribution $P(\text{Age})$ in Fig. 4.2b. We have:

$$F(\text{Age}, L_1) = \frac{\left(O_{<18}^{L_1} - E_{<18}\right)^2}{E_{<18}} + \ldots + \frac{\left(O_{\geq 55}^{L_1} - E_{\geq 55}\right)^2}{E_{\geq 55}} = 104.532750$$

Similarly, we obtain: $F(\text{Age}, L_2) = 878.201780$, $F(\text{Age}, L_3) = 30.837391$, $F(\text{Age}, L_4) = 17.340740$, and $F(\text{Age}, L_5) = 39.875054$.

The lower the distance between $P(X|y)$ and $P(X)$ in the released dataset, the more the correlation between variables X and Y has been obfuscated. To determine when the distance between the y-conditioned distribution $P(X|y)$ and the baseline distribution $P(X)$ can be considered significant (and then exploited to infer a possible dependency between X and Y), we can adopt either an *absolute* or a *relative* approach. The absolute approach compares the distance between $P(X|y)$ and $P(X)$ for each value y of Y with a fixed threshold. The relative approach compares instead the distance between $P(X|y)$ and $P(X)$ for a given value y, with the distances obtained for the other values of Y.

Both the strategy based on statistical independence and the strategy based on minimizing the distance between distributions described above for obfuscating the correlation between X and Y can be concretely applied through specific metrics. Before describing such metrics in the following section, it is important to note that an external observer can only see and learn the distribution of values computed on tuples that have been released. In the remainder of this chapter, we will then use R_{rel} to denote the set of tuples released to the external world at a given point in time, and P_{rel} to denote the value distributions observable on R_{rel} (in contrast to the P observable on R). The knowledge of an external observer includes the different observations $P_{rel}(X|y)$ she can learn by collecting all the released tuples (i.e., R_{rel}), and the baseline distribution $P(X)$ publicly available.

4.5 Statistical Tests for Assessing Inference Exposure

In this section, we describe four statistical tests that can be adopted for verifying whether the release of a set of tuples is safe, that is, a potential observer can neither identify the entities associated with a sensitive value (e.g., an observer cannot identify that L_2 is a headquarter), nor improperly associate sensitive values with released entities in the dataset (i.e., false positives). Figure 4.4 summarizes such tests, classifying them depending on the strategy they follow to obfuscate the dependency between statistical variables X and Y, as illustrated in Sect. 4.4.

The statistical tests described in this section are based on the definition of a metric to measure how much the release of a subset R_{rel} of tuples of R is exposed

		Test	Safe release control
Statistical Independence		MIS (Section 4.5.1)	$I_{rel}(X, Y) < I_{rc}$
Distance	Absolute	KLD (Section 4.5.2)	$\forall y \in Y, \Delta_{rel}(X, y) < \Delta_{rc}(y)$
		CST (Section 4.5.3)	$\forall y \in Y, F_{rel}(X, y) < F_{rc}$
	Relative	DQT (Section 4.5.4)	$Q_{rel}(X) < Q_{rc}$

Fig. 4.4 Statistical tests and safe release control

to inferences (*inference exposure*), and on the computation of a threshold that this measure should not exceed to guarantee that the data release is safe. In the following, we define different properties that the released dataset should satisfy to guarantee that a potential observer cannot infer the existence of a dependency between the random variables X and Y.

4.5.1 Significance of the Mutual Information

This statistical test aims at ensuring that mutual information $I_{rel}(X, Y)$ characterizing the released dataset R_{rel} is *statistically not significant*. The rationale is that the mutual information between X and Y, as illustrated in Sect. 4.4, measures the average amount of knowledge about Y that an observer acquires looking at X (and vice-versa). In other words, the mutual information $I_{rel}(X, Y)$ between X and Y quantifies the (linear or non linear) dependency between the considered statistical variables. When $I_{rel}(X, Y)$ is close to zero an observer does not have enough confidence on the existence of a dependency between X and Y in the released dataset R_{rel}. Hence, the observer cannot infer anything about the sensitive property $s(y)$ associated with a target y that belongs to the released dataset.

From a practical point of view, to verify when the release of a given subset R_{rel} of R can be considered safe, it is sufficient to check whether the mutual information $I_{rel}(X, Y)$ of R_{rel} is below a predefined threshold I_{rc} close enough to zero. For instance, the release of a set R_{rel} of tuples related to a subset of the soldiers in our running example does not disclose information on the dependency between Age and Location if $I_{rel}(\text{Age}, \text{Location}) < I_{rc}$. A safe release is formally defined as follows.

Definition 4.3 (Safe Release w.r.t. Mutual Information—MIS). Let R be a relation over attributes A, X and Y be two subsets of A such that $X \leadsto Y$, R_{rel} be a subset of tuples in R, and I_{rc} be the critical value for the mutual information. The release of R_{rel} is *safe* iff $I_{rel}(X, Y) < I_{rc}$.

The problem becomes now how to compute I_{rc}. The solution we propose is based on the following property [22].

Property 4.1. Let R be a relation over attributes A, X and Y be two subsets of A such that $X \leadsto Y$, and R_{rel} be a subset of tuples in R. Under the independence hypothesis between X and Y:

$$2N_{rel} \log(2) I_{rel}(X, Y) \sim \chi^2((N_{X_{rel}} - 1)N_{Y_{rel}})$$

where $N_{rel} = |R_{rel}|$ is the number of released tuples, $N_{X_{rel}}$ is the number of values of X in R_{rel}, and $N_{Y_{rel}}$ is the number of values of Y in R_{rel}.

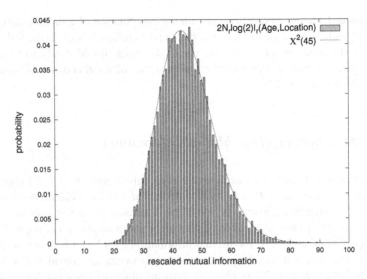

Fig. 4.5 Comparison between the chi-square distribution with 45 degrees of freedom and the distribution of $2N_{rel} \log(2) I_{rel}(\text{Age}, \text{Location})$

Property 4.1 states that under the hypothesis of independence between X and Y, $2N_{rel} \log(2) I_{rel}(X, Y)$ is asymptotically chi-square distributed with $(N_{X_{rel}} - 1) N_{Y_{rel}}$ degrees of freedom.[1]

Example 4.7. Figure 4.5 compares the distribution of the rescaled[2] mutual information $I_{rel}(\text{Age}, \text{Location})$ of our dataset, with the chi-square distribution with $(10 - 1)5 = 45$ degrees of freedom, where 10 is the number of different values for attribute Age and 5 is the number of different values for attribute Location. The histogram in the figure has been obtained with 10000 Monte Carlo iterations, considering the baseline distribution $P(\text{Age})$ and the distribution $P(\text{Location})$ of the sensitive information of our running example. From the figure, it is easy to see that the approximation of our rescaled mutual information to the chi-square distribution nicely holds.

Since, by Property 4.1, $I_{rel}(X, Y)$ is distributed as a chi-square distribution with $(N_{X_{rel}} - 1) N_{Y_{rel}}$ degrees of freedom, we propose to compute the critical value

---

[1] In [22] the mutual information was computed by comparing each y-conditioned distribution $P(X|y)$ with a sample distribution $P(X)$ estimated on the same dataset. Hence, the number of degrees of freedom was $(N_{X_{rel}} - 1)(N_{Y_{rel}} - 1)$. In this chapter, the baseline distribution $P(X)$ is assumed to be known to the observer. Coherently, Property 4.1 is derived under the assumption that the observer tests the mutual information at hand by comparing it to the case where samples (x, y) are drawn from the distribution $P(X, Y) = P(X)P(Y)$. Then, the number of degrees of freedom increases to $(N_{X_{rel}} - 1) N_{Y_{rel}}$.

[2] Rescaled by factor $2N_{rel} \log(2)$, with $N_{rel} = 5000$.

I_{rc} for the mutual information by selecting a *significance level* α (i.e., a residual probability) and imposing $P(I_{rel}(X,Y) > I_{rc}) = \alpha$ (i.e., the probability that $I_{rel}(X,Y)$ is greater than threshold I_{rc} should be equal to α). As a consequence, I_{rc} can be obtained by constraining $\int_0^{2N_{rel}\,\log(2)I_{rc}} \chi^2[(N_{X_{rel}} - 1)N_{Y_{rel}}](x)\mathrm{d}x = 1 - \alpha$. The significance level α represents the confidence in the result of a statistical analysis. Indeed, the higher the value of α, the more restrictive the condition that a release must satisfy to be considered safe. In fact, a lower value for α represents a low probability of error in drawing conclusions starting from the mutual information measured on the data. The value of the significance level α must be chosen in such a way to limit the confidence that an observer can have in the test results, thus preventing the observer from exploiting this test for drawing inferences. For instance, if an observer can evaluate the statistical test with significance level $\alpha = 5\,\%$, the inference she can draw from the result obtained has a high probability of being right (i.e., a high mutual information is due to chance only in 5 % of the cases). The value chosen for α by the data holder should then be higher than the risk that an observer is willing to take when trying to guess the sensitive property $s(y)$ of a target y in Y. If the cost of the observer for her attack is low (e.g., the observer is interested in detecting which location is a headquarter for curiosity), she will be probably willing to take a high risk of making a wrong guess and she will therefore choose a high significance level for her analysis. In this case, α should be high to guarantee a better protection of the sensitive property (e.g., 15–20 %). On the other hand, if the cost of an observer for her attack is high (e.g., the observer wants to destroy headquarters), she will be probably willing to take a low risk of error, and α could be lower, thus permitting the release of a larger subset of tuples (e.g., 5 % represents the typical value adopted in statistical hypothesis testing). Since it is unlikely for the data holder to know the significance level considered by a possible observer in the analysis, the data holder should estimate it and choose a value for α trying to balance the need for data protection on one side and the need for data release on the other side. In fact, the released dataset is protected against those analyses that assume a risk of error lower than α.

Once the data holder has fixed the significance level and computed the critical value I_{rc} for the mutual information, she can decide whether to release a tuple when its respondent requires it. Let R_{rel} be a safe set of released tuples and t be a tuple in R that needs to be released. To decide whether to release t, it is necessary to check if the mutual information $I_{rel}(X,Y)$ associated with $R_{rel} \cup \{t\}$ is lower than critical value I_{rc}. If this is the case, tuple t can be safely released; otherwise tuple t cannot be released since it may cause leakage of sensitive information.

Example 4.8. Consider the military dataset in Fig. 4.2a, the release of the subset R_{rel} of tuples in Fig. 4.6a, and assume that the data holder chooses a significance level $\alpha = 20\,\%$. The mutual information $I_{rel}(\texttt{Age}, \texttt{Location})$ of R_{rel} is 0.025522, while the critical value I_{rc} is 0.025527. Since $I_{rel}(\texttt{Age}, \texttt{Location}) < I_{rc}$, the release of R_{rel} is safe.

Consider the release of the whole dataset R in Fig. 4.2a, and assume that the data holder adopts a less restrictive significance level $\alpha = 5\,\%$. The mutual information

a

Age	Number of tuples					
	L1	L2	L3	L4	L5	Total
<18	9	5	7	8	11	40
18-19	23	11	12	19	29	94
20-24	80	30	68	70	109	357
25-29	71	18	55	58	88	290
30-34	51	30	43	47	74	245
35-39	55	28	46	50	76	255
40-44	25	24	23	25	38	135
45-49	2	10	11	11	13	47
50-54	2	8	4	5	6	25
≥55	1	1	0	0	0	2
Total	319	165	269	293	444	1490

b

Age	$P_{rel}($Age$|Li)$					
	L1	L2	L3	L4	L5	$P_{rel}($Age$)$
<18	2.82	3.03	2.60	2.73	2.48	2.68
18-19	7.21	6.67	4.46	6.49	6.53	6.31
20-24	25.08	18.18	25.28	23.89	24.55	23.96
25-29	22.26	10.91	20.45	19.80	19.81	19.46
30-34	15.99	18.18	15.98	16.04	16.67	16.44
35-39	17.24	16.97	17.10	17.06	17.12	17.11
40-44	7.84	14.55	8.55	8.53	8.56	9.07
45-49	0.63	6.06	4.09	3.75	2.93	3.15
50-54	0.63	4.85	1.49	1.71	1.35	1.69
≥55	0.30	0.60	0.00	0.00	0.00	0.13

c

L_i	$P_{rel}(L_i)$
L_1	21.41
L_2	11.08
L_3	18.05
L_4	19.66
L_5	29.80

Fig. 4.6 Number of tuples by Age and Location in a safe dataset R_{rel} w.r.t. mutual information significance with $\alpha = 20\%$ (**a**), L_i-conditioned distributions $P_{rel}($Age$| L_i)$, $i = 1,\dots,5$, over R_{rel} (**b**), and location frequencies (**c**)

$I($Age, Location$)$ of the whole dataset is 0.063285 (see Example 4.4) and its critical value I_{rc} is 0.004448. Therefore, as expected, the release of the whole dataset is not safe.

4.5.2   Significance of the Distance Between Distributions

The evaluation of the significance of the distance between distributions aims at verifying whether there are specific targets in the released dataset that can be considered as *outliers*, that is, whose y-conditioned distribution is far from the expected distribution represented by the baseline $P(X)$. The rationale is that peculiarities of the y-conditioned distribution can be exploited for inferring the sensitive property $s(y)$. This statistical test, operating on the single values y of Y, works at a finer granularity level than the previous one, based on the mutual information.

As already noted in Sect. 4.4, a possible way for the data holder to verify whether the y-conditioned distribution presents some peculiarities consists in computing the Kullback-Leibler distance $\Delta_{rel}(X, y)$ between the y-conditioned distribution

$P_{rel}(X|y)$ of the released dataset and the baseline distribution $P(X)$. Following an approach similar to that illustrated in Sect. 4.5.1, the disclosure of the sensitive property $s(y)$ can be prevented by ensuring that $\Delta_{rel}(X, y)$ is *statistically not significant*, for all targets y in the released dataset.

From a practical point of view, we can verify if the release of a given subset R_{rel} of R can be considered safe by checking whether the distance $\Delta_{rel}(X, y)$ is smaller than a predefined threshold $\Delta_{rc}(y)$ for all targets y. A safe release is formally defined as follows.

Definition 4.4 (Safe Release w.r.t. KL Distance—KLD). Let R be a relation over attributes A, X and Y be two subsets of A such that $X \leadsto Y$, R_{rel} be a subset of tuples in R, and $\Delta_{rc}(y)$ be the critical value for $\Delta_{rel}(X, y)$, for all values y of Y in R_{rel}. The release of R_{rel} is *safe* iff for all values y of Y in R_{rel}, $\Delta_{rel}(X, y) < \Delta_{rc}(y)$.

According to Definition 4.4, if $\Delta_{rel}(X, y) < \Delta_{rc}(y)$ for all released targets y, the release of R_{rel} is safe. If there exists at least a target y' such that $\Delta_{rel}(X, y') \geq \Delta_{rc}(y')$, the release of R_{rel} is not safe and y' is considered exposed.

The approach we propose to compute threshold $\Delta_{rc}(y)$ is based on the observation that the mutual information $I_{rel}(X, Y)$ by definition equals to $\sum_{y \in Y} p(y) \Delta_{rel}(X, y)$, and that Property 4.1 can be adapted for the Kullback-Leibler distance $\Delta_{rel}(X, y)$ as follows.

Property 4.2. Let R be a relation over attributes A, X and Y be two subsets of A such that $X \leadsto Y$, y be a value of Y, and R_{rel} be a subset of tuples in R. Under the independence hypothesis between X and Y:

$$2N_{rel}(y) \log(2) \Delta_{rel}(X, y) \sim \chi^2(N_{X_{rel}} - 1)$$

where $N_{rel}(y)$ is the number of released tuples with $Y = y$, and $N_{X_{rel}}$ is the number of values of X in R_{rel}.

Property 4.2 states that under the hypothesis of independence between X and Y, $2N_{rel}(y) \log(2) \Delta_{rel}(X, y)$ is asymptotically chi-square distributed with $(N_{X_{rel}} - 1)$ degrees of freedom.

Example 4.9. Figures 4.7a–e compare the distribution of the rescaled (by factor $2N_{rel}(y) \log(2)$ with $N_{rel}(L_1) = 1014$, $N_{rel}(L_2) = 649$, $N_{rel}(L_3) = 826$, $N_{rel}(L_4) = 1003$, and $N_{rel}(L_5) = 1506$) Kullback-Leibler distance $\Delta_{rel}(\text{Age}, L_i)$, $i = 1, \ldots, 5$, with the chi-square distribution with $10 - 1 = 9$ degrees of freedom. The histograms in the figures have been obtained with 10000 Monte Carlo iterations, considering the baseline distribution $P(\text{Age})$ and the distribution $P(\text{Location})$ of the sensitive information of our running example. From the figures, it is easy to see that our rescaled $\Delta_{rel}(\text{Age}, L_i)$ fit the considered chi-square distribution.

For each target y, Property 4.2 can be used to compute the critical value $\Delta_{rc}(y)$ for $\Delta_{rel}(X, y)$ by selecting a *significance level* α and requiring $P(\Delta_{rel}(X, y) > \Delta_{rc}(y)) = \alpha$. $\Delta_{rc}(y)$ can then be obtained by constraining

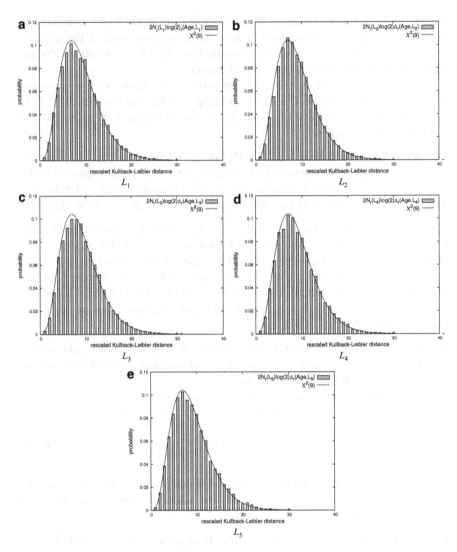

Fig. 4.7 Comparison between the chi-square distribution with 9 degrees of freedom and the distribution of $2N_{rel}(L_1)\log(2)\Delta_{rel}(\text{Age}, L_1)$ **(a)**, $2N_{rel}(L_2)\log(2)\Delta_{rel}(\text{Age}, L_2)$ **(b)**, $2N_{rel}(L_3)\log(2)\Delta_{rel}(\text{Age}, L_3)$ **(c)**, $2N_{rel}(L_4)\log(2)\Delta_{rel}(\text{Age}, L_4)$ **(d)**, and $2N_{rel}(L_5)\log(2)\Delta_{rel}(\text{Age}, L_5)$ **(e)**

$\int_0^{2N_{rel}(y)\log(2)\Delta_{rel}(X,y)} \chi^2(N_{X_{rel}} - 1)(x)\mathrm{d}x = 1 - \alpha$. As already observed for the mutual information, higher values of α guarantee better protection against inference exposure of the sensitive property.

Once the data holder has fixed the significance level and computed the critical values $\Delta_{rc}(y)$ for each target y, she can decide whether to release a tuple when its

a

Age	Number of tuples					
	L1	L2	L3	L4	L5	Total
<18	12	4	6	5	16	43
18-19	25	11	18	18	43	115
20-24	86	29	90	72	141	418
25-29	66	19	65	67	112	329
30-34	56	31	37	49	94	267
35-39	57	29	55	51	115	307
40-44	19	18	19	27	47	130
45-49	9	8	8	4	13	42
50-54	2	4	6	2	7	21
≥55	0	1	1	1	0	3
Total	332	154	305	296	588	1675

b

Age	P_{rel}(Age$\mid$Li)					
	L1	L2	L3	L4	L5	P_{rel}(Age)
<18	3.61	2.60	1.97	1.69	2.72	2.57
18-19	7.53	7.14	5.90	6.08	7.31	6.87
20-24	25.90	18.83	29.51	24.32	23.98	24.96
25-29	19.89	12.34	21.31	22.64	19.05	19.64
30-34	16.87	20.13	12.13	16.55	15.99	15.94
35-39	17.17	18.83	18.03	17.23	19.56	18.33
40-44	5.72	11.69	6.23	9.12	7.99	7.75
45-49	2.71	5.19	2.62	1.35	2.21	2.51
50-54	0.60	2.60	1.97	0.68	1.19	1.25
≥55	0.00	0.65	0.33	0.34	0.00	0.18

c

L_i	$P_{rel}(L_i)$
L_1	19.82
L_2	9.20
L_3	18.21
L_4	17.67
L_5	35.10

Fig. 4.8 Number of tuples by Age and Location in a safe dataset R_{rel} w.r.t. Kullback-Leibler distance with $\alpha = 20\,\%$ (**a**), L_i-conditioned distributions P_{rel}(Age$\mid L_i$), with $i = 1, \ldots, 5$, over R_{rel} (**b**), and location frequencies (**c**)

respondent requires it. Let R_{rel} be a safe set of released tuples and t be a tuple in R whose release has been requested. To decide whether to release t, it is necessary to check if the distance $\Delta_{rel}(X, y)$ for target $y = t[Y]$, computed on $R_{rel} \cup \{t\}$, is lower than the critical value $\Delta_{rc}(y)$. If such a control succeeds, the release of t, that is, the disclosure of $T_{rel} \cup \{t\}$, is considered safe. Otherwise, target y is considered exposed (i.e., y is an outlier) and the release of t is blocked. Note that condition $\Delta_{rel}(X, y) < \Delta_{rc}(y)$ is certainly satisfied for all the targets different from $t[Y]$ because R_{rel} is assumed to be safe.

Example 4.10. Consider the military dataset in Fig. 4.2a and the release of the subset R_{rel} of tuples in Fig. 4.8a, and assume that the data holder adopts a significance level $\alpha = 20\,\%$. The distances between each L_i-conditioned distribution P_{rel}(Age$\mid L_i$), $i = 1, \ldots, 5$, and the baseline distribution P(Age) are: Δ_{rel}(Age$, L_1$) $= 0.026582$, Δ_{rel}(Age$, L_2$) $= 0.056478$, Δ_{rel}(Age$, L_3$) $= 0.028935$, Δ_{rel}(Age$, L_4$) $= 0.029818$, and Δ_{rel}(Age$, L_5$) $= 0.014996$. The critical values are: $\Delta_{rc}(L_1) = 0.026599$, $\Delta_{rc}(L_2) = 0.057343$, $\Delta_{rc}(L_3) = 0.028954$, $\Delta_{rc}(L_4) = 0.029834$, and $\Delta_{rc}(L_5) = 0.015018$. Since the distance Δ_{rel}(Age$, L_i$) computed for each location L_i, $i = 1, \ldots, 5$, is lower than the corresponding critical value, the release of R_{rel} is safe.

Consider the release of the whole dataset R in Fig. 4.2a and assume that the data holder adopts a less restrictive significance level $\alpha = 5\%$. The distances between each L_i-conditioned distribution and the baseline distribution are: $\Delta(\text{Age}, L_1) = 0.047349$, $\Delta(\text{Age}, L_2) = 0.358836$, $\Delta(\text{Age}, L_3) = 0.013967$, $\Delta(\text{Age}, L_4) = 0.007375$, and $\Delta(\text{Age}, L_5) = 0.010879$ (see Example 4.5). Their critical values are: $\Delta_{rc}(L_1) = 0.006015$, $\Delta_{rc}(L_2) = 0.009395$, $\Delta_{rc}(L_3) = 0.007388$, $\Delta_{rc}(L_4) = 0.006081$, $\Delta_{rc}(L_5) = 0.004051$. Since the distance $\Delta(\text{Age}, L_i)$ of each location L_i, $i = 1, \ldots, 5$, exceeds the corresponding critical value, the release of R is, as expected, not safe.

By comparing the two metrics discussed so far, it is easy to see that the metric based on the mutual information does not distinguish the exposures of the different targets. Hence, if for a given y, $p_{rel}(y)$ represents a small portion of the released dataset, a high value for $\Delta_{rel}(X, y)$ has a limited influence on the decision of whether the release of R_{rel} is safe or not, since the contribution of $\Delta_{rel}(X, y)$ in the computation of $I_{rel}(X, Y)$ is limited. On the contrary, the test based on the Kullback-Leibler distance results more restrictive than the evaluation of the significance of the mutual information since the safety control is performed at the level of each single target y of Y.

4.5.3 Chi-Square Goodness-of-Fit Test

The *chi-square goodness-of-fit* test aims at verifying, like the statistical test described in Sect. 4.5.2, whether the released dataset includes a target y that can be considered an *outlier*. The chi-square goodness-of-fit test [90] is a well known statistical test, traditionally used to determine whether a probability distribution $(P_{rel}(X|y))$ fits into another (theoretical) probability distribution $(P(X))$, that is, if the two probability distributions are similar. The test is based on the computation of Pearson's cumulative statistic $F_{rel}(X, y)$ that measures how "close" the observed y-conditioned distribution $P_{rel}(X|y)$ is to the expected (baseline) distribution $P(X)$. When $F_{rel}(X, y)$ is close to zero, $P_{rel}(X|y)$ appears as a distribution that fits $P(X)$ (i.e., the values of $P_{rel}(X|y)$ appear as randomly extracted from the baseline distribution $P(X)$) and therefore nothing can be inferred about the sensitive property $s(y)$ associated with target y.

From a practical point of view, we verify if the release of a given subset R_{rel} of R can be considered safe by checking whether the Pearson's cumulative statistic $F_{rel}(X, y)$ is smaller than a predefined threshold F_{rc}. Formally, a safe release is defined as follows.

Definition 4.5 (Safe Release w.r.t. Chi-Square Goodness-of-Fit—CST). Let R be a relation over attributes A, X and Y be two subsets of A such that $X \rightsquigarrow Y$, R_{rel} be a subset of tuples in R, and F_{rc} be the critical value for $F_{rel}(X, y)$. The release of R_{rel} is *safe* iff for all values y of Y in R_{rel}, $F_{rel}(X, y) < F_{rc}$.

According to Definition 4.5, if all the released targets y satisfy condition $F_{rel}(X, y) < F_{rc}$, the release of R_{rel} is safe; if there exists at least a target y' that violates the condition, the release of R_{rel} is not safe and y' is considered exposed.

The threshold F_{rc} is computed by exploiting the following statistical property enjoyed by the chi-square goodness-of-fit test [90].

Property 4.3. Let R be a relation over attributes A, X and Y be two subsets of A such that $X \rightsquigarrow Y$, y be a value of Y, and R_{rel} be a subset of tuples in R. Under the independence hypothesis between X and Y:

$$F_{rel}(X, y) = \sum_{x \in X} \frac{(O_x^y - E_x)^2}{E_x} \sim \chi^2(N_{X_{rel}}(y) - 1)$$

where $N_{X_{rel}}(y)$ is the number of values of X for the tuples in R_{rel} with $Y = y$.

Property 4.3 states that, under the hypothesis of independence between X and Y, the Pearson's cumulative statistic $F_{rel}(X, y)$ is asymptotically chi-square distributed with $(N_{X_{rel}}(y) - 1)$ degrees of freedom. Like for the metrics already discussed, we compute the critical value $F_{rc}(y)$ for the Pearson's cumulative statistic by selecting a *significance level* α and requiring $P(F_{rel}(X, y) > F_{rc}(y)) = \alpha$. As a consequence, $F_{rc}(y)$ can be obtained by constraining $\int_0^{\sum_{x \in X} \frac{(O_x^y - E_x)^2}{E_x}} \chi^2(N_{X_{rel}}(y) - 1)(x)dx = 1 - \alpha$. It is important to note that the number of degrees of freedom of the chi-square distribution depends on the number $N_{X_{rel}}$ of values of variable X that have been released for target y, which may be different from the number of values in the domain of attribute X (for more details see Sect. 4.6).

Once the data holder has fixed the significance level and computed the critical value F_{rc}, she can decide whether to release a tuple when its respondent requires it. Let R_{rel} be a safe set of tuples and t be a requested tuple in R. To evaluate whether the release of tuple t is safe, it is necessary to check whether the Pearson's cumulate statistic $F_{rel}(X, y)$ for target $y = t[Y]$, computed on $R_{rel} \cup \{t\}$ is lower than the fixed threshold F_{rc}. If this is the case, tuple t can be safely released; otherwise the release of t is blocked since it reveals that y is an outlier. We note that it is not necessary to check the Pearson's cumulate statistics of the other targets in R_{rel}, since they are not affected by the release of t, and their associated $F_{rel}(X, y)$ are lower than F_{rc}, as R_{rel} is supposed to be safe.

Example 4.11. Consider the military dataset in Fig. 4.2a and the release of the subset R_{rel} of tuples in Fig. 4.9a and assume that the data holder adopts a significance level $\alpha = 20\%$. The Pearson's cumulative statistics for the five locations are: $F_{rel}(\text{Age}, L_1) = 8.550683$, $F_{rel}(\text{Age}, L_2) = 0.961415$, $F_{rel}(\text{Age}, L_3) = 9.717669$, $F_{rel}(\text{Age}, L_4) = 8.293681$, and $F_{rel}(\text{Age}, L_5) = 8.554984$. The critical values are: $F_{rc}(L_1) = 8.558059$, $F_{rc}(L_2) = 1.642374$, $F_{rc}(L_3) = 9.803249$, $F_{rc}(L_4) = 11.030091$, and $F_{rc}(L_5) = 8.558059$. It is immediate to see that $F_{rel}(\text{Age}, L_i) < F_{rc}(L_i)$, for all $i = 1, \ldots, 5$. As a consequence, the release of R_{rel} is safe.

a

Age	Number of tuples					
	L1	L2	L3	L4	L5	Total
<18	13	0	8	6	4	31
18-19	25	1	13	35	35	109
20-24	92	0	80	100	135	407
25-29	74	0	76	94	117	361
30-34	65	3	55	63	98	284
35-39	64	38	48	71	94	315
40-44	32	7	21	29	41	130
45-49	3	3	11	13	18	48
50-54	0	0	3	8	4	15
≥55	0	0	0	0	0	0
Total	368	52	315	419	546	1700

b

Age	$P_{rel}(Age\|L_i)$					
	L1	L2	L3	L4	L5	$P_{rel}(Age)$
<18	3.53	0.00	2.53	1.43	0.73	1.82
18-19	6.79	1.92	4.13	8.35	6.41	6.41
20-24	25.00	0.00	25.4	23.87	24.73	23.94
25-29	20.11	0.00	24.13	22.43	21.43	21.24
30-34	17.66	5.77	17.46	15.04	17.95	16.71
35-39	17.39	73.08	15.24	16.95	17.21	18.53
40-44	8.70	13.46	6.67	6.92	7.51	7.65
45-49	0.82	5.77	3.49	3.10	3.3	2.82
50-54	0.00	0.00	0.95	1.91	0.73	0.88
≥55	0.00	0.00	0.00	0.00	0.00	0.00

c

L_i	$P_{rel}(L_i)$
L_1	21.65
L_2	3.06
L_3	18.52
L_4	24.65
L_5	32.12

Fig. 4.9 Number of tuples by Age and Location in a safe dataset R_{rel} w.r.t. Chi-Square Goodness-of-Fit with $\alpha = 20\%$ (**a**), L_i-conditioned distributions $P_{rel}(Age\| L_i)$, $i = 1,\dots,5$, over R_{rel} (**b**), and location frequencies (**c**)

Consider the release of the whole dataset R in Fig. 4.2a and assume that the data holder adopts a less restrictive significance level $\alpha = 5\%$. The Pearson's cumulative statistics for the five locations are: $F(Age, L_1) = 104.532750$, $F(Age, L_2) = 878.201780$, $F(Age, L_3) = 30.837391$, $F(Age, L_4) = 17.340740$, and $F(Age, L_5) = 39.875054$ (see Example 4.6). The critical values are: $F_{rc}(L_1) = 15.507313$, $F_{rc}(L_2) = 16.918978$, $F_{rc}(L_3) = F_{rc}(L_4) = F_{rc}(L_5) = 15.507313$. Therefore, $P(Age\|L_i)$, $i = 1,\dots,5$, is not close enough to $P(Age)$ and the release of the whole dataset is not safe. This result is not surprising since none of the L_i-conditioned distribution $P(Age\|L_i)$, $i = 1,\dots,5$, in our running example exactly fits the baseline distribution $P(Age)$.

4.5.4 Dixon's Q-Test

The Dixon's Q-test, similarly to the statistical tests described in Sects. 4.5.2 and 4.5.3, aims at verifying whether there is one target in the released dataset that can be considered an *outlier*. The Dixon's Q-test is a well-known solution for outlier detection in a given dataset that can be adopted whenever there is at most one outlier and at least three targets in the considered dataset [48]. This statistical test differs from the ones illustrated in Sects. 4.5.2 and 4.5.3 since, instead of comparing each distance between $P_{rel}(X|y)$ and $P(X)$ against a fixed threshold, it evaluates if one of the distances between $P_{rel}(X|y)$ and $P(X)$ is significantly higher than the others. The Dixon's Q-test can be applied considering any definition of distance between distributions (e.g., Kullback-Leibler distance, or Pearson's cumulative statistic). In line with the rest of the chapter, we apply the Dixon's Q-test to the Kullback-Leibler distance $\Delta_{rel}(X, y)$ between $P_{rel}(X|y)$ and $P(X)$. We note that different versions of this test have been proposed in the literature, and we adopt r_{10} [48]. This test assumes the presence of at most one outlier at the upper hand of the dataset (i.e., one outlier characterized by a high value for the distance between distributions) and no outlier at the lower hand of the dataset (i.e., no outlier is characterized by a low distance between distributions).

The Dixon's Q-test requires to first organize the values on which it needs to be evaluated (i.e., $\Delta_{rel}(X, y)$ in our scenario) in ascending order. Starting from the last two values in the ordered sequence (i.e., the two highest values), it computes coefficient $Q_{rel}(X)$ as their relative distance. More formally, Dixon's coefficient is computed as:

$$Q_{rel}(X) = \frac{\Delta_{rel}(X, y_n) - \Delta_{rel}(X, y_{n-1})}{\Delta_{rel}(X, y_n) - \Delta_{rel}(X, y_1)},$$

where $\Delta_{rel}(X, y_1), \ldots, \Delta_{rel}(X, y_n)$ is the sequence, in ascending order, of distance values.

The Dixon's Q-test is not able to identify any outlier in the dataset if $Q_{rel}(X)$ is close enough to zero, since the distance between each pair of subsequent values in the sequence is almost the same. In this case, there is no target y such that the distance between its y-conditioned distribution $P_{rel}(X|y)$ and the baseline $P(X)$ stands out from the other distances.

From a practical point of view, we verify if the release of a given subset R_{rel} of R can be considered safe by checking whether the Dixon's coefficient $Q_{rel}(X)$ is smaller than a predefined threshold Q_{rc}. The critical value Q_{rc} is computed by fixing a *significance level* α and imposing $P(Q_{rel}(X) > Q_{rc}) = \alpha$. Figure 4.10 summarizes the critical values Q_{rc} when the number of distinct values in the domain of Y ranges between 3 and 10 and the significance level is fixed to 20 %, 10 %, 5 %,

Significance	Number of elements							
	3	4	5	6	7	8	9	10
20%	0.781	0.560	0.451	0.386	0.344	0.314	0.290	0.273
10%	0.886	0.679	0.557	0.482	0.434	0.399	0.370	0.349
5%	0.941	0.765	0.642	0.560	0.507	0.468	0.437	0.412
1%	0.988	0.889	0.780	0.698	0.637	0.590	0.555	0.527

Fig. 4.10 Critical values Q_c for the Dixon's Q-test with significance levels 20 %, 10 %, 5 %, 1 % and [3–10] distinct values in Y domain [49]

and 1 %, respectively. If $Q_r(X) < Q_{rc}$, the release of R_{rel} does not reveal the presence of any outlier and the release of R_{rel} is *safe*. A safe release is formally defined as follows.

Definition 4.6 (Safe Release w.r.t. Dixon's Q-Test—DQT). Let R be a relation over attributes A, X and Y be two subsets of A such that $X \rightsquigarrow Y$, R_{rel} be a subset of tuples in R, and Q_{rc} be a critical value for $Q_{rel}(X)$. The release of R_{rel} is *safe* iff $Q_r(X) < Q_{rc}$.

If condition $Q_r(X) < Q_{rc}$ does not hold, an observer can infer that the target y characterized by the maximum distance $\Delta_{rel}(X, y)$ between $P_{rel}(X|y)$ and $P(X)$ is an outlier.

Once the data holder has fixed the significance level and computed the critical value Q_{rc} for the Dixon's Q-test, she can decide whether to release a tuple when its respondent requires it. Let R_{rel} be a safe set of released tuples and t be a requested tuple in R. To decide whether to release t, it is necessary to check if Dixon's coefficient $Q_r(X)$ associated with $R_{rel} \cup \{t\}$ is lower than critical value Q_{rc}. If this is the case, tuple t can be safely released; otherwise tuple t is not released since it may cause leakage of sensitive information.

Example 4.12. Consider the military dataset in Fig. 4.2a and the release of the subset R_{rel} of tuples in Fig. 4.11a, and assume that the data holder adopts a significance level $\alpha = 20\%$. The distance values between $P_{rel}(\text{Age}|L_i)$, $i = 1, \ldots, 5$, and the baseline $P(\text{Age})$ are equal to: $\Delta_{rel}(\text{Age}, L_1) = 0.209188$, $\Delta_{rel}(\text{Age}, L_2) = 0.361504$, $\Delta_{rel}(\text{Age}, L_3) = 0.037932$, $\Delta_{rel}(\text{Age}, L_4) = 0.018421$, and $\Delta_{rel}(\text{Age}, L_5) = 0.021103$. To apply the Dixon's Q-test, these distance values are considered in ascending order and the Dixon's coefficient is computed as $Q_{rel}(X) = \frac{0.361504 - 0.209188}{0.361504 - 0.018421} = 0.443963$. Since attribute Location has 5 distinct values in its domain, we consider the third column in the table in Fig. 4.10 for the definition of critical value Q_{rc}. In particular, the critical value is fixed to 0.451 for the considered significance level. Since Dixon's coefficient is lower than the critical value, the release of R_{rel} is safe.

Consider the release of the whole dataset R in Fig. 4.2a and assume that the data holder adopts a less restrictive significance level $\alpha = 5\%$. The distance values in Example 4.5 are considered in ascending order and Dixon's coefficient is computed as $Q_{rel}(X) = \frac{0.358836 - 0.047349}{0.358836 - 0.07375} = 0.886263$, which is greater than 0.642. Therefore, the release of the whole dataset of our running example is not safe, since it discloses that L_2 is an outlier.

4.6   Controlling Exposure and Regulating Releases

We now illustrate how the incremental release of tuples is controlled and regulated according to the metrics discussed in the previous section.

a

Age	Number of tuples					
	L1	L2	L3	L4	L5	Total
<18	14	3	5	8	15	45
18-19	36	10	10	34	43	133
20-24	104	30	77	84	176	471
25-29	96	18	73	76	134	397
30-34	69	50	48	77	109	353
35-39	64	32	49	64	120	329
40-44	0	36	18	30	42	126
45-49	0	34	17	10	18	79
50-54	3	14	5	6	4	32
≥55	1	3	0	1	0	5
Total	387	230	302	390	661	1970

b

Age	$P_{rel}(\text{Age}\|Li)$					
	L1	L2	L3	L4	L5	$P_{rel}(\text{Age})$
<18	3.62	1.30	1.66	2.05	2.27	2.28
18-19	9.30	4.35	3.30	8.72	6.51	6.75
20-24	26.87	13.04	25.50	21.54	26.63	23.91
25-29	24.81	7.83	24.17	19.49	20.27	20.15
30-34	17.83	21.75	15.89	19.74	16.49	17.92
35-39	16.54	13.91	16.23	16.41	18.15	16.70
40-44	0.00	15.65	5.96	7.69	6.35	6.40
45-49	0.00	14.78	5.63	2.56	2.72	4.01
50-54	0.78	6.09	1.66	1.54	0.61	1.63
≥55	0.25	1.30	0.00	0.26	0	0.25

c

L_i	$P_{rel}(L_i)$
L_1	19.64
L_2	11.68
L_3	15.33
L_4	19.80
L_5	33.55

Fig. 4.11 Number of tuples by Age and Location in a safe dataset R_{rel} w.r.t. Dixon's Q-test with $\alpha = 20\%$ (**a**), L_i-conditioned distributions $P_{rel}(\text{Age}| L_i)$, $i = 1, \ldots, 5$, over R_{rel} (**b**), and location frequencies (**c**)

The data holder first chooses the metric and the significance level α she wants to adopt. Every time a tuple t is requested, it is necessary to check if the release of t, combined with all the tuples already released and potentially known to an observer R_{rel}, may cause the unintended disclosure of sensitive information. In particular, if $R_{rel} \cup \{t\}$ satisfies the definition of safe release for the considered metric (see Sect. 4.5), t is released. If tuple t cannot be released when it is requested, its release might simply be denied. However, this choice represents a restrictive solution, since it does not take into consideration the fact that if a tuple cannot be released when it is requested, it may be safely released at a later time (i.e., after the release of other tuples in the dataset). Indeed, the grant or denial of the release of a tuple depends on the set of tuples that has already been released. Exploiting this observation, we propose to insert the tuples that cannot be released when requested into a queue. Every time a tuple t is released, the tuples in the queue are analyzed to check whether a subset of them can be safely released.

Particular attention has to be paid on the release of the first few tuples because they will produce random value distributions that usually do not resemble the actual distributions existing in the dataset. Such random distributions may characterize the data release as not safe, thus blocking any further release and raising many false alarms (since also targets that are not outliers will have a random initial distribution that will differ from the baseline). However, no observer could put confidence on statistics computed over a few releases as they cannot be considered accurate and their distribution can be completely random. With reference to the release of the first few tuples, it is also important to note that the metrics illustrated in Sect. 4.5 are based on approximation properties that hold only when a sufficient number of tuples has been released. There is therefore a starting time at which the data holder should define an alternative condition for determining if a release should be considered safe. In the following we discuss, for each of the metrics in Sect. 4.5, how to check whether the release of a tuple t is safe when only few tuples have been released.

Significance of the Mutual Information and Significance of the Kullback-Leibler Distance Between Distributions The definition of the critical value for the mutual information described in Sect. 4.5.1 is based on Property 4.1, which is an asymptotic approximation of $I_{rel}(X, Y)$ to a chi-square distribution that holds only if a sufficient number of tuples has been released. Using the traditional Monte Carlo approach, we propose to compute the critical value of the mutual information for the release of a small number n of tuples as the α-th percentile of the mutual information obtained by extracting a sufficient number of samples (10000 in our experimental evaluation) of n tuples each from a simulated dataset composed of $|R|$ tuples, where X is distributed following $P(X)$, and X and Y are statistically independent. Indeed, if the mutual information of the released dataset is close to the mutual information of a sample of the same size extracted from a dataset where X and Y are statistically independent, the observer cannot exploit the released tuples for drawing inferences. The remaining aspect to consider is when to start adopting the critical value computed exploiting Property 4.1. A nice approximation is represented by $2N_X N_Y$ tuples (100 in our example), which is confirmed by our experimental evaluation illustrated in Fig. 4.12. In this figure, the curve representing the critical value for the mutual information, corresponding to the value computed through the Monte Carlo method in the interval [0–100] and exploiting Property 4.1 in interval [100–10000], presents a smooth trend. This result also confirms that Property 4.1 holds in our framing of the problem.

The same approach can be adopted for the metric based on the Kullback-Leibler distance since Property 4.2 derives from Property 4.1, and the mutual information is a weighted average of the Kullback-Leibler distances for the different targets y in the dataset.

Chi-Square Goodness-of-Fit Test The approximation on which this statistical test is based holds on a data collection only if, for each target y and for each $x \in X$, a sufficient number of tuples (typically 5 [90]) has been released. In other words, considering a target y, for each $x \in X$, there must be at least 5 tuples in R_{rel} with $t[Y] = y$ and $t[X] = x$. If, for a given target y, there are less than 5 tuples with value x for attribute X, we can combine x with either its preceding or subsequent value in the domain of X and sum their relative frequencies. With reference to our example, if only 2 soldiers located at L_2 in the age range [20–24] have been released, range [20–24] for L_2 can be combined either with [18–19] or with [25–29] for the same location. Suppose now that the relative frequency for age range [25–29] is 4. By merging [20–24] with [25–29] for location L_2, we obtain a new value [20–29] of the domain of attribute Age for location L_2, with relative frequency equal to 6. This process is iteratively applied, possibly combining a set of contiguous values for attribute X, until all the relative frequencies of the values in the domain of X are greater than or equal to 5. If all the values in X are combined in a unique value, the test cannot be applied and the release is considered safe. If at least 2 values in the domain of X are maintained, the test can be evaluated. We note however that when multiple original values of X are combined, the approximation in Property 4.3 should be revised to consider the correct number of degrees of freedom, which is equal to the number of values in the domain of X in R_{rel} after the possible merge operation. For instance, with reference to our example, suppose that the values for attribute Age for location L_2 have been combined obtaining the following domain values: ≤ 24, [25–39], [40–44], [45, 49], ≥ 50. The critical value of Pearson's cumulative statistic for L_2 should be computed considering a chi-square distribution with 4 (instead of 9) degrees of freedom.

Dixon's Q-Test As already noted, this statistical test can be applied only on data collections that include at least 3 elements [48]. In our scenario, it can then be used only if 3 different distances between the y-conditioned distributions and the baseline can be computed. Consequently, datasets with less than 3 different distance values are considered safe since an observer could not gain any information.

4.7 Experimental Results

To evaluate the behavior of the metrics presented in Sect. 4.5, we implemented the data release strategy described in Sect. 4.6 with a Matlab prototype and executed a series of experiments. For the experiments, we considered the dataset R introduced in Example 4.2, which has been obtained by randomly extracting 10000 tuples from the baseline distribution $P(\text{Age})$ of the age of soldiers of the UK Regular Forces as at 1 April 2006 [103] (Fig. 4.3a). The experiments evaluated the inference exposure (computed as the mutual information, Kullback-Leibler distance between distributions, Pearson's cumulative statistic, or Dixon's coefficient), and the information loss (i.e., the number of tuples not released upon request) caused by our privacy protection technique. We also compared the results obtained adopting the different metrics.

4.7.1 Inference Exposure

We evaluated how the metrics discussed in Sect. 4.5 vary with the release of tuples and compared them with the corresponding critical values. The experiments have been conducted on 20 randomly extracted sequences of 10000 requests each. For the sake of readability, in this section we illustrate the graphs showing the evolution

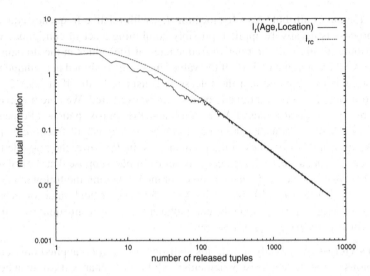

Fig. 4.12 Evolution of the mutual information and its critical value

of the inference exposure and of its critical value for one of the 20 sequences; the results obtained with the other sequences present a similar trend.

Mutual Information Figure 4.12 shows the evolution of both the mutual information, and the corresponding critical value, varying the number of released tuples (the scale of the axis in Fig. 4.12 is logarithmic). The two curves are close to each other and their distance decreases as the number of released tuples increases. It is easy to see that the mutual information of released data is always lower than the critical value. The figure also shows a smooth trend for the curve representing the critical value, confirming that the approximation in Property 4.1 nicely holds in our scenario. In fact, the discontinuity in the critical value of the mutual information when the 100th tuple is released, due to the fact that the critical value is computed using the Monte Carlo based approach in the interval [1–100] and the approach using Property 4.1 in the interval [100–10000], is small and cannot be noticed in the figure.

Kullback-Leibler Distance Figures 4.13a–e show the evolution of both the Kullback-Leibler distance between $P_{rel}(\text{Age}|L_i)$ and $P(\text{Age})$, $i = 1, \ldots, 5$, and the corresponding critical values, varying the number of released tuples (the scale of the axis in Figs. 4.13a–e is logarithmic). It is not surprising that the trends shown in these figures are similar to that illustrated in Fig. 4.12. Indeed, the mutual information is the weighted average of the Kullback-Leibler distance values of all the locations in the dataset. It is interesting to note that all the locations present a similar trend for the evolution of both the Kullback-Leibler distance and its critical value. Also, like for the mutual information, Figs. 4.13a–e present a smooth trend in the curves representing the critical values for the five locations, confirming that the

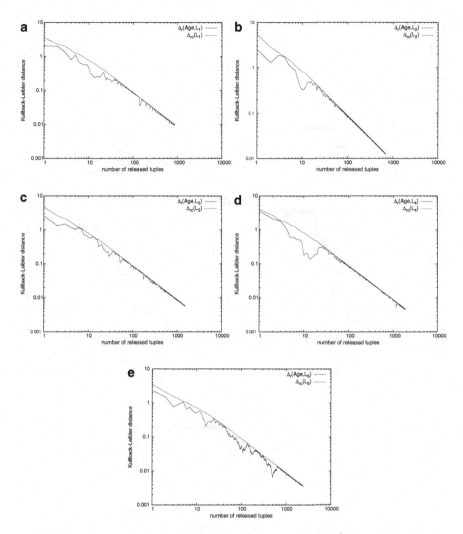

Fig. 4.13 Evolution of the Kullback-Leibler distance between $P_{rel}(\text{Age}|L_i)$ and $P(\text{Age})$ and its critical value for each location. (**a**) L_1, (**b**) L_2, (**c**) L_3, (**d**) L_4, (**e**) L_5

approximation in Property 4.2 holds. In fact, the discontinuity in the critical value of the Kullback-Leibler distance when the 100th tuple is released cannot be noticed from the figure.

Chi-Square Goodness-of-Fit Figures 4.14a–e show the evolution of both the Pearson's cumulative statistic of each location, and the corresponding critical values, varying the number of released tuples. As discussed in Sect. 4.5.3, when a sufficient number of tuples have been released the critical value F_{rc} is the same for all the locations. On the contrary, when a limited number of tuples have been released, the

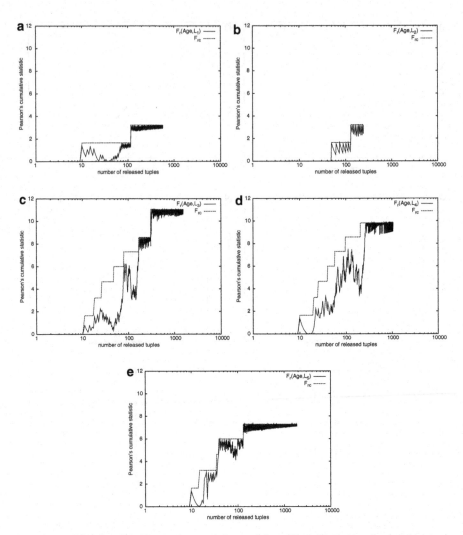

Fig. 4.14 Evolution of the Pearson's cumulative statistic and its critical value for each location. (a) L_1, (b) L_2, (c) L_3, (d) L_4, (e) L_5

critical value may be different for each location, depending on the number of distinct values in the domain of attribute X for each location. As it is visible from Fig. 4.14, the curve representing the critical value has different steps. Each step corresponds to a change in the number of values in the domain of X and therefore a different (higher) number of degrees of freedom of the chi-square distribution in Property 4.3. When the number of released tuples does not permit to correctly evaluate if the Chi-square goodness-of-fit test is passed or not, the release is considered safe since an observer cannot gain knowledge by looking at the released data. This is the reason why the Pearson's cumulative statistic and its critical value are not computed

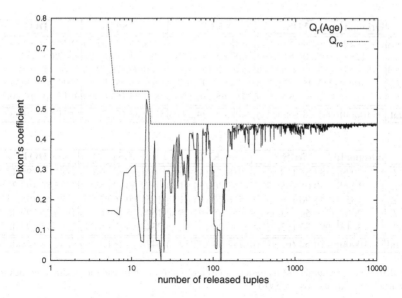

Fig. 4.15 Evolution of the Dixon's coefficient and its critical value

for the first few (about 10) released tuples in Figs. 4.14a–e. For all the locations, the value of the Pearson's cumulative statistic increases while tuples are released. In particular, this growing trend is more visible when less than 100 tuples have been released. Also in this case, as expected, the distance between the Pearson's cumulative statistic and its critical value decreases while data are released.

Dixon's Q-Test Figure 4.15 shows the evolution of both the Dixon's coefficient and the corresponding critical value, varying the number of released tuples. The distance between Dixon's coefficient and the critical value decreases while tuples are released. As it is visible from Fig. 4.15, the Dixon's coefficient and its critical value are not reported for the first 5 tuples released. This is due to the fact that, for the first 5 tuples, it is not possible to compute 3 different distance values between y-conditioned distributions and the baseline. The curve representing the critical value presents three steps. Each step corresponds to the release of a tuple that permits to compute an additional difference. In other words, it corresponds to the release of a tuple t such that $t[Y]$ is a target that either was not represented in R_{rel} or that was characterized by a distance from the baseline equal to the distance of another target.

We note that, for all the considered metrics, the distance between the exposure and its critical value decreases as more data are released, since the fluctuations in the value distribution characterize the release of the first few tuples. In fact, as the number of tuples in the released dataset increases, the impact of the release of a single tuple on the distribution of released values decreases.

a

	Original	MIS	KLD	CST	DQT
L_1	2029	1156.00 (56.97%)	871.85 (42.97%)	994.55 (49.02%)	1935.85 (95.41%)
L_2	1299	705.20 (54.29%)	697.65 (53.71%)	255.35 (19.66%)	1262.65 (97.20%)
L_3	1652	1119.00 (67.74%)	1549.75 (93.81%)	1300.00 (78.69%)	1565.45 (94.76%)
L_4	2007	1256.95 (62.63%)	1874.75 (93.41%)	1361.85 (67.86%)	1990.20 (99.16%)
L_5	3013	1876.65 (62.29%)	2415.65 (80.17%)	1899.25 (63.04%)	3013.00 (100.00%)
Total	10000	6095.78 (60.96%)	7408.67 (74.09%)	5119.88 (51.20%)	9631.55 (96.32%)

b

	Original	MIS	KLD	CST	DQT
L_1	2029	1187.55 (58.53%)	918.35 (45.26%)	1021.85 (50.36%)	1996.90 (98.42%)
L_2	1299	720.05 (55.43%)	713.30 (54.91%)	322.30 (24.81%)	1275.80 (98.21%)
L_3	1652	1145.90 (69.36%)	1576.20 (95.41%)	1151.90 (69.73%)	1571.80 (95.15%)
L_4	2007	1283.50 (63.95%)	1951.85 (97.25%)	1698.15 (84.61%)	1996.25 (99.46%)
L_5	3013	1907.85 (63.32%)	2530.20 (83.98%)	2344.55 (77.81%)	2996.75 (99.46%)
Total	10000	6290.58 (62.91%)	7757.14 (77.57%)	6478.14 (64.78%)	9846.14 (98.46%)

Fig. 4.16 Average number of requested tuples released by each metric for the different locations with $\alpha = 20\%$ (**a**) and $\alpha = 5\%$ (**b**)

4.7.2   Information Loss

To evaluate the quality of the results obtained adopting our metrics, we consider the number of released and discarded tuples. Figures 4.16a,b summarize the average number of tuples released by each of our metrics with significance level α equal to 20 % and 5 %, respectively, for the 20 sequences of 10000 requests that we generated for our experiments, distinguishing also how many requests for each location have been fulfilled.

Comparing the results in Figs. 4.16a,b we note that, as expected, a lower significance level permits to release a higher number of tuples for all the considered metrics. Indeed, most of the cells in the table in Fig. 4.16b have higher values than the corresponding cells in Fig. 4.16a. It is also easy to see that there is not a metric that is always better than the others in terms of the number of tuples released. For instance, Dixon's Q-test is less restrictive that the other metrics, since it releases the highest number of tuples as a whole and for each locations when $\alpha = 20\%$, and as a whole and for each locations but L_3 when $\alpha = 5\%$. From our analysis of the results reported in the two tables, we can conclude that the considered metrics adopt a different approach to protect the released data: CST and KLD block the release of the tuples of the outlier, while MIS and DQT block the release of the tuples from all the locations.

The location with the fewest released tuples is L_2 for both MIS and CST metrics, and for DQT in the case $\alpha = 20\%$. This is a non-surprising result, since L_2 is the headquarter (i.e., the outlier that needs to be protected). On the contrary, metric KLD blocks more tuples from L_1 than from L_2, and DQT, for $\alpha = 5\%$, blocks more tuples from location L_3 than from L_2. The location that enjoys the largest

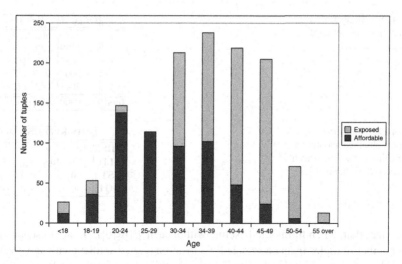

Fig. 4.17 Fitting the baseline distribution within the L_2-conditioned distribution

number of tuples released with $\alpha = 20\%$ is L_3 for all the metrics but DQT, which privileges location L_5. With $\alpha = 5\%$, the location with the highest percentage of released tuples is L_4 for all the metrics but MIS, which privileges location L_3.

It is interesting to note that all the metrics proposed in this chapter to evaluate if a release is safe permit to release a considerable number of tuples, especially if compared with the (more intuitive) approach of *fitting the baseline distribution* within each L_i-conditioned distribution. Fitting the baseline within an L_i-conditioned distribution forces a maximum number of tuples that could be released for each age range in L_i, since the relative frequency of the tuples in each age range must be exactly that of the baseline for each location in the released dataset. For instance, in the baseline distribution almost 19.67% soldiers are in the range [25–29], while in L_2 only 8.78% of tuples (140 tuples) fall in such range. Respecting the baseline distribution requires, even in the case where all tuples in the range [25–29] of L_2 are released to not release tuples in other ranges (so that the 140 tuples above actually correspond to 19.67%). Figure 4.17 graphically depicts this reasoning of fitting the baseline distribution (in black) within the L_2-conditioned distribution (gray going over the black). For each value range, no more than the number reached by the baseline distribution should be released. Figure 4.18 summarizes the number of tuples for each location that would be released adopting the approach of fitting the baseline within each L_i-conditioned distribution, $i = 1, \ldots, 5$. It is easy to see that this approach is far more restrictive than our solution and blocks the release of a larger number of tuples. Each of the proposed metrics permits to release a higher number of tuples for most of the locations (but for CST in the case of location L_4 with $\alpha = 20\%$ and L_3 with $\alpha = 5\%$). In particular, our approach permits to release in most cases more than twice the number of tuples that would be released by fitting the baseline distribution within each L_i-conditioned distribution. This is mainly due

Fig. 4.18 Number of requested tuples released fitting the baseline

	Original	Released	
L_1	2029	500	(24.6%)
L_2	1299	580	(44.6%)
L_3	1652	952	(57.7%)
L_4	2007	952	(47.5%)
L_5	3013	952	(31.6%)
Total	10000	3937	(39.37%)

Fig. 4.19 Number of datasets obtained adopting a metric that are safe also with respect to the other metrics

	MIS	KLD	CST	DQT
MIS	100	0	0	54
KLD	1	100	1	61
CST	0	0	100	45
DQT	0	0	0	100

to the fact that, when fitting the baseline within each $P(\text{Age}|L_i)$, the presence of a low number of tuples in an age-range for a location (e.g., 2 soldiers with age greater than 55 in L_3, L_4, and L_5) hardly constraints the release of the tuples in all the other age ranges. In our example, the two tuples representing soldiers older than 55 must represent the 0.21 % of all the tuples released for locations L_3, L_4, and L_5. As a consequence, the data holder can release at most 952 tuples of L_3, L_4, and L_5. Our metrics try to loosen this constraint, by evaluating the distance (or its average) between the distributions, instead of the value that the distribution has at each age value.

4.7.3 Comparison

To further compare the behavior of the metrics proposed, we have randomly generated 100 request sequences of 5000 tuples each, out of the 10000 in our dataset of the UK Regular Forces. For each of the metrics proposed in the chapter, and for each of the 100 random request sequences, we run our algorithm. For this series of experiments, we fixed the significance level α to 20 %, which represents the most restrictive release scenario. We then checked, for each of the metrics, how many of the 100 safe releases obtained running our algorithm with the considered metric represents a safe release also with respect to each of the other three metrics. Figure 4.19 summarizes the number of datasets obtained adopting each metric (on the row) that are safe also with respect to the other metrics (on the column). It is immediate to see that DQT is the less restrictive metric, confirming the results illustrated in the previous subsection. In fact, none of the 100 datasets obtained adopting DQT metric is safe with respect to the other three metrics (fourth row in Fig. 4.19). On the contrary, 54 (61 and 45, respectively) datasets obtained using MIS metric (KLD and CST metrics, respectively) also satisfy the definition of safe release of Dixon's Q-test. The most restrictive metric is instead KLD, since no dataset obtained adopting a different metric resulted safe with respect to KLD metric (second column in Fig. 4.19) while at least one dataset obtained adopting KLD metric is safe with respect to each of the other three metrics (second row in Fig. 4.19). It is interesting to note that this result is different from the conclusions drawn in the previous subsection, where we noted that MIS and CST are the metrics that minimize the release of tuples. It is however not surprising since the analysis illustrated in Fig. 4.19 is different from the one summarized in Figs. 4.16a,b. In fact, the results illustrated in Fig. 4.19 are obtained analyzing a dataset that is considered safe by one metric with respect to the other metrics introduced in Sect. 4.5. On the contrary, the results in Figs. 4.16a,b are obtained analyzing the safe datasets produced by each of the metrics of interest, starting from the same original data collection and considering the same order in the request of tuple. The results in Fig. 4.19 confirm the fact that the considered metrics measure the exposure of the released dataset in different ways and that the considered metrics obtain a different result if applied to the same sequence of tuple requests. Each metric is therefore suited for protecting a different statistical characteristic of the data that could be exploited for inference purposes. For instance, MIS metric is the ideal solution to protect the released data against attacks that exploit the mutual information between X and Y (i.e., their statistical dependency) to gain information about the sensitive property. To decide the metric and the value for α to be adopted for protecting the release of her dataset, the data holder needs to estimate the attacks that a possible observer could exploit to gain sensitive information. If the data holder wants to achieve a higher protection for her data, she can combine (a subset of) the metrics introduced in Sect. 4.5. This approach, while better preserving privacy of sensitive data, has the drawback of limiting the number of tuples released, since the released dataset must satisfy all the conditions in Fig. 4.4 (or a subset thereof). Analogously, to take a safe approach, the data holder can choose a high value for the significance level.

4.8 Chapter Summary

In this chapter, we considered the problem of protecting sensitive information in an incremental data release scenario, where the data holder releases non sensitive data on demand. As more and more data are released, an external observer can aggregate such data and infer the sensitive information by exploiting the dependency between the distribution of the non sensitive released data and the sensitive information itself. We presented an approach for characterizing when data can be released without incurring to such inference. To this purpose, we defined different metrics that can be considered to determine when the released data can be exploited for inference, and introduced the concept of safe release according to such metrics. We also discussed how to enforce the information release control at run-time, and provided an experimental evaluation of the proposed solution, proving its efficacy.

Chapter 5
Enforcing Dynamic Read and Write Privileges

As illustrated in Chap. 1, users and companies are more and more resorting on external providers for storing their data and making them available to others. When the release is selective, meaning that different users are authorized by the data owner to access different portions of the released data, there is the problem of ensuring that accesses to resources be allowed to authorized users only. Recent approaches based on selective encryption provide convenient enforcement of read privileges over outsourced resources, but are not directly applicable for supporting write privileges. In addition, they cannot easily support the enforcement of a subscription-based authorization policy where, due to new subscriptions and the publication of new resources, both the set of users who can access a resource and the set of resources change frequently over time. In this chapter, we build upon the selective encryption approach to propose an efficient solution for enforcing dynamic read and write privileges over outsourced data. We also define an effective mechanism for checking data integrity. Finally, we enhance our solution to effectively support the definition of subscription-based authorizations.

Part of this chapter is reprinted from Computers & Security, vol. 39, issue A: S. De Capitani di Vimercati, S. Foresti, S. Jajodia, G. Livraga, S. Paraboschi, and P. Samarati, "Enforcing Dynamic Write Privileges in Data Outsourcing", pp. 47–63 [41], ©2013, with permission from Elsevier.
Part of this chapter is reprinted with kind permission from Springer Science+Business Media: Data and Applications Security and Privacy XXVI, Lecture Notes in Computer Science, vol. 7371: S. De Capitani di Vimercati, S. Foresti, S. Jajodia, and G. Livraga, "Enforcing Subscription-Based Authorization Policies in Cloud Scenarios", 2012, pp. 314–329 [40], and any original (first) copyright notice displayed with material.

© Springer International Publishing Switzerland 2015
G. Livraga, *Protecting Privacy in Data Release*, Advances in Information Security 57, DOI 10.1007/978-3-319-16109-9_5

5.1 Introduction

The advances in the Information and Communication Technologies (ICTs) have driven the users into the Globalization era, where the techniques for processing, storing, and accessing information have radically changed. New emerging computing paradigms (e.g., data outsourcing and cloud computing) offer enormous advantages to both users and organizations. Users can now subscribe to a variety of services, and access them anywhere anytime: at home from their laptop, on the train from their tablet, or while waiting in a queue from their smartphone. Organizations are more and more resorting to external elastic storage and computational services for creating and running business over the Internet in new ways. Organizations can then provide large-scale cloud data services widely accessible to a variety of users. A common requirement is that data should remain confidential to both unauthorized users and the external server storing them, which is considered *honest-but-curious* (i.e., trustworthy for managing resources but not for accessing their content). To provide such confidentiality guarantee, existing proposals typically assume data to be encrypted before being sent to the external server, and associate with the encrypted data additional indexing information that can be used by the server to perform queries on encrypted data. For efficiency reasons, encryption is based on symmetric keys. Earlier proposals typically consider data to be encrypted with a single key, assuming either all users to have complete visibility of the resources in the data collection, or the data owner to mediate access requests to the data to enforce read authorizations. More recent proposals, addressing the problem of allowing users to have *selective* visibility over the data (so that different sets of users be able to access different resources), have proposed the application of a 'selective encryption' approach. Intuitively, different keys are used to encrypt different resources, and users have visibility on subsets of resources depending on the keys they know. Proper modeling and key derivation techniques have been devised to ensure limited key management overhead in approaches based on selective encryption.

While interesting and promising, traditional solutions remain limited for a variety of reasons. First, they assume outsourced resources to be read-only. In other words, they assume that only the owner be authorized to modify resources, while all other users can only read them. Such an assumption can result restrictive in all those scenarios where a data owner wants to authorize other users, again selectively, to write and update the outsourced resources. Moreover, traditional techniques cannot easily support a dynamic subscription-based scenario, where both the set of users who can access a resource and the set of resources change frequently over time, due to new subscriptions and the publication of new resources. In this regard, they cannot be directly applied to emerging real-world scenarios in which, for example, users pay for a service and can access the resources made available during their subscriptions: to access resources after the expiration of their subscriptions, users would be forced to download them to their local machine.

In this chapter, we extend selective encryption approaches to overcome these two limitations. By relying on selective encryption for enforcing both read and write access restrictions, our solution has efficiency and manageability as primary goals. Before being stored at the external server, resources are encrypted, and an ad-hoc key derivation structure is built to avoid expensive re-keying and re-encryption operations. Our contribution is therefore multifold. First, we propose an efficient solution for enforcing both read and write authorizations on encrypted resources undergoing selective release. Second, we complement our solution with the definition of a subscription-based authorization policy, allowing users to maintain the right to access the resources made available during their subscriptions without the worry that they will lose this right after the expiration of their subscriptions (for instance, so that users who have purchased an annual subscription for 2012 for a magazine be able to access all and only the issues of the magazine published in 2012, even after December 31, 2012). More in details, our contributions can be summarized as follows.

As for the enforcement of read and write authorizations, we build upon an earlier proposal [39] to support grant and revoke of write authorizations, providing a general solution applicable to scenarios where static write authorizations may result limiting. A key feature of our solution is that it delegates the enforcement of updates on the write access control policy to the external server, reducing the burden left at the data owner side. We also propose a mechanism allowing both the data owner and the authorized writers to verify the integrity of the resources externally stored (i.e., to verify that resources have not been modified by unauthorized users or by the server), applicable also in case of updates to the write access policy.

As for the enforcement of subscription-based authorizations, we take once more advantage of selective encryption to guarantee that users who subscribe for a service can access all and only the resources published during their subscriptions, while allowing the resources to self-enforce the subscription-based restrictions. The key derivation structure is updated whenever new resources are published, new subscriptions are received, or users withdraw from their subscriptions.

By taking into consideration different data release scenarios (i.e., both traditional and subscription-based scenarios), we provide a solution for enforcing access restrictions on externally stored resources, easily applicable by a data owner depending on her specific release needs.

5.1.1 Chapter Outline

The remainder of this chapter is organized as follows. Section 5.2 illustrates some basic concepts on selective encryption, and motivates the need for enforcing write privileges on selectively released resources. Section 5.3 illustrates our solution for enforcing write authorizations exploiting selective encryption. Section 5.4 discusses our approach for enforcing grant and revoke of write privileges. Section 5.5 presents a mechanism for allowing the data owner and writers to check the write operations executed and detect possible misbehaviors by the server or by the users. Section 5.6 extends the integrity check mechanism to support updates to the write access policy. Section 5.7 motivates our extended subscription-based scenario, illustrates the specific protection requirements to be guaranteed, and formalizes the concept of subscription-based policy. Section 5.8 presents our techniques for enforcing a subscription-based policy. Section 5.9 illustrates how new resources can be published and subscriptions managed. Finally, Sect. 5.10 gives our final remarks and concludes the chapter.

5.2 Basic Concepts and Problem Statement

Our work builds upon traditional proposals (e.g., [37]) for confidential data out-sourcing, according to which a data owner outsourcing data to a honest-but-curious server and wishing to provide selective visibility over them to other users encrypts resources before sending them to the external server for storage, and reflects the authorization policy in the encryption itself. Therefore, each resource o is encrypted with a key to be made known only to the users authorized to read o, that is, to users who belong to the access control list of o. Symmetric encryption is used and different keys are assumed: the adoption of a *key derivation technique* based on public tokens allows users to access the resources of the system while having to manage only one key. In further detail, each key k_i is identified by a public label l_i and, given keys k_i and k_j, token $d_{i,j}$ is computed as $k_j \oplus h(k_i, l_j)$, with $\oplus$ the bitwise xor operator, and h a deterministic cryptographic function. Token $d_{i,j}$ permits to derive key k_j from the knowledge of key k_i and public label l_j [5]. All keys with which resources are encrypted are then connected in a graph structure, that is, a DAG whose nodes correspond to keys of the system and whose edges correspond to tokens that ensure that each user can-via a sequence of public tokens-derive the keys corresponding to the sets to which she belongs. Each user is then communicated the key of the node representing herself in the graph. Each resource is encrypted with a key that can be derived only by authorized users according to the access control policy set by the data owner. Encrypted resources as well as the tokens are outsourced to the server. In particular, for each resource o, the external server stores the encrypted version of the resource together with the resource identifier and the label of the key with which the resource is encrypted. A user authorized to read a resource can, via the tokens available on the server, derive the key used for encrypting the resource and decrypt it.

Example 5.1. Consider a system with four users $\mathscr{U} = \{A, B, C, D\}$ and four resources $\mathscr{O} = \{o_1, o_2, o_3, o_4\}$, whose access control lists are reported in Fig. 5.1a. Figure 5.1b illustrates the encrypted resources stored at the server, where: *r_label* is the label of the key used to encrypt the resource (i.e., the key associated with its access control list); *o_id* is the resource identifier; and *encr_resource* is the encrypted resource. Figure 5.1c illustrates the key derivation graph enforcing the

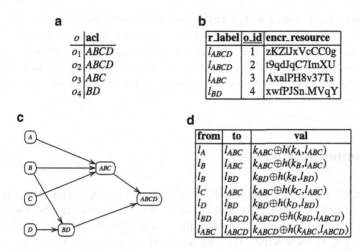

a

o	acl
o_1	ABCD
o_2	ABCD
o_3	ABC
o_4	BD

b

r_label	o_id	encr_resource
l_{ABCD}	1	zKZlJxVcCC0g
l_{ABCD}	2	t9qdJqC7ImXU
l_{ABC}	3	AxalPH8v37Ts
l_{BD}	4	xwfPJSn.MVqY

c

d

from	to	val
l_A	l_{ABC}	$k_{ABC} \oplus h(k_A, l_{ABC})$
l_B	l_{ABC}	$k_{ABC} \oplus h(k_B, l_{ABC})$
l_B	l_{BD}	$k_{BD} \oplus h(k_B, l_{BD})$
l_C	l_{ABC}	$k_{ABC} \oplus h(k_C, l_{ABC})$
l_D	l_{BD}	$k_{BD} \oplus h(k_D, l_{BD})$
l_{BD}	l_{ABCD}	$k_{ABCD} \oplus h(k_{BD}, l_{ABCD})$
l_{ABC}	l_{ABCD}	$k_{ABCD} \oplus h(k_{ABC}, l_{ABCD})$

Fig. 5.1 An example of four resources with their acls (**a**), encrypted resources (**b**), key derivation graph (**c**), and tokens (**d**)

authorizations. For the sake of readability, in the key derivation graph we denote a key corresponding to a given acl U (i.e., a key with label l_U and value k_U) with U. Figure 5.1d illustrates the tokens corresponding to the key derivation graph in Fig. 5.1c.

The encryption-based model described in this section nicely fits a scenario in which the authorization policy regulates only read access privileges, selectively restricting resource visibility to subsets of users. The support of read accesses without consideration of write privileges may result however limiting in emerging data sharing scenarios (e.g., document sharing), where the data owner may wish to grant other users the privilege to modify some of her resources. Unfortunately, the keys associated with resources for regulating the read accesses to them cannot be used for restricting write accesses as well. As a matter of fact, we can imagine that in many situations the set of users authorized to write a resource is different from (typically being a subset of) the set of users authorized to read it. A straightforward solution for enforcing write authorizations might consist in simply outsourcing to the external server the authorization policy (for write privileges) as is. The server would then perform traditional (authorization-based) access control, adopting user authentication and policy enforcement. This solution would however present the main drawback of requesting a considerable management overhead. Also, it would not be in line with the goal pursued by outsourcing approaches, aimed at minimizing the server's involvement and responsibility in access control enforcement. Our goal is to enforce write privileges following the same spirit of the proposal in [37]: for this reason, we propose to exploit selective encryption for the enforcement also of write authorizations. As a matter of fact, having resources tied to access restrictions by means of cryptographic solutions can provide a more robust and flexible control, whose enforcement is less exposed to server misbehaviors. However, while the

encryption of a resource with a key known to all and only the users authorized
to read it suffices for enforcing read authorizations, enforcement of write privileges
requires cooperation from the external server. In the following sections, we will
describe an approach, based on selective encryption, for the effective outsourcing to
the external server of the enforcement of both read and write privileges, as well as
of grant and revoke operations.

5.3 Authorization Policy

The basic idea of our approach for the enforcement of both read and write privileges
consists in associating each resource with a *write tag* defined by the data owner,
and in adopting selective encryption techniques to regulate both access to resource
contents and to their write tags. Our intuition is to encrypt the tag of a given
resource with a key known only by the users authorized to write the resource and
by the external server. In this way, only the server and authorized writers will have
access to the plaintext write tag of each resource. The server will then accept a
write operation on a resource when the requesting user shows knowledge of the
corresponding write tag. Since the key used for encrypting the write tag has to
be shared by the server and the writers, we leverage on the underlying structure
already in place for regulating the necessary read operations. In this section, we
illustrate our key derivation structure for managing the encryption keys of the system
(Sect. 5.3.1), and we discuss how to use it for enforcing read and write access
restrictions (Sect. 5.3.2).

5.3.1 Key Derivation Structure

Elaborating on the approach in [37], and adapting it to our context, we introduce a
set-based key derivation graph as follows.

Definition 5.1 (Set-Based Key Derivation Graph). Let $\mathscr{U}$ be a set of users and
$\mathrm{U} \subseteq 2^{\mathscr{U}}$ be a family of subsets of users in $\mathscr{U}$ such that $\forall u \in \mathscr{U}$, $\{u\} \in \mathrm{U}$. A *set-based
key derivation graph* over $\mathscr{U}$ and U is a triple $\langle \mathscr{K}, \mathscr{L}, \mathscr{D} \rangle$, with $\mathscr{K}$ a set of keys, $\mathscr{L}$
the set of corresponding labels, and $\mathscr{D}$ a set of tokens, such that:

1. $\forall U \in \mathrm{U}$, there exist a *derivation key* $k_U \in \mathscr{K}$;
2. $\forall u \in \mathscr{U}$, $\forall U \in \mathrm{U} \setminus \{u\}$ s.t. $u \in U$, there exists either a token $d_{\{u\},U}$ or a sequence
   $\langle d_{\{u\},U_i}, \dots, d_{U_j,U} \rangle$ of tokens in $\mathscr{D}$, with $d_{w,z}$ following $d_{x,y}$ in the sequence if
   $y = w$.

Definition 5.1 ensures that, for each set $U \in \mathrm{U}$ of users, there exists a derivation
key, and that each user u in the system can derive (through either a single token or a
chain of tokens) all the derivation keys of all the groups $U \in \mathrm{U}$ to which she belongs.

Since our approach requires each resource to be associated with a write tag that must be encrypted with a key shared by the server and the authorized writers of the resource, we extend the set-based key derivation graph in Definition 5.1 with the external server. However, since the server cannot access the plaintext of the outsourced resources, it cannot be treated the same way as authorized users (i.e., considering it as an additional user). We then define a *key derivation structure* by extending the set-based key derivation graph to include also the keys that will be shared with the server, and will be used to encrypt the write tags for enforcing write privileges (see Sect. 5.3.2). These additional keys are defined in such a way that authorized users can compute them applying a secure hash function h^s to a key they already know (or can derive via a sequence of tokens), while the server can derive them through a token specifically added to the key derivation structure. Compared with the set-based key derivation graph in Definition 5.1, in the key derivation structure we also distinguish between two kinds of keys (possibly associated with each set of users): *derivation keys* and *access keys*. Access keys are actually used to encrypt resources, while derivation keys are used to provide the derivation capability via tokens, that is, tokens can be defined only with derivation keys as starting points. Each set of users in U is therefore associated with a derivation key k and, when needed, also with an access key k^a obtained by applying a secure hash function h^a to k (i.e., $k^a = h^a(k)$). The rationale for this evolution is to distinguish the two roles associated with keys, namely: enabling key derivation (by applying the corresponding tokens) and enabling access to resources.

Formally, a key derivation structure is defined as follows.

Definition 5.2 (Key Derivation Structure). Let $\mathcal{U}$ be a set of users, $\mathcal{S}$ be an external server, $\mathsf{U} \subseteq 2^{\mathcal{U}}$ be a family of subsets of users in $\mathcal{U}$ such that $\forall u \in \mathcal{U}$, $\{u\} \in \mathsf{U}$, U^s and U^a be two subsets of U, and $\langle \mathcal{K}', \mathcal{L}', \mathcal{D}' \rangle$ be a set-based key derivation graph over $\mathcal{U}$ and U. A *key derivation structure* implied by U^s and U^a over $\langle \mathcal{K}', \mathcal{L}', \mathcal{D}' \rangle$ is a triple $\langle \mathcal{K}, \mathcal{L}, \mathcal{D} \rangle$, with $\mathcal{K}$ a set of keys, $\mathcal{L}$ the set of corresponding labels, and $\mathcal{D}$ a set of tokens, such that:

1. $\mathcal{K} = \mathcal{K}' \cup \{k_{\mathcal{S}}\} \cup \{k_{U \cup \{\mathcal{S}\}} = h^s(k_U) \mid U \in \mathsf{U}^s\} \cup \{k_U^a = h^a(k_U) \mid U \in \mathsf{U}^a\}$, with h^s and h^a two secure hash functions;
2. $\mathcal{D} = \mathcal{D}' \cup \{d_{\mathcal{S}, U \cup \{\mathcal{S}\}} \mid U \in \mathsf{U}^s\}$.

A key derivation structure therefore extends a set-based key derivation graph by including: (1) a derivation key $k_{\mathcal{S}}$ assigned to the server; (2) a key $k_{U \cup \{\mathcal{S}\}}$ shared by the users in U and the server, for each set U of users in U^s; (3) an access key k_U^a shared by the users in U, for each set U of users in U^a; and (4) a token $d_{\mathcal{S}, U \cup \{\mathcal{S}\}}$ that allows the server to derive key $k_{U \cup \{\mathcal{S}\}}$ starting from its key $k_{\mathcal{S}}$, for each set U of users in U^s. For each set U of users in U^s, both a derivation key k_U and a key $k_{U \cup \{\mathcal{S}\}}$ shared with the server belong to $\mathcal{K}$. Analogously, for each set U of users in U^a, both a derivation key k_U and an access key k_U^a belong to the set $\mathcal{K}$ of keys in the key derivation structure.

Figure 5.2 illustrates function **Define_Key_Derivation_Structure** that builds a key derivation structure. The function receives as input a set $\mathcal{U}$ of users, an

INPUT

$\mathcal{U}$: users of the system

$\mathcal{S}$: external server

$\mathsf{U} \subseteq 2^{\mathcal{U}}$: family of subsets of users in $\mathcal{U}$

$\mathsf{U}^s \subseteq \mathsf{U}$, $\mathsf{U}^a \subseteq \mathsf{U}$: subsets of U

h^s, h^a : secure hash functions

OUTPUT

$\langle \mathcal{K}, \mathcal{L}, \mathcal{D} \rangle$: key derivation structure implied by U^s and U^a over $\langle \mathcal{K}', \mathcal{L}', \mathcal{D}' \rangle$

DEFINE_KEY_DERIVATION_STRUCTURE

1: /* **Step 1**: define the set-based key derivation graph */
2: $\mathcal{K}' := \emptyset$
3: $\mathcal{L}' := \emptyset$
4: $\mathcal{D}' := \emptyset$
5: **for each** $U \in \mathsf{U}$ **do** /* generate a derivation key for each $U \in \mathsf{U}$ (C1 in Def. 5.1) */
6:      generate a derivation key k_U and a label l_U
7:      $\mathcal{K}' := \mathcal{K}' \cup \{k_U\}$
8:      $\mathcal{L}' := \mathcal{L}' \cup \{l_U\}$
9: /* define a set of tokens s.t. $\forall U \in \mathsf{U}$ and $\forall u \in \mathcal{U}$, k_u is derivable from k_U iff $u \in U$ (C2 in Def. 5.1) */
10: **for each** $U_j \in \mathsf{U}, |U_j| > 1$ **do**
11:     $cover_j := \{U_1, \ldots, U_n \in \mathsf{U} \mid \bigcup_{i=1}^{n} U_i = U_j\}$
12:     $\mathcal{D}' := \mathcal{D}' \cup \{d_{U_i, U_j} = k_{U_j} \oplus h(k_{U_i}, l_{U_j}) \mid U_i \in cover_j\}$
13: /* **Step 2**: define a key derivation structure */
14: generate a key $k_{\mathcal{S}}$ and a label $l_{\mathcal{S}}$ /* generate a key for the external server (C1 in Def. 5.2) */
15: $\mathcal{K} := \mathcal{K}' \cup \{k_{\mathcal{S}}\}$
16: $\mathcal{L} := \mathcal{L}' \cup \{l_{\mathcal{S}}\}$
17: $\mathcal{D} := \mathcal{D}'$
18: **for each** $U \in \mathsf{U}^s$ **do** /* for each $U \in \mathsf{U}^s$, compute $k_{U \cup \{\mathcal{S}\}}$ as the result of h^s over k_U (C1 in Def. 5.2) */
19:     $k_{U \cup \{\mathcal{S}\}} := h^s(k_U)$
20:     generate a label $l_{U \cup \{\mathcal{S}\}}$
21:     $\mathcal{K} := \mathcal{K} \cup \{k_{U \cup \{\mathcal{S}\}}\}$
22:     $\mathcal{L} := \mathcal{L} \cup \{l_{U \cup \{\mathcal{S}\}}\}$
23:     $\mathcal{D} := \mathcal{D} \cup \{d_{\mathcal{S}, U \cup \{\mathcal{S}\}} = k_{U \cup \{\mathcal{S}\}} \oplus h(k_{\mathcal{S}}, l_{U \cup \{\mathcal{S}\}})\}$ /* token from $k_{\mathcal{S}}$ to $k_{U \cup \{\mathcal{S}\}}$ (C2 in Def. 5.2) */
24: **for each** $U \in \mathsf{U}^a$ **do** /* for each $U \in \mathsf{U}^a$, compute k_U^a as the result of h^a over k_U (C1 in Def. 5.2) */
25:     $k_U^a := h^a(k_U)$
26:     generate a label l_U^a
27:     $\mathcal{K} := \mathcal{K} \cup \{k_U^a\}$
28:     $\mathcal{L} := \mathcal{L} \cup \{l_U^a\}$
29: **return**($\langle \mathcal{K}, \mathcal{L}, \mathcal{D} \rangle$)

Fig. 5.2 Function that defines a key derivation structure

external server $\mathcal{S}$, three families U, U^s, and U^a of subsets of users in $\mathcal{U}$, with $\mathsf{U}^s \subseteq \mathsf{U}$ and $\mathsf{U}^a \subseteq \mathsf{U}$, and two secure hash functions h^s and h^a. It returns the key derivation structure $\langle \mathcal{K}, \mathcal{L}, \mathcal{D} \rangle$ implied by U^s and U^a over $\langle \mathcal{K}', \mathcal{L}', \mathcal{D}' \rangle$ (Definition 5.2). The function operates in two steps: the first step defines the set-based key derivation graph over $\mathcal{U}$ and U; the second step extends the key derivation graph with the server, for defining the key derivation structure of interest. In the first step, the function leverages on the algorithms in [37] to define the set-based key derivation graph $\langle \mathcal{K}', \mathcal{L}', \mathcal{D}' \rangle$. To this aim, for each set $U \in \mathsf{U}$ of users the function generates a derivation key and the corresponding label, and inserts them into the sets $\mathcal{K}'$ of keys and $\mathcal{L}'$ of labels, respectively (lines 5–8). The function then defines a set $\mathscr{D}'$ of tokens such that, for each user u in the set $\mathscr{U}$, there is a token (or a sequence of tokens) in $\mathscr{D}'$ that permits to derive, starting from k_u, all those keys k_U associated with a set $U \in \mathsf{U}$ of users with $u \in U$ (lines 10–12). In the second step, function **Define_Key_Derivation_Structure** extends the set-based key derivation graph computed in the previous step to obtain the key derivation structure of interest. To this aim, the function first generates a derivation key $k_{\mathscr{S}}$ for the server and the corresponding label $l_{\mathscr{S}}$, and inserts them into sets $\mathscr{K}$ and $\mathscr{L}$, respectively (lines 14–16). The set $\mathscr{D}$ of tokens is initialized to the set $\mathscr{D}'$ of tokens in the set-based key derivation graph (line 17). For each set U of users in U^s, the function computes key $k_{U \cup \{\mathscr{S}\}}$ (shared by the server and U) applying secure hash function h^s to k_U, generates the corresponding label, and inserts them into the set $\mathscr{K}$ of keys and into the set $\mathscr{L}$ of labels in the key derivation structure, respectively (lines 18–22). The set $\mathscr{D}$ of tokens is then updated by inserting a token that permits to derive $k_{U \cup \{\mathscr{S}\}}$ from $k_{\mathscr{S}}$ for each set U of users in U^s (line 23). The function generates an access key k_U^a (and the corresponding label) for each set U of users in U^a by applying secure hash function h^a to the derivation key k_U associated with the same set of user, and inserts the key and the label into $\mathscr{K}$ and $\mathscr{L}$, respectively (lines 24–28). The function terminates returning the resulting key derivation structure $\langle \mathscr{K}, \mathscr{L}, \mathscr{D} \rangle$ (line 29). The following theorem formally shows that function **Define_Key_Derivation_Structure** correctly computes a key derivation structure.

Theorem 5.1 (Correctness of Procedure Define_Key_Derivation_Structure). *Let $\mathscr{U}$ be a set of users, $\mathscr{S}$ be an external server, $\mathsf{U} \subseteq 2^{\mathscr{U}}$ be a family of subsets of users in $\mathscr{U}$ such that $\forall u \in \mathscr{U}$, $\{u\} \in \mathsf{U}$, and U^s and U^a be two subsets of U. Triple $\langle \mathscr{K}, \mathscr{L}, \mathscr{D} \rangle$ computed by function **Define_Key_Derivation_Structure** in Fig. 5.2 is a key derivation structure (Definition 5.2).*

Proof. We prove that the two conditions in Definition 5.2 are satisfied by a triple $\langle \mathscr{K}, \mathscr{L}, \mathscr{D} \rangle$ computed by function **Define_Key_Derivation_Structure**.

- Condition 1 is satisfied since in Step 1 the function generates a key for each set of users in U and inserts it into $\mathscr{K}'$ (lines 6–7). The set $\mathscr{K}'$ of keys resulting from Step 1 then corresponds to the set of keys of the set-based key derivation graph. In Step 2, the function generates a key $k_{\mathscr{S}}$ for the server (line 14) and inserts both key $k_{\mathscr{S}}$ and all the keys in $\mathscr{K}'$ into $\mathscr{K}$ (line 15). For each set U of users in U^s, the function computes the key for $U \cup \{\mathscr{S}\}$ as $h^s(k_U)$ (lines 18–19), where h^s is a secure hash function, and inserts $k_{U \cup \{\mathscr{S}\}}$ into $\mathscr{K}$ (line 21). Similarly, for each set U of users in U^a, the function computes the access key k_U^a as $h^a(k_U)$ (lines 24–25), where h^a is a secure hash function, and inserts k_U^a into $\mathscr{K}$ (line 27).
- Condition 2 is satisfied since in Step 1 the function defines a set $\mathscr{D}'$ of tokens that guarantees that each key k_U in $\mathscr{K}$ can be directly derived from a set $\{k_{U_1}, \ldots, k_{U_n}\}$ of keys in $\mathscr{K}'$ such that $U_1 \cup \ldots \cup U_n = U$ (lines 10–12). As proved in [37], this property is equivalent to Condition 2 in Definition 5.1. Therefore the set of tokens $\mathscr{D}'$ resulting from Step 1 corresponds to the set of tokens of the set-

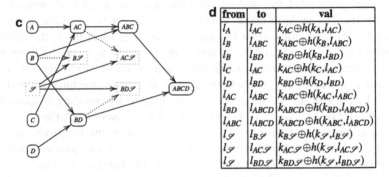

a

o	r[o]	w[o]
o_1	ABCD	BD
o_2	ABCD	BD
o_3	ABC	AC
o_4	BD	B

b

r_label	w_label	o_id	encw_tag	encr_resource
l_{ABCD}	$l_{BD.\mathscr{S}}$	1	α	zKZlJxVcCrC0g
l_{ABCD}	$l_{BD.\mathscr{S}}$	2	β	t9qdJqC7AImXU
l_{ABC}	$l_{AC.\mathscr{S}}$	3	γ	AxalPH8Kv37Ts
l_{BD}	$l_{B.\mathscr{S}}$	4	δ	xwfPJSLn.MVqY

d

from	to	val
l_A	l_{AC}	$k_{AC} \oplus h(k_A, l_{AC})$
l_B	l_{ABC}	$k_{ABC} \oplus h(k_B, l_{ABC})$
l_B	l_{BD}	$k_{BD} \oplus h(k_B, l_{BD})$
l_C	l_{AC}	$k_{AC} \oplus h(k_C, l_{AC})$
l_D	l_{BD}	$k_{BD} \oplus h(k_D, l_{BD})$
l_{AC}	l_{ABC}	$k_{ABC} \oplus h(k_{AC}, l_{ABC})$
l_{BD}	l_{ABCD}	$k_{ABCD} \oplus h(k_{BD}, l_{ABCD})$
l_{ABC}	l_{ABCD}	$k_{ABCD} \oplus h(k_{ABC}, l_{ABCD})$
$l_{\mathscr{S}}$	$l_{B.\mathscr{S}}$	$k_{B.\mathscr{S}} \oplus h(k_{\mathscr{S}}, l_{B.\mathscr{S}})$
$l_{\mathscr{S}}$	$l_{AC.\mathscr{S}}$	$k_{AC.\mathscr{S}} \oplus h(k_{\mathscr{S}}, l_{AC.\mathscr{S}})$
$l_{\mathscr{S}}$	$l_{BD.\mathscr{S}}$	$k_{BD.\mathscr{S}} \oplus h(k_{\mathscr{S}}, l_{BD.\mathscr{S}})$

Fig. 5.3 An example of read and write acls (**a**), encrypted resources (**b**), key derivation structure (**c**), and tokens (**d**)

based key derivation graph. In Step 2 the function inserts into $\mathscr{D}$ all the tokens in $\mathscr{D}'$ (line 17) and, for each set U of users in U^s, it defines and inserts into $\mathscr{D}$ token $d_{\mathscr{S},U \cup \{\mathscr{S}\}}$ that permits to derive $k_{U \cup \{\mathscr{S}\}}$ from $k_{\mathscr{S}}$ (line 23). □

Example 5.2. Consider a system with four users $\mathscr{U} = \{A, B, C, D\}$, a family $\mathsf{U} = \{A, B, C, D, AC, BD, ABC, ABCD\}$ of subsets of users, and two subsets $\mathsf{U}^s = \{B, AC, BD\}$ and $\mathsf{U}^a = \{BD, ABC, ABCD\}$ of U. Figure 5.3c illustrates the key derivation structure computed by function **Define_Key_Derivation_Structure** in Fig. 5.2. In the figure, nodes drawn with a continuous line represent derivation keys, and nodes drawn with a dotted line represent keys shared with the external server (for the sake of readability, access keys are not reported in the figure). Continuous edges represent tokens, and dotted edges correspond to hash-based derivations computed via secure hash function h^s.

5.3.2 Access Control Enforcement

We now illustrate our proposal for enforcing both read and write access restrictions. Each resource o is associated with two (possibly different) access control lists: (1) a read access list $r[o]$ reporting the set of users authorized to read o, and (2) a write access list $w[o]$ reporting the set of users authorized to write o. Consistently with most real-world scenarios, we assume the users authorized to write a resource to also read it, that is, $\forall o \in \mathcal{O}: w[o] \subseteq r[o]$.

Read authorizations are enforced through selective encryption. Each resource o in the set $\mathcal{O}$ of resources is then encrypted with the *access key* corresponding to the set of users in its read access list $r[o]$, which is known or can be derived by all and only the users authorized to view the resource content.

Enforcement of write authorizations, as mentioned at the beginning of this section, relies on the definition of a write tag for each resource and on the cooperation with the external server. Each resource $o \in \mathcal{O}$ is associated with a write tag $tag[o]$, defined by the data owner using a secure random function to ensure independence of the tag from both the resource identifier and its content. To guarantee that only the server $\mathcal{S}$ and the set $w[o]$ of authorized writers know the plaintext value of the write tag of resource o, $tag[o]$ is encrypted with a key that is known or can be derived only by the users in $w[o]$ and by the server.

Each resource $o \in \mathcal{O}$ is stored at the external server in encrypted form, together with the following metadata.

- r_label: label of the key with which the resource is encrypted, which is the access key of the set $r[o]$ of users authorized to read o (i.e., $l^a_{r[o]}$).
- w_label: label of the key shared by the set $w[o]$ of users authorized to write o and the server $\mathcal{S}$ (i.e., $l_{w[o] \cup \{\mathcal{S}\}}$).
- encw_tag: write tag $tag[o]$ of resource o, which is used by the server to enforce restrictions on write privileges. The tag is encrypted with the key identified by the label in w_label (i.e., $E(tag[o], k_{w[o] \cup \{\mathcal{S}\}})$, where E is a symmetric encryption function computed over $tag[o]$ with key $k_{w[o] \cup \{\mathcal{S}\}}$).
- encr_resource: encrypted version of resource o, encrypted with the access key identified by the label in r_label (i.e., $E(o, k^a_{r[o]})$).

Given the set $\mathcal{U}$ of users and the set $\mathcal{O}$ of resources in the system, where each resource is associated with read and write access control lists as mentioned above, the data owner must compute keys and tokens composing the key derivation structure before outsourcing resources in $\mathcal{O}$. To this aim, it calls procedure **Initialize_System** in Fig. 5.4, which in turn calls function **Define_Key_Derivation_Structure** in Fig. 5.2 to properly define the key derivation structure. The procedure receives as input the set $\mathcal{U}$ of users and the set $\mathcal{O}$ of resources in the system, an external server $\mathcal{S}$, and two secure hash functions h^s and h^a. The procedure first needs to define three families U, U^s, and U^a of subsets of users in $\mathcal{U}$. U corresponds to the set of groups of users whose keys must be represented in the system for the correct enforcement of the authorizations. It then includes the singleton sets $\{u\}$ of users u in $\mathcal{U}$, and the sets U of users representing read and write access lists ($r[o]$ and $w[o]$, respectively) of resources o in $\mathcal{O}$. U^s is the subset of U representing those sets of users that have to share a key with the external server. It then includes all the sets of users corresponding to the write access lists $w[o]$ of resources o in $\mathcal{O}$. U^a is the subset of U representing those sets of users for which an access key needs to be defined. It then includes all the sets corresponding to the read access lists $r[o]$ of resources o in $\mathcal{O}$ (lines 2–4). The procedure then calls function **Define_Key_Derivation_Structure**, which returns a key derivation structure (line 5). Finally, the procedure:

INPUT
$\mathscr{U}$: users of the system
$\mathscr{O}$: resources of the system
$\mathscr{S}$: external server
h^s, h^a : secure hash functions

INITIALIZE_SYSTEM

1:   /* **Step 1**: define the key derivation structure */
2:   $U^s := \bigcup_{o \in \mathscr{O}} w[o]$
3:   $U^a := \bigcup_{o \in \mathscr{O}} r[o]$
4:   $U := U^s \cup U^a \cup \{\{u\} \mid u \in \mathscr{U}\}$
5:   $\langle \mathscr{K}, \mathscr{L}, \mathscr{D} \rangle :=$ **Define_Key_Derivation_Structure**$(\mathscr{U}, \mathscr{S}, U, U^s, U^a, h^s, h^a)$
6:   /* **Step 2**: distribute keys */
7:   **for each** $u \in \mathscr{U}$ **do** /* communicate derivation keys to users */
8:       send k_u to u
9:   send $k_{\mathscr{S}}$ to $\mathscr{S}$ /* communicate the derivation key to the server */
10: /* **Step 3**: outsource resources and tokens */
11: $\mathscr{O}^k := \emptyset$ /* outsourced relation */
12: **for each** $o \in \mathscr{O}$ **do** /* define the outsourced relation */
13:      create a new tuple t
14:      $t[\texttt{r\_label}] := l_{r[o]}$
15:      $t[\texttt{w\_label}] := l_{w[o] \cup \{\mathscr{S}\}}$
16:      $t[\texttt{o\_id}] := \textbf{Id}(o)$
17:      randomly generate a value for $tag[o]$
18:      $t[\texttt{encw\_tag}] := E(tag[o], k_{w[o] \cup \{\mathscr{S}\}})$
19:      $t[\texttt{encr\_resource}] := E(o, k_{r[o]})$
20:      insert t into $\mathscr{O}^k$
21: send relation $\mathscr{O}^k$ to the server
22: TOKEN $:= \emptyset$ /* relation storing public tokens */
23: **for each** $d_{i,j} \in \mathscr{D}$ **do**
24:      create a new tuple t
25:      $t[\texttt{from}] := l_i$
26:      $t[\texttt{to}] := l_j$
27:      $t[\texttt{val}] := d_{i,j}$
28:      insert t into TOKEN
29: send relation TOKEN to the server

Fig. 5.4 Procedure that enforces the access control policy defined by the data owner before outsourcing resources

1. communicates to each user u derivation key k_u, and to the external server derivation key $k_{\mathscr{S}}$ (lines 7–9);
2. computes and stores at the external server the encrypted resources and the associated metadata (lines 11–21);
3. stores at the external server all the tokens in the key derivation structure (i.e., tokens in $\mathscr{D}$) as a set of triples of the form $\langle l_i, l_j, d_{i,j} \rangle$ indicating that the key with label l_j can be directly derived from the key with label l_i through token $d_{i,j}$ (lines 22–29).

Example 5.3. Consider a system with four users $\mathcal{U}=\{A,B,C,D\}$ and four resources $\mathcal{O}=\{o_1,o_2,o_3,o_4\}$, and assume read and write acls of resources to be as in Fig. 5.3a (read acls are the same as in Example 5.1). Figure 5.3c illustrates the key derivation structure computed as described in Example 5.2. Figures 5.3b and d illustrate the encrypted resources and associated metadata, and the tokens outsourced to the external server, respectively.

It is easy to see that our approach guarantees: (1) correct *read authorization enforcement*; (2) correct *write authorization enforcement*; and (3) *write control* by the server. Read authorization enforcement is guaranteed as each resource $o \in \mathcal{O}$ is encrypted with an access key (i.e., $k^a_{r[o]}$) that only authorized readers in $r[o]$ know or can derive. In fact, each user u can compute any access key k^a_U such that $u \in U$ by applying hash function h^a to derivation key k_U, which u knows or can derive as she belongs to U. Write authorization enforcement is guaranteed since the write tag $tag[o]$ of each resource $o \in \mathcal{O}$ is encrypted with a key (i.e., $k_{w[o] \cup \{\mathcal{S}\}}$) that only authorized writers in $w[o]$ (and the server) can derive. Also, the server is assumed to be *honest-but-curious* and therefore not interested in tampering with resources (see Sects. 5.5 and 5.6). Write control by the server is guaranteed since the server has visibility over the write tag of all resources, which is encrypted with a key that the server can directly derive.

The correct enforcement of the authorization policy is formally proved by the following theorem.

Theorem 5.2 (Correct Enforcement of Authorizations). *Let $\mathcal{U}$ be a set of users, $\mathcal{S}$ be an external server, $\mathcal{O}$ be a set of resources such that $\forall o \in \mathcal{O}$ $r[o]$ and $w[o]$ are the read and write access lists of o, respectively. Our access control system satisfies the following conditions:*

1. $\forall u \in \mathcal{U}$ *and* $\forall o \in \mathcal{O}$, *u can decrypt* encr_resource[o] *iff* $u \in r[o]$ *(read authorization enforcement);*
2. $\forall u \in \mathcal{U}$ *and* $\forall o \in \mathcal{O}$, *u can decrypt* encw_tag[o] *iff* $u \in w[o]$ *(write authorization enforcement);*
3. $\forall o \in \mathcal{O}$, $\mathcal{S}$ *can decrypt* encw_tag[o] *(write control).*

Proof. The proof is based on the fact that, by Theorem 5.1, triple $\langle \mathcal{K}, \mathcal{L}, \mathcal{D} \rangle$ computed by function **Define_Key_Derivation_Structure** is a key derivation structure. We first note that, by procedure **Initialize_System** in Fig. 5.4, $\mathcal{K}$ includes a derivation key k_u for each user $u \in \mathcal{U}$, and a derivation key k_U for each set U of users representing a read or write access list of a resource $o \in \mathcal{O}$. In fact, function **Define_Key_Derivation_Structure** is called over $\mathcal{U}$, $\mathcal{S}$, U, U^s, U^a, h^s, and h^a, with U^s the set of write access lists, U^a the set of read access lists, and U the result of U$^a \cup$ U^s together with all the singleton sets $\{u\}$ of users in $\mathcal{U}$ (lines 2–5). We now prove that each condition in Theorem 5.2 holds.

1. *u can decrypt* encr_resource[o] $\implies u \in r[o]$.
   Assume, by contradiction, that $u \notin r[o]$ can decrypt encr_resource[o]. Since encr_resource[o] is computed by encrypting o with access key $k^a_{r[o]}$

(line 19), u can either compute or derive $k^a_{r[o]}$. $\mathscr{D}$ does not include any token that permits to derive access keys, therefore u needs to know derivation key $k_{r[o]} \in \mathscr{K}$ with which $k^a_{r[o]} \in \mathscr{K}$ has been computed. However, $\mathscr{D}$ includes a token (or a sequence thereof) from derivation key k_u of user u (lines 7–8) to derivation key k_U iff $u \in U$ (Condition 2 in Definition 5.1). This implies that $\{u\} \subseteq r[o]$, which contradicts our hypothesis.

$u \in r[o] \implies u$ can decrypt encr_resource[o].
By Condition 2 in Definition 5.1, there exists a token (or a sequence thereof) in $\mathscr{D}$ that permits to derive derivation key k_U from k_u iff $u \in U$. Therefore, if $u \in r[o]$, there exists a token (or a sequence thereof) in $\mathscr{D}$ from k_u to $k_{r[o]} \in \mathscr{K}$. Since u can derive $k_{r[o]}$ and h^a is public, she can also compute access key $k^a_{r[o]} = h^a(k_{r[o]})$ and decrypt encr_resource[o].

2. u can decrypt encw_tag[o] $\implies u \in w[o]$.
   Assume, by contradiction, that $u \notin w[o]$ can decrypt encw_tag[o]. encw_tag[o] is computed by encrypting $tag[o]$ with key $k_{w[o] \cup \{\mathscr{S}\}}$ (line 18). Therefore, u can compute or derive $k_{w[o] \cup \{\mathscr{S}\}}$. Since all tokens in $\mathscr{D}$ that permit to derive key $k_{w[o] \cup \{\mathscr{S}\}}$ shared with the server have $k_\mathscr{S}$ as starting point (Condition 2 in Definition 5.2), u must know (or be able to derive) derivation $k_{w[o]}$. However, $\mathscr{D}$ includes a token (or a sequence thereof) from derivation key k_u of user u (lines 7–8) to derivation key $k_U \in \mathscr{K}$, iff $u \in U$ (Condition 2 in Definition 5.1). This implies that $\{u\} \subseteq w[o]$, which contradicts our hypothesis.

   $u \in w[o] \implies u$ can decrypt encw_tag[o].
   By Condition 2 in Definition 5.1, there exists a token (or a sequence thereof) in $\mathscr{D}$ that permits to derive derivation key k_U from k_u iff $u \in U$. Therefore, if $u \in w[o]$, there exists a token (or a sequence thereof) in $\mathscr{D}$ from k_u to $k_{w[o]}$. Since u can derive $k_{w[o]}$ and h^s is public, she can also compute key $k_{w[o] \cup \{\mathscr{S}\}} = h^s(k_{w[o]})$ and decrypt encw_tag[o].

3. $\mathscr{S}$ can decrypt encw_tag[o].
   As noted above, encw_tag[o] is computed by encrypting $tag[o]$ with key $k_{w[o] \cup \{\mathscr{S}\}}$. Since $\mathscr{S}$ knows key $k_\mathscr{S}$ and, for each key $k_{U \cup \{\mathscr{S}\}}$ in $\mathscr{K}$, $\mathscr{D}$ includes token $d_{\mathscr{S}, U \cup \{\mathscr{S}\}}$ (Condition 2 in Definition 5.2), $\mathscr{S}$ can derive $k_{w[o] \cup \{\mathscr{S}\}}$ and decrypt encw_tag[o]. $\square$

5.4 Policy Updates

Policy updates must be managed with special care in our scenario, since they might require expensive re-encryption and/or key re-distribution operations by the data owner, thus limiting the advantages of data outsourcing. The problem of granting and revoking read authorizations with limited overhead for the data owner has been already investigated, and we can therefore assume to solve it by using the proposal in [37], which is based on over-encryption. In this section, we will focus on the management of write privileges, with the goal of outsourcing the enforcement of grant and revoke operations to the external server. Since both grant and revoke operations translate into the insertion of keys (and tokens) in the key derivation structure, we first illustrate how to manage this operation (Sect. 5.4.1). We then describe how grants and revokes of privileges can be enforced to correctly reflect updates in the write authorizations (Sect. 5.4.2).

5.4.1 Updates to the Key Derivation Structure

The basic operations on the key derivation structure necessary to manage grant and revoke operations consist in the retrieval/insertion of derivation and access keys.

Function **Get_Key** in Fig. 5.5 receives as input a set $U \subseteq \mathcal{U}$ of users and returns the derivation key associated with it. The function first checks whether the set $\mathcal{K}$ of keys in the key derivation structure already includes a derivation key for U (line 1). If this is not the case, the function generates a new derivation key for the set of users together with its label, and computes the corresponding access key together with its label. It then inserts keys and labels in the sets $\mathcal{K}$ and $\mathcal{L}$ of keys and labels of the key derivation structure (lines 2–7). The function then updates the set $\mathcal{D}$ of tokens in the key derivation structure by inserting the tokens necessary to guarantee that each user u in U can derive k_U from her key k_u (lines 8–12). The function then updates relation TOKEN at the server side accordingly (lines 13–17). Finally, the function returns derivation key k_U (line 18).

Function **Get_Shared_Key** in Fig. 5.5 receives as input a set $U \subseteq \mathcal{U}$ of users and returns the key shared by the server and U. The function first checks whether the set $\mathcal{K}$ of keys already includes the key of interest (line 19). If this is not the case, the function first retrieves the derivation key associated with the set U of users by calling function **Get_Key** over U (lines 20–21). It then computes the hash of k_U through secure hash function h^s, obtaining $k_{U \cup \{\mathcal{S}\}}$ (line 22). The function then generates the corresponding label and inserts the key into $\mathcal{K}$ and the label into $\mathcal{L}$ (lines 23–25). The function inserts into $\mathcal{D}$ a token that permits the server to derive $k_{U \cup \{\mathcal{S}\}}$ from $k_{\mathcal{S}}$ (line 26). The function then updates relation TOKEN at the server side accordingly (lines 27–31). Finally, the function returns $k_{U \cup \{\mathcal{S}\}}$ (line 32).

Example 5.4. Consider the key derivation structure of Fig. 5.3c, and assume that a key has to be shared by the server $\mathcal{S}$ and the set ABD of users. Figure 5.6 illustrates the key derivation structure, and the corresponding set of tokens, resulting from the call to function **Get_Shared_Key** in Fig. 5.5 over ABD. Since $\mathcal{K}$ does not include a key shared by $\mathcal{S}$ and ABD, function **Get_Shared_Key** calls function **Get_Key** over ABD, which inserts derivation key k_{ABD} and access key k_{ABD}^a into $\mathcal{K}$, labels l_{ABD} and l_{ABD}^a into $\mathcal{L}$, and tokens $d_{A,ABD}$ and $d_{BD,ABD}$ into $\mathcal{D}$. It returns the derivation key of ABD. Function **Get_Shared_Key** then computes key $k_{ABD\mathcal{S}}$ by applying secure hash function h^s to k_{ABD}, inserts $k_{ABD\mathcal{S}}$ into $\mathcal{K}$, the corresponding label $l_{ABD\mathcal{S}}$ into $\mathcal{L}$, and token $d_{\mathcal{S},ABD\mathcal{S}}$ into $\mathcal{D}$. In Fig. 5.6b and in the following figures, we denote tokens inserted by functions **Get_Key** and **Get_Shared_Key** with a bullet •.

GLOBAL VARIABLES
$\mathcal{U}$: users of the system
$\mathcal{S}$: external server
$\langle \mathcal{K}, \mathcal{L}, \mathcal{D} \rangle$: key derivation structure
h^s, h^a : secure hash functions

GET_KEY(U)

1: let k_U be the key in $\mathcal{K}$ associated with U
2: **if** k_U = NULL **then** /* if $\mathcal{K}$ does not include a derivation key for U */
3:      generate k_U and label l_U
4:      $k_U^a := h^a(k_U)$ /* compute k_U^a as the result of h^a over k_U */
5:      generate a label l_U^a
6:      $\mathcal{K} := \mathcal{K} \cup \{k_U, k_U^a\}$
7:      $\mathcal{L} := \mathcal{L} \cup \{l_U, l_U^a\}$
8:      let $\mathcal{U}'$ be the family of subsets of $2^{\mathcal{U}}$ such that $\forall U \in \mathcal{U}', k_U \in \mathcal{K}$
9:      $cover := \{U_1, \ldots, U_n \subseteq \mathcal{U}' \mid \bigcup_{i=1}^{n} U_i = U_j\}$
10:     **for each** $U_i \in cover$ **do**
11:         $d_{U_i,U} := k_U \oplus h(k_{U_i}, l_U)$
12:         $\mathcal{D} := \mathcal{D} \cup \{d_{U_i,U}\}$
13:         create a new tuple t
14:         $t[\text{from}] := l_{U_i}$
15:         $t[\text{to}] := l_U$
16:         $t[\text{val}] := d_{U_i,U}$
17:         insert t into TOKEN /* at the server side */
18: **return**(k_U)

GET_SHARED_KEY(U)

19: let $k_{U \cup \{\mathcal{S}\}}$ be the key in $\mathcal{K}$ shared by U and $\mathcal{S}$
20: **if** $k_{U \cup \{\mathcal{S}\}}$ = NULL **then** /* if $\mathcal{K}$ does not include a key shared by U and $\mathcal{S}$ */
21:      $k_U := \textbf{Get\_Key}(U)$ /* retrieve or create the derivation key associated with U */
22:      $k_{U \cup \{\mathcal{S}\}} := h^s(k_U)$ /* compute $k_{U \cup \{\mathcal{S}\}}$ as the result of h^s over k_U */
23:      generate a label $l_{U \cup \{\mathcal{S}\}}$
24:      $\mathcal{K} := \mathcal{K} \cup \{k_{U \cup \{\mathcal{S}\}}\}$
25:      $\mathcal{L} := \mathcal{L} \cup \{l_{U \cup \{\mathcal{S}\}}\}$
26:      $\mathcal{D} := \mathcal{D} \cup \{d_{\mathcal{S}, U \cup \{\mathcal{S}\}} = k_{U \cup \{\mathcal{S}\}} \oplus h(k_{\mathcal{S}}, l_{U \cup \{\mathcal{S}\}})\}$ /* insert into $\mathcal{D}$ the token from $k_{\mathcal{S}}$ to $k_{U \cup \{\mathcal{S}\}}$ */
27:      create a new tuple t
28:      $t[\text{from}] := l_{\mathcal{S}}$
29:      $t[\text{to}] := l_{U \cup \{\mathcal{S}\}}$
30:      $t[\text{val}] := d_{\mathcal{S}, U \cup \{\mathcal{S}\}}$
31:      insert t into TOKEN /* at the server side */
32: **return**($k_{U \cup \{\mathcal{S}\}}$)

Fig. 5.5 Pseudocode of functions **Get_Key** and **Get_Shared_Key**

5.4.2 Grant and Revoke

Despite effective for enforcing changes to read authorizations, over-encryption falls short when it is necessary to grant or revoke write privileges. In fact, in a worst case scenario, users are not oblivious (i.e., they have the ability to store and keep indefinitely all information they have been entitled to access), and the users in the write access list of a resource have knowledge of the value of the corresponding

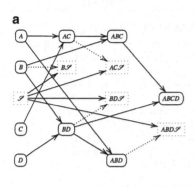

b

from	to	val
l_A	l_{AC}	$k_{AC} \oplus h(k_A, l_{AC})$
l_A	l_{ABD}	$k_{ABD} \oplus h(k_A, l_{ABD})$ •
l_B	l_{ABC}	$k_{ABC} \oplus h(k_B, l_{ABC})$
l_B	l_{BD}	$k_{BD} \oplus h(k_B, l_{BD})$
l_C	l_{AC}	$k_{AC} \oplus h(k_C, l_{AC})$
l_D	l_{BD}	$k_{BD} \oplus h(k_D, l_{BD})$
l_{AC}	l_{ABC}	$k_{ABC} \oplus h(k_{AC}, l_{ABC})$
l_{BD}	l_{ABD}	$k_{ABD} \oplus h(k_{BD}, l_{ABD})$ •
l_{BD}	l_{ABCD}	$k_{ABCD} \oplus h(k_{BD}, l_{ABCD})$
l_{ABC}	l_{ABCD}	$k_{ABCD} \oplus h(k_{ABC}, l_{ABCD})$
$l_{\mathscr{S}}$	$l_{B\mathscr{S}}$	$k_{B\mathscr{S}} \oplus h(k_{\mathscr{S}}, l_{B\mathscr{S}})$
$l_{\mathscr{S}}$	$l_{AC\mathscr{S}}$	$k_{AC\mathscr{S}} \oplus h(k_{\mathscr{S}}, l_{AC\mathscr{S}})$
$l_{\mathscr{S}}$	$l_{BD\mathscr{S}}$	$k_{BD\mathscr{S}} \oplus h(k_{\mathscr{S}}, l_{BD\mathscr{S}})$
$l_{\mathscr{S}}$	$l_{ABD\mathscr{S}}$	$k_{ABD\mathscr{S}} \oplus h(k_{\mathscr{S}}, l_{ABD\mathscr{S}})$ •

Fig. 5.6 Key derivation structure (**a**) and tokens (**b**) after the insertion of key $k_{ABD\mathscr{S}}$ in the key derivation structure in Fig. 5.3c

write tag. These users can therefore exploit such knowledge to modify the resource even when they lost the write privilege. To illustrate, consider a resource o with write access list $w[o]$ and assume that, at a given point in time, the data owner revokes from user $u \in w[o]$ the write privilege for o. To enforce the revoke operation, write tag $tag[o]$ should be encrypted with a key known only to the users in $w[o] \setminus \{u\}$. However, since u was previously included in $w[o]$ she might know the plaintext value of the write tag $tag[o]$. Even without being able to decrypt the encrypted write tag sent by the server, user u would then still be able to correctly reply to the challenge of the server, thus violating the write access policy defined by the data owner. For instance, consider the key derivation structure in Fig. 5.3c, and suppose that the data owner revokes the write privilege over resource o_2 from user B. If B already knows the plaintext value of $tag[o_2]$, she can still answer the challenge of the server, and then improperly modify o_2. Since this problem depends on previous knowledge of the revoked user and not on her ability to decrypt the write tag received from the server, it is necessary to associate a fresh write tag with the revoked resource to effectively enforce the policy change.

We now illustrate in details how write authorizations can be granted and revoked upon decision of the data owner.

Grant We consider the case of the data owner granting user u write privilege over resource o. Note that, if u is not a reader of o, the access control policy is first modified granting u read access to o. To ensure that write requests by u are accepted by the server, the data owner must encrypt the write tag associated with o with a key known to: the server, the authorized writers in $w[o]$, and the user u who is being granted the write privilege. In other words, $tag[o]$ must be encrypted with a key shared by the server and the new set $w[o] \cup \{u\}$ of writers. Clearly, if the key derivation structure does not include a key known by the server and by all and only the users in $w[o] \cup \{u\}$, then the data owner must first update the key derivation structure to include it.

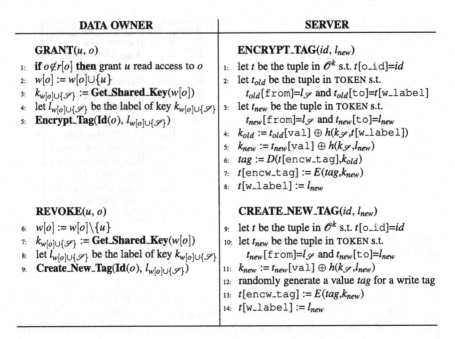

DATA OWNER	SERVER
GRANT(*u*, *o*)	**ENCRYPT_TAG**(*id*, l_{new})
1: **if** $o \notin r[o]$ **then** grant *u* read access to *o*	1: let *t* be the tuple in $\mathcal{O}^k$ s.t. $t[\texttt{o\_id}]=id$
2: $w[o] := w[o] \cup \{u\}$	2: let t_{old} be the tuple in TOKEN s.t.
3: $k_{w[o] \cup \{\mathscr{S}\}} :=$ **Get_Shared_Key**($w[o]$)	$t_{old}[\texttt{from}]=l_{\mathscr{S}}$ and $t_{old}[\texttt{to}]=t[\texttt{w\_label}]$
4: let $l_{w[o] \cup \{\mathscr{S}\}}$ be the label of key $k_{w[o] \cup \{\mathscr{S}\}}$	3: let t_{new} be the tuple in TOKEN s.t.
5: **Encrypt_Tag**(Id(*o*), $l_{w[o] \cup \{\mathscr{S}\}}$)	$t_{new}[\texttt{from}]=l_{\mathscr{S}}$ and $t_{new}[\texttt{to}]=l_{new}$
	4: $k_{old} := t_{old}[\texttt{val}] \oplus h(k_{\mathscr{S}}, t[\texttt{w\_label}])$
	5: $k_{new} := t_{new}[\texttt{val}] \oplus h(k_{\mathscr{S}}, l_{new})$
	6: $tag := D(t[\texttt{encw\_tag}], k_{old})$
	7: $t[\texttt{encw\_tag}] := E(tag, k_{new})$
	8: $t[\texttt{w\_label}] := l_{new}$
REVOKE(*u*, *o*)	**CREATE_NEW_TAG**(*id*, l_{new})
6: $w[o] := w[o] \setminus \{u\}$	9: let *t* be the tuple in $\mathcal{O}^k$ s.t. $t[\texttt{o\_id}]=id$
7: $k_{w[o] \cup \{\mathscr{S}\}} :=$ **Get_Shared_Key**($w[o]$)	10: let t_{new} be the tuple in TOKEN s.t.
8: let $l_{w[o] \cup \{\mathscr{S}\}}$ be the label of key $k_{w[o] \cup \{\mathscr{S}\}}$	$t_{new}[\texttt{from}]=l_{\mathscr{S}}$ and $t_{new}[\texttt{to}]=l_{new}$
9: **Create_New_Tag**(Id(*o*), $l_{w[o] \cup \{\mathscr{S}\}}$)	11: $k_{new} := t_{new}[\texttt{val}] \oplus h(k_{\mathscr{S}}, l_{new})$
	12: randomly generate a value *tag* for a write tag
	13: $t[\texttt{encw\_tag}] := E(tag, k_{new})$
	14: $t[\texttt{w\_label}] := l_{new}$

Fig. 5.7 Pseudocode of the procedures operating at the data owner and at the server side to grant and revoke write privileges

Procedure **Grant** in Fig. 5.7 receives as input a user *u* and a resource *o* and grants *u* the privilege of modifying *o*. The procedure first updates the read access list (if necessary) and the write access list of the resource (lines 1–2). It then retrieves the derivation key (and the corresponding label) that will be used to encrypt the write tag of the resource (i.e., the key shared by the authorized writers of *o*, including *u*, and the server) by calling function **Get_Shared_Key** on the updated write access list of the resource (lines 3–4). The procedure then calls procedure **Encrypt_Tag**, which is executed by the server, to update the representation of the resource at the server side (line 5). Procedure **Encrypt_Tag** in Fig. 5.7 receives as input a resource identifier *id* and a label l_{new} and encrypts the write tag of the resource identified by *id* with the key identified by l_{new}. To this purpose, it first determines the tuple *t* in the outsourced table representing resource *o* with identifier *id* (line 1). It then finds the token that permits to derive key k_{old} with which $t[\texttt{encw\_tag}]$ is currently encrypted (i.e., the token from $l_{\mathscr{S}}$ to $t[\texttt{w\_label}]$), and the token that permits to derive key k_{new} with which the write tag must be encrypted to reflect the policy change (i.e., the token from $l_{\mathscr{S}}$ to l_{new}) (lines 2–3). The procedure then uses these tokens to derive both k_{old} and k_{new} (lines 4–5). It decrypts $t[\texttt{encw\_tag}]$ with k_{old}, re-encrypts the write tag with k_{new}, and updates $t[\texttt{w\_label}]$, setting it to l_{new} to reflect the policy update (lines 6–8).

a

o	r[o]	w[o]
o_1	$ABCD$	BD
o_2	$ABCD$	ABD
o_3	ABC	AC
o_4	BD	BD

b

r_label	w_label	o_id	encw_tag	encr_resource
l_{ABCD}	$l_{BD\mathscr{S}}$	1	α	zKZlJxVcCrC0g
l_{ABCD}	$l_{ABD\mathscr{S}}$	2	ε	t9qdJqC7AImXU
l_{ABC}	$l_{AC\mathscr{S}}$	3	γ	AxalPH8Kv37Ts
l_{BD}	$l_{BD\mathscr{S}}$	4	ζ	xwfPJSLn.MVqY

c

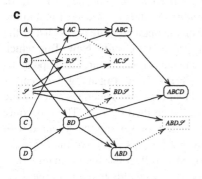

d

from	to	val
l_A	l_{AC}	$k_{AC} \oplus h(k_A, l_{AC})$
l_A	l_{ABD}	$k_{ABD} \oplus h(k_A, l_{ABD})$ •
l_B	l_{ABC}	$k_{ABC} \oplus h(k_B, l_{ABC})$
l_B	l_{BD}	$k_{BD} \oplus h(k_B, l_{BD})$
l_C	l_{AC}	$k_{AC} \oplus h(k_C, l_{AC})$
l_D	l_{BD}	$k_{BD} \oplus h(k_D, l_{BD})$
l_{AC}	l_{ABC}	$k_{ABC} \oplus h(k_{AC}, l_{ABC})$
l_{BD}	l_{ABD}	$k_{ABD} \oplus h(k_{BD}, l_{ABD})$ •
l_{BD}	l_{ABCD}	$k_{ABCD} \oplus h(k_{BD}, l_{ABCD})$
l_{ABC}	l_{ABCD}	$k_{ABCD} \oplus h(k_{ABC}, l_{ABCD})$
$l_{\mathscr{S}}$	$l_{B\mathscr{S}}$	$k_{B\mathscr{S}} \oplus h(k_{\mathscr{S}}, l_{B\mathscr{S}})$
$l_{\mathscr{S}}$	$l_{AC\mathscr{S}}$	$k_{AC\mathscr{S}} \oplus h(k_{\mathscr{S}}, l_{AC\mathscr{S}})$
$l_{\mathscr{S}}$	$l_{BD\mathscr{S}}$	$k_{BD\mathscr{S}} \oplus h(k_{\mathscr{S}}, l_{BD\mathscr{S}})$
$l_{\mathscr{S}}$	$l_{ABD\mathscr{S}}$	$k_{ABD\mathscr{S}} \oplus h(k_{\mathscr{S}}, l_{ABD\mathscr{S}})$ •

Fig. 5.8 Read and write acls (**a**), encrypted resources (**b**), key derivation structure (**c**), and tokens (**d**) of Fig. 5.3 after B is granted write permission over o_2 and D is granted write permission over o_4

Example 5.5. Consider the key derivation structure, outsourced resources, and tokens in Fig. 5.3 and assume that the data owner grants A write privilege over o_2 (i.e., $w[o_2]=w[o_2]\cup\{A\}=ABD$). Since the key derivation structure includes neither a key shared by ABD and $\mathscr{S}$, nor a derivation key for ABD, the structure is first updated to accommodate the new keys (see Example 5.4). Then, the write tag of o_2 is re-encrypted by the server with $k_{ABD\mathscr{S}}$.

Assume now that the data owner grants D write privilege over o_4 (i.e., $w[o_4]= w[o_4]\cup\{D\}=BD$). Since the key derivation structure already contains a key for the updated write access list of o_4, no update is necessary to the key derivation structure. Hence, the only operation performed to enforce this authorization update consists in encrypting the write tag of o_4 with key $k_{BD\mathscr{S}}$. Figure 5.8 illustrates the read and write access lists, the encrypted resources, the key derivation structure, and the tokens after these two grant operations.

Revoke We consider the case of the data owner revoking from user u the write privilege over resource o. To ensure that u cannot exploit her knowledge of the plaintext write tag $tag[o]$ of the revoked resource to perform unauthorized write operations on o, a new write tag must be defined for o, whose value must be independent from the former value of $tag[o]$ (i.e., it has to be chosen adopting a secure random function). Since the server is authorized to know the write tag of each and every resource in the system to correctly enforce write privileges, the data owner can delegate to the external server both the generation and encryption with the correct key of the write tag of resource o. In fact, the data owner does not need to known or keep track of the write tag of her resources.

Procedure **Revoke** in Fig. 5.7 receives as input a user u and a resource o and revokes u the privilege of modifying o. The procedure first updates the write access list $w[o]$ of the resource by removing user u (line 6). It then retrieves the derivation key (and the corresponding label) that will be used to encrypt the write tag of the resource (i.e., the key shared by the authorized writers of o, except u, and the server) by calling function **Get_Shared_Key** on the updated write access list of the resource (lines 7–8). The procedure then calls procedure **Create_New_Tag**, which is executed by the server, to generate a new write tag for the resource and update its representation at the server (line 9). Procedure **Create_New_Tag** in Fig. 5.7 receives as input the identifier id of resource o and a label l_{new}, and generates a new write tag for o, which is then encrypted with the key identified by l_{new}. The procedure first determines the tuple t in the outsourced table representing the resource with identifier id (line 9). It then finds the token that permits to derive the key k_{new} with which the new write tag must be encrypted to reflect the policy change (i.e., the token from $l_{\mathscr{S}}$ to l_{new}) (line 10). The procedure uses this token to derive k_{new} (line 11), randomly generates a value for the write tag (line 12), and encrypts this value with key k_{new} (line 13). Finally, the procedure updates $t[\texttt{w\_label}]$, setting it to l_{new} to reflect the policy update (line 14).

Example 5.6. Consider the key derivation structure, outsourced resources, and tokens in Fig. 5.8, and assume that the data owner revokes from A the write privilege over resource o_3 (i.e., $w[o_3]=w[o_3]\setminus\{A\}=C$). Since the key derivation structure does not include a key shared by the server and C, such a key is first computed as the hash of derivation key k_C with secure hash function h^s. Then, a new write tag is generated for o_3 and encrypted with $k_{C\mathscr{S}}$. Figure 5.9 illustrates the read an write access lists, the encrypted resources, the key derivation structure, and the tokens after this revocation.

The following theorem formally proves that procedures **Grant** and **Revoke** correctly enforce updates to the write authorizations in the system.

Theorem 5.3 (Correct Enforcement of Policy Updates). *Let $\mathscr{U}$ be a set of users, $\mathscr{S}$ be an external server, $\mathscr{O}$ be a set of resources with $r[o]$ and $w[o]$ the read and write access lists of o, respectively, and $\langle \mathscr{K},\mathscr{L},\mathscr{D}\rangle$ a key derivation structure. Procedures **Grant** and **Revoke** in Fig. 5.7 guarantee that the following conditions are satisfied:*

1. *$\forall u \in \mathscr{U}$ and $\forall o \in \mathscr{O}$, u can decrypt $\texttt{encr\_resource}[o]$ iff $u \in r[o]$ (read authorization enforcement);*
2. *$\forall u \in \mathscr{U}$ and $\forall o \in \mathscr{O}$, u can decrypt $\texttt{encw\_tag}[o]$ iff $u \in w[o]$ (write authorization enforcement);*
3. *$\forall o \in \mathscr{O}$, $\mathscr{S}$ can decrypt $\texttt{encw\_tag}[o]$ (write control).*

a

o	r[o]	w[o]
o_1	ABCD	BD
o_2	ABCD	ABD
o_3	ABC	C
o_4	BD	BD

b

r_label	w_label	o_id	encw_tag	encr_resource
l_{ABCD}	$l_{BD\mathcal{S}}$	1	α	zKZlJxVcCrC0g
l_{ABCD}	$l_{ABD\mathcal{S}}$	2	ε	t9qdJqC7AImXU
l_{ABC}	$l_{C\mathcal{S}}$	3	η	AxalPH8Kv37Ts
l_{BD}	$l_{BD\mathcal{S}}$	4	ζ	xwfPJSLn.MVqY

c

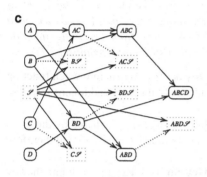

d

from	to	val
l_A	l_{AC}	$k_{AC}\oplus h(k_A,l_{AC})$
l_A	l_{ABD}	$k_{ABD}\oplus h(k_A,l_{ABD})$
l_B	l_{ABC}	$k_{ABC}\oplus h(k_B,l_{ABC})$
l_B	l_{BD}	$k_{BD}\oplus h(k_B,l_{BD})$
l_C	l_{AC}	$k_{AC}\oplus h(k_C,l_{AC})$
l_D	l_{BD}	$k_{BD}\oplus h(k_D,l_{BD})$
l_{AC}	l_{ABC}	$k_{ABC}\oplus h(k_{AC},l_{ABC})$
l_{BD}	l_{ABD}	$k_{ABD}\oplus h(k_{BD},l_{ABD})$
l_{BD}	l_{ABCD}	$k_{ABCD}\oplus h(k_{BD},l_{ABCD})$
l_{ABC}	l_{ABCD}	$k_{ABCD}\oplus h(k_{ABC},l_{ABCD})$
$l_{\mathcal{S}}$	$l_{B\mathcal{S}}$	$k_{B\mathcal{S}}\oplus h(k_{\mathcal{S}},l_{B\mathcal{S}})$
$l_{\mathcal{S}}$	$l_{C\mathcal{S}}$	$k_{C\mathcal{S}}\oplus h(k_{\mathcal{S}},l_{C\mathcal{S}})$
$l_{\mathcal{S}}$	$l_{AC\mathcal{S}}$	$k_{AC\mathcal{S}}\oplus h(k_{\mathcal{S}},l_{AC\mathcal{S}})$
$l_{\mathcal{S}}$	$l_{BD\mathcal{S}}$	$k_{BD\mathcal{S}}\oplus h(k_{\mathcal{S}},l_{BD\mathcal{S}})$
$l_{\mathcal{S}}$	$l_{ABD\mathcal{S}}$	$k_{ABD\mathcal{S}}\oplus h(k_{\mathcal{S}},l_{ABD\mathcal{S}})$

Fig. 5.9   Read and write acls (**a**), encrypted resources (**b**), key derivation structure (**c**), and tokens (**d**) of Fig. 5.8 after A is revoked write permission over o_3

Proof. To prove Theorem 5.3, we must first show that both function **Get_Key** and function **Get_Shared_Key**, which possibly update the key derivation structure, do not compromise its correctness (Definition 5.2), as proved by the following two lemmas.

Lemma 5.1 (Correctness of Function Get_Key). *Let $\mathcal{U}$ be a set of users, U be a subset of $\mathcal{U}$, $\mathcal{S}$ be an external server, and $\langle \mathcal{K},\mathcal{L},\mathcal{D}\rangle$ be a key derivation structure. Triple $\langle \mathcal{K}',\mathcal{L}',\mathcal{D}'\rangle$ resulting from the execution of function **Get_Key**(U) in Fig. 5.5 is a key derivation structure (Definition 5.2).*

Proof. Since we assume that $\langle \mathcal{K},\mathcal{L},\mathcal{D}\rangle$ is a key derivation structure when function **Get_Key** is called, we need to consider only the keys and tokens inserted, updated, or removed by the function.

If the key derivation structure already includes a key k_U known to all and only the users in U, the function does not modify $\langle \mathcal{K},\mathcal{L},\mathcal{D}\rangle$ and therefore the lemma holds (lines 1–2).

If, on the contrary, $k_U\notin\mathcal{K}$, function **Get_Key** inserts it into the key derivation structure. We then need to prove that such an insertion does not violate the conditions in Definition 5.2.

- Condition 1 is satisfied since function **Get_Key** generates a derivation k_U (and a label l_U) and computes the corresponding access key k_U^a (and a label l_U^a). It then inserts k_U, k_U^a into $\mathcal{K}$ and l_U, l_U^a into $\mathcal{L}$ (lines 3–7). The function then inserts access key k_U^a into $\mathcal{K}$ only when the corresponding derivation key k_U has been inserted into $\mathcal{K}$.

- Condition 2 is satisfied as the set of tokens inserted into $\mathcal{D}$ by function **Get_Key** guarantees that k_U can be directly derived from a set $\{k_{U_1}, \ldots, k_{U_n}\}$ of keys in $\mathcal{K}$ such that $U_1 \cup \ldots \cup U_n = U$ (lines 8–12). As proved in [37], this property is equivalent to Condition 2 in Definition 5.1.   □

Lemma 5.2 (Correctness of Function Get_Shared_Key). *Let $\mathcal{U}$ be a set of users, U be a subset of $\mathcal{U}$, $\mathcal{S}$ be an external server, and $\langle \mathcal{K}, \mathcal{L}, \mathcal{D} \rangle$ be a key derivation structure. Triple $\langle \mathcal{K}', \mathcal{L}', \mathcal{D}' \rangle$ resulting from executing function* **Get_Shared_Key**(U) *in Fig. 5.5 is a key derivation structure (Definition 5.2).*

Proof. Since we assume that $\langle \mathcal{K}, \mathcal{L}, \mathcal{D} \rangle$ is a key derivation structure when function **Get_Shared_Key** is called, we need to consider only the keys and tokens inserted, updated, or removed by the function.

If the key derivation structure already includes a key $k_{U \cup \{\mathcal{S}\}}$ shared by the users in U and the external server, the function does not modify $\langle \mathcal{K}, \mathcal{L}, \mathcal{D} \rangle$ and therefore the lemma holds (lines 19–20).

If, on the contrary, $k_{U \cup \{\mathcal{S}\}} \notin \mathcal{K}$, function **Get_Shared_Key** inserts it into the key derivation structure. We then need to prove that such an insertion does not violate the conditions in Definition 5.2.

- Condition 1 is satisfied since function **Get_Shared_Key** computes key $k_{U \cup \{\mathcal{S}\}}$ as the result of hash function h^s over k_U (line 22) and it obtains k_U by calling function **Get_Key** (line 21), which does not compromise the correctness of the key derivation structure (as proved by Lemma 5.1). Function **Get_Shared_Key** then inserts $k_{U \cup \{\mathcal{S}\}}$ and the corresponding label into $\mathcal{K}$ and $\mathcal{L}$, respectively (lines 24–25). The function then inserts key $k_{U \cup \{\mathcal{S}\}}$ into $\mathcal{K}$ only when derivation key k_U has been inserted into $\mathcal{K}$.
- Condition 2 is satisfied since function **Get_Shared_Key** inserts a token $d_{\mathcal{S}, U \cup \{\mathcal{S}\}}$, which permits the server to derive $k_{U \cup \{\mathcal{S}\}}$ from $k_{\mathcal{S}}$ (line 26).   □

Having proved that both function **Get_Key** and function **Get_Shared_Key** do not compromise the correctness of a key derivation structure (Definition 5.2), we can now proceed with proving Theorem 5.3, as follows.

Since we assume that all the conditions are satisfied when procedure **Grant** (**Revoke**, respectively) is called, we need to consider only users and resources for which the policy changes. Also, Condition 1 is not affected by procedures **Grant** and **Revoke** as they neither modify the read access list of resources nor re-encrypt resources content.

- **Grant**(u, R). The procedure inserts u into $w[o]$ (line 2), therefore Condition 2 is satisfied iff u can decrypt `encw_tag[o]`. The write tag $tag[o]$ of resource o is encrypted by procedure **Encrypt_Tag** with the key k_{new} associated with label l_{new}. Since procedure **Grant** calls procedure **Encrypt_Tag** with $l_{w[o] \cup \{\mathcal{S}\}}$

as input, the server encrypts $tag[o]$ with key $k_{w[o]\cup\{\mathscr{S}\}}$ (line 5). This key belongs to the key derivation structure, since procedure **Grant** calls function **Get_Shared_Key** with $w[o]$ as input (line 3). By Lemma 5.2, key $k_{w[o]\cup\{\mathscr{S}\}}$ can be derived by all and only users in $w[o]$ and by the server. Therefore, procedure **Grant** satisfies both Condition 2 and Condition 3.

- **Revoke**(u,R). The procedure removes u from $w[o]$ (line 6), therefore Condition 2 is satisfied iff u cannot decrypt `encw_tag[o]`. Procedure **Create_New_Tag** generates a new tag for o and encrypts it with the key k_{new} associated with label l_{new}. Since procedure **Revoke** calls procedure **Create_New_Tag** with $l_{w[o]\cup\{\mathscr{S}\}}$ as input, the server encrypts the new value of the tag with key $k_{w[o]\cup\{\mathscr{S}\}}$ (line 9). This key belongs to the key derivation structure, since procedure **Revoke** calls function **Get_Shared_Key** with $w[o]$ as input (line 7). By Lemma 5.2, key $k_{w[o]\cup\{\mathscr{S}\}}$ can be derived by all and only users in $w[o]$ and by the server. Therefore, procedure **Revoke** satisfies both Condition 2 and Condition 3. $\square$

5.5 Write Integrity Control

Although the server can be assumed trustworthy to manage resources and delegated actions, it is important to provide a means to the data owner to verify that the server and users are behaving properly (e.g., [44]). Providing such a control has a double advantage: (1) it allows detecting resource tampering, due to the server not performing the required check on the write tags or directly tampering with resources, and (2) it discourages improper behavior by the server and by the users since they know that their improper behavior can be easily detected, and their updates recognized as invalid and discarded. In this section, we illustrate our approach for providing the data owner with a means to verify that modifications to a resource have been produced only by users authorized to write the resource. In the following section, we will extend our solution to the management of updates to write privileges. As discussed in previous sections, if the server performs the correct control on the write tags, data integrity is automatically guaranteed. We therefore illustrate how to perform a write integrity control to detect misbehavior (or laziness) by the server as well as misbehavior by users that can happen with the help of the server (not enforcing the control on the write tags since it is either colluding with the user or just behaving lazily) or without the help of the server (if the user improperly acquires the write tag for a resource by others).

A straightforward approach to provide such a write integrity control would be to apply a signature-based approach. This requires each user to have a pair ⟨`private`,`public`⟩ of keys and, when updating a resource, to sign the new resource content with her private key. The data owner can then check the write integrity by verifying that the signature associated with a resource correctly reflects the resource content and that it has been produced by a user authorized for the operation. Such an approach, while intuitive and simple, has however the main drawback of being computationally expensive (asymmetric encryption is

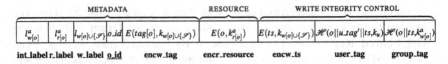

Fig. 5.10 Structure of outsourced resources

considerably less efficient than symmetric encryption) and not well aligned with our approach, which-as a matter of fact-exploits symmetric encryption, tokens, and hash functions to provide efficiency in storage and processing. In the spirit of our approach, we then build our solution for controlling write integrity on HMAC functions [10]. In fact, for common platforms, the ratio between the execution times of digital signatures and of HMAC is more than three orders of magnitude. We then associate with each resource the following three integrity control fields (namely, `encw_ts`, `user_tag`, and `group_tag`) and metadata field (namely, `int_label`) to the fields introduced in Sect. 5.3 (see Fig. 5.10).

- `encw_ts`: timestamp of the write operation, encrypted with the key $k_{w[o] \cup \{\mathscr{S}\}}$ corresponding to the group including the server and all the users in the write access list of o (i.e., $E(ts, k_{w[o] \cup \{\mathscr{S}\}})$);
- `user_tag`: HMAC $\mathscr{H}$ computed with the key k_u of the user who performed the write operation over the resource, concatenated with the `user_tag` u_tag' of the resource prior to the write operation,[1] and the timestamp ts of the write operation (i.e., $\mathscr{H}(o||u\_tag'||ts, k_u)$);
- `group_tag`: HMAC $\mathscr{H}$ computed with the access key $k_{w[o]}^a$ corresponding to the write access list of o over the resource, concatenated with the timestamp of the write operation (i.e., $\mathscr{H}(o||ts, k_{w[o]}^a)$).
- `int_label`: label of the key used to compute the `group_tag` (i.e., $l_{w[o]}^a$).

At time zero, when the data owner outsources her resources to the server, the values of the `user_tag` and of the `group_tag` are those computed by the owner with her own key for the `user_tag`, and with the key of the write access list of the resource (to which the owner clearly belongs) for the `group_tag`. Every time a user updates a resource, it also updates its `user_tag`, `group_tag`, and `int_label`.

A `user_tag` is considered valid if it matches the resource content and it is produced by a user in the write access list of the resource. The `user_tag` provides write integrity (meaning the resource has been written by an authorized user) and accountability of user actions (i.e., the user cannot repudiate her write actions). In fact, since the data owner knows the key k_u of every user u (which she generated and distributed), she can check the validity of the `user_tag` and detect

---

[1]The reason for including the `user_tag` of the resource prior to the write operation is to provide the data owner with a hash chain connecting all the resource versions (we assume the server to never overwrite resources but to maintain all their versions).

possible mismatches, corresponding to unauthorized writes. In addition, every write operation considered valid (according to the control on the user_tag) cannot be repudiated by the user u whose key k_u generated the HMAC. The consideration of group_tag extends the ability of checking the validity of the write operations (i.e., write integrity) also to all the users in the write access list of the resource. Note that allowing writers to check resource integrity is not less important than allowing the data owner to perform the check, as it guarantees that, even in cases of data owner absence, all write operations are performed on resources that have not been improperly modified. Indeed, before modifying a resource content, the writer will check its integrity to be sure that she is operating on genuine data.

While we assume the server to be trustworthy and therefore not interested in tampering with the resources, we note that the user_tag would allow also to detect possible tampering of the server with the resource (since not being an authorized writer, the server will not be able to produce a valid user_tag). The server could also tamper with the write authorizations, by decrypting the write tag and encrypting it with the key corresponding to a different write access list. However, the improper inclusion of a user in the write access list does not have any different effect than when the server does not perform the control, since the user improperly included in the write access list will not be able to produce a valid user_tag. Analogously, the improper removal of a user from the write access list has the same effects as when the server refuses its services.

Unauthorized write operations, in the case of a well behaving server, can only happen if a user has improperly acquired or received from other authorized users the write tag of a resource. Whichever the case, the user will be able to provide neither a valid user_tag nor a valid group_tag for the resource. Also, the data owner and any user authorized to write the resource will be able to detect the invalidity of the group_tag, since the key used to compute the HMAC will not correspond to the access key of $w[o]$.

5.6   Write Integrity Control with Policy Updates

A change in the write authorizations of a resource also requires a change in the write integrity fields associated with the resource. In particular, when user u gains the privilege of writing resource o as a consequence of a grant operation, the set $w[o] \cup \{u\}$ of users should be able to generate and check the group_tag of o. If this were not the case, u would not be able to verify the integrity of the resource before modifying its content. Analogously, when u is revoked the write privilege over o, the set $w[o] \setminus \{u\}$ of users should be able to generate and check the group_tag of o. If this were not the case, u could possibly collude with the server to modify the content of resource o without being detected by the other writers of the resource. A naive strategy to compute a group_tag that guarantees the correct enforcement of integrity checks would require the data owner, when granting/revoking a write privilege, to: (1) download the encrypted resource from the external server, (2) decrypt its content, (3) compute the HMAC of the resource with the access key of the new set of writers, and (4) send the new value of the `group_tag` back to the server. However, this approach causes a high computation and communication overhead for the data owner, who should interact with the external server at every update of the write authorizations. To reduce this overhead, we put forward the idea of modifying the key derivation structure to prevent the re-computation of the `group_tag`, and therefore the need for the data owner to download the resource at every policy update. In the remainder of this section, we first describe our approach for efficiently supporting integrity verification in case of policy updates (Sect. 5.6.1), and we then discuss its exposure to integrity violations (Sect. 5.6.2).

5.6.1 Integrity Keys

Let us assume that the data owner grants user u the write privilege for resource o. Since the `group_tag` of o is computed using key $k^a_{w[o]}$ that u does neither know nor can derive, a straightforward approach that would permit u to verify the integrity of o consists in inserting into the key derivation structure a token from k_u to $k^a_{w[o]}$. This solution has however two drawbacks: (1) it does not handle revoke operations; and (2) it permits u to derive access key $k^a_{w[o]}$ used to encrypt resources o' with $r[o']=w[o]$ (and to generate the `group_tag` of resources o' with $w[o']=w[o]$). With respect to the first drawback, we note that the data owner can always detect the misbehavior of users who modify revoked resources since they are not able to generate correct user tags for these resources. With respect to the second drawback, this solution has the side effect of permitting used u to access the content of resources she is not authorized to read. For instance, with reference to Example 5.5, granting A write access to o_2 causes the insertion of a token from k_A to k^a_{BD}, used to compute the `group_tag` of o_2. However, k^a_{BD} is also used to encrypt o_4 ($r[o_4]=BD$), which A is not authorized to read. This confidentiality breach is due to the fact that the same key is used for two different purposes: protect data confidentiality (when encrypting the content of resources), and provide integrity guarantees to outsourced data (when computing the `group_tag` of resources). A simple and effective solution to this problem consists in using two different keys for protecting data confidentiality and for providing integrity. We then associate an *integrity key* (and corresponding label) with a derivation key whenever needed, and we use integrity keys to compute group tags. We note that, like access keys, integrity keys do not provide derivation capability via tokens (i.e., tokens cannot have integrity keys as starting point). Given derivation key k_U associated with a group U of users, the corresponding integrity key k^i_U is obtained by applying a secure hash function h^i to k_U (i.e., $k^i_U=h^i(k_U)$). The `group_tag` of a resource o is then the HMAC, computed with the integrity key $k^i_{w[o]}$ of the write access list of o, over the resource concatenated with the timestamp of the write operation (see Fig. 5.11). When user u is granted the privilege of modifying o, the data owner inserts into the key derivation structure a token that

METADATA					RESOURCE	WRITE INTEGRITY CONTROL		
$l^i_{w[o]}$	$l^a_{r[o]}$	$l_{w[o]\cup\{\mathscr{S}\}}$	o_id	$E(tag[o],k_{w[o]\cup\{\mathscr{S}\}})$	$E(o,k^a_{r[o]})$	$E(ts,k_{w[o]\cup\{\mathscr{S}\}})$	$\mathscr{H}(o||u\_tag'||ts,k_u)$	$\mathscr{H}(o||ts,k^i_{w[o]})$
int_label	r_label	w_label	o_id	encw_tag	encr_resource	encw_ts	user_tag	group_tag

Fig. 5.11 Structure of outsourced resources adopting integrity keys

permits u to derive integrity key $k^i_{w[o]}$. With reference to the example above, when A is granted write access to o_2, the data owner inserts a token from k_A to k^i_{BD}, which permits A to verify the integrity of o_2 without compromising the confidentiality of o_4.

It is interesting to note that, when inserting a token from k_u to k^i_U, the set of users who know or can derive k^i_U becomes $U\cup\{u\}$, and is therefore different from the set of users who know or can derive the corresponding derivation key k_U. As a consequence, when granting u write access to o, the integrity field int_label of o remains unchanged and is equal to l^i_U, where U corresponds to the write access list of resource o before the grant operation (i.e., $u\notin U$). To limit this mismatch between $w[o]$ and the label of the key used for the group_tag, at each write operation the user who modifies the resource content generates a new group_tag using the integrity key associated with the current write access list of the resource, which reflects the grant/revoke operation. For instance, with reference to Example 5.5, after granting A write privilege over o_2 (but before any further update to o_2), integrity field int_label for resource o_2 has value l^i_{BD} since the group_tag had been computed using the integrity key of $w[o_2]$ before inserting A into the write access list of the resource. Assume now that user B modifies resource o_2. She will compute the group_tag for the resource as $\mathscr{H}(o_2||ts,k^i_{ABD})$ and, when uploading the new resource content and the corresponding group_tag, she will also update the value of int_label, setting it to l^i_{ABD}.

5.6.2 Exposure Risk

We now discuss two cases of possible exposure of data integrity that might occur as a consequence of a policy update.

Revoke According to the mechanism illustrated above, when the data owner revokes u write access to o neither the group_tag of the resource nor the key derivation structure are modified. As a consequence, u is able to verify and to generate a valid group_tag for o till the first update of the resource content by an authorized writer. In this time window, u is not able to decrypt encw_tag for o but, colluding with the server, she could possibly modify the resource content and compute a valid group_tag for o (i.e., a tag that authorized writers would accept). In fact, u can derive the integrity key identified by int_label, and then compute a `group_tag` that is compliant with the new resource content, using the key identified by `int_label`. Note that this collusion has the effect that we have when the server does not check write requests.

Policy Split A similar situation can happen when a user u is granted the write privilege for a resource o that has the same write access list of other resources. In fact, the integrity key k^i used to compute the `group_tag` of o is also used to compute the `group_tag` of all the resources o' with $w[o']=w[o]$ before the grant operation. Since u, as a consequence of the grant operation, can derive k^i to verify the integrity of o, she can (as a side-effect) also verify and compute a valid `group_tag` for all those resources with the same `int_label`. Also in this situation, u can collude with the server (or exploit the laziness of the server not checking write requests) to modify the content of o without being detected by authorized users.

The misbehaviors described above for the revoke and policy split cases do not go undetected by the data owner. In fact, users cannot compute a valid user tag for a resource that she is not authorized to write. Also, exposure to integrity violations is limited and well identifiable. The data owner can then counteract them by explicitly recomputing the `group_tag` of the resource subject to the revoke/grant operation when she considers the communication and computation overhead worth to protect the exposed resources. The risk of integrity violations caused by policy splits can be mitigated by a proper organization of the resources, that is, adopting the same integrity key only if the write access list of the resources is likely to evolve in the same way.

5.7 Supporting User Subscriptions

The solution illustrated in the previous sections of this chapter nicely fits a general scenario in which read authorizations are set by the data holder, and the set of resources of the system does not undergo frequent updates. In the reminder of this chapter, we complement the solution illustrated so far with the definition of a *subscription-based* access control policy regulating access to resources in a subscription-based scenario. In this section, we motivate our extension and formalize the concept of subscription-based policy. We then present how to enforce a subscription-based policy (Sect. 5.8), and we finally illustrate how resources and subscriptions can be managed (Sect. 5.9).

5.7.1 Motivations

In a subscription-based scenario, accesses to resources should be regulated by a *subscription-based access control policy* according to which users are authorized to access all and only the resources that have been published by the resource provider during their subscribed periods. A peculiarity of those scenarios is that user authorizations remain valid also after the expiration of their subscriptions. The subscription-based access control policy takes then into consideration both the subscriptions of the users and the time when resources have been published. Existing solutions result limited for such a scenario. We can classify existing solutions in two main categories.

- *Account-based.* Traditional access control solutions (e.g., [95]), including those emerging in the data outsourcing scenario (e.g., [37]), are based on the assumption that when users leave the system their authorizations terminate and they cannot access the resources anymore. Furthermore, access control solutions for data outsourcing cannot easily support a dynamic scenario where resources are continuously created, and new users can join the system and old users can leave the system at any time.
- *Time-based.* Temporal-based access control solutions (e.g., [11]) enforce time restrictions in a way that is different from what we need. In fact, these solutions consider a scenario where resources are stored and managed by the party who creates them, and assume that authorizations apply only to specific time intervals and/or that authorizations can be applied following a periodic pattern (e.g., a user can access a file only during the working days from 8:00 a.m. to 5:00 p.m.).

We then put forward the idea of extending our solution for enforcing access restrictions illustrated in the previous sections to enforce a subscription-based access control policy without delegating it to the cloud storage server, combining authorization-based access control and cryptographic protection. Our solution should guarantee the correct enforcement of the subscription-based access control policy (i.e., users should be able to access the resources made available during their subscribed periods also after the expiration of their subscriptions) and the *forward* and *backward* protection requirements. Forward protection means that users cannot access resources published before the beginning of their subscriptions (e.g, users who subscribe to a magazine for 2012 cannot access the issues of the magazine published before January 1, 2012). Backward protection means that users cannot access resources published after the expiration of their subscriptions (e.g., users who subscribe to a magazine for 2012 cannot access the issues of the magazine published during 2013). Like for traditional data outsourcing scenario, with our solution the published resources are encrypted so that they self-enforce the subscription-based access restrictions. In addition to the correct enforcement of the subscription-based policy and the satisfaction of the forward and backward protection requirements mentioned above, our solution should avoid re-encryption of resources and re-distribution of keys whenever users subscribe to services or withdraw from their subscriptions.

5.7.2 Subscription-Based Policy

In our subscription-based scenario, a resource provider offers a service consisting of a period of publication of resources, and each user subscribing to the service can access all the resources published during her subscription. We denote with $\mathscr{U}$ and $\mathscr{O}$ the set of users subscribed to the service and the set of published resources, respectively. We note that, although in this chapter we consider time-based subscriptions, our approach can be easily adapted to other scenarios where subscriptions to a service can be defined on the basis of different criteria (e.g., topic of interest, geographical region).

Given a *time domain* $(\mathbb{TS},\leq)$, with $\mathbb{TS}$ a set of time instants and $\leq$ a total order relationship on $\mathbb{TS}$ [12], the resource provider assigns to each resource $o \in \mathscr{O}$ a timestamp $o.t$ in $\mathbb{TS}$ that represents the time when the resource has been published. The resource provider may combine contiguous time instants into time windows, defined on arbitrary granularities, forming a *time hierarchy*. Intuitively, these time windows represent the periods of time for which the resource provider allows users to subscribe to the service offered. Formally, a time hierarchy $\mathscr{H}_{\mathscr{T}}$ is a pair $(\mathscr{T},\succeq)$, where $\mathscr{T}$ is a set of time windows, and $\succeq$ is a partial order relationship over $\mathscr{T}$. A time window T_i in $\mathscr{T}$ is a pair $[t_i^s,t_i^e]$ of time instants and represents the set of time instants $t \in \mathbb{TS}$ such that $t_i^s \leq t \leq t_i^e$. Given two time windows T_i and T_j in $\mathscr{T}$, T_i *dominates* T_j, denoted $T_i \succeq T_j$, if $t_i^s \leq t_j^s$ and $t_j^e \leq t_i^e$ (i.e., the time instants in T_j represent a subset of the time instants in T_i). The leaves of the time hierarchy correspond to time instants in $\mathbb{TS}$, which can be seen as time windows with $t^s = t^e$. The time hierarchy can be graphically represented as a directed acyclic graph with vertices representing time windows in $\mathscr{T}$ and edges representing direct dominance relationships. For simplicity, but without loss of generality, in this chapter we assume $\mathscr{H}_{\mathscr{T}}$ to be a tree. As an example, consider resource provider Condé Nast, monthly publishing magazine *Glamour* and offering the possibility to buy subscriptions for a month (single issue), a trimester, a semester, or a year. Figure 5.12 illustrates the time hierarchy defined by the resource provider. For the sake of readability, in the figure we denote leaves with the time instant they represent. Each user $u \in \mathscr{U}$ can subscribe to the service offered by the resource provider for an arbitrary set, denoted $u.\mathscr{S}$, of time windows in $\mathscr{H}_{\mathscr{T}}$ (i.e., $u.\mathscr{S} \subseteq \mathscr{T}$).

The timestamps assigned to resources along with the user subscriptions establish the set of resources that each user can access: user $u \in \mathscr{U}$ can access resource $o \in \mathscr{O}$ if she subscribed for a time window including $o.t$. Formally, the subscription-based policy regulating access to the resources is defined as follows.

Definition 5.3 (Subscription-Based Policy). Let $\mathscr{H}_{\mathscr{T}}(\mathscr{T},\succeq)$ be a time hierarchy defined on time domain $(\mathbb{TS},\leq)$, $\mathscr{U}$ be a set of users with $u.\mathscr{S} \subseteq \mathscr{T}$ for all $u \in \mathscr{U}$, and $\mathscr{O}$ be a set of resources with $o.t \in \mathbb{TS}$ for all $o \in \mathscr{O}$. The *subscription-based policy* $\mathscr{A}$ on $\mathscr{U}$ and $\mathscr{O}$ grants $u \in \mathscr{U}$ access to $o \in \mathscr{O}$ iff $\exists [t^s,t^e] \in u.\mathscr{S}$ s.t. $t^s \leq o.t \leq t^e$.

Example 5.7. Suppose that three issues of magazine *Glamour* have been published with timestamp Jan'12, Feb'12, and Mar'12, respectively (i.e., $\mathscr{O} = \{$*Glam-01,Glam-*

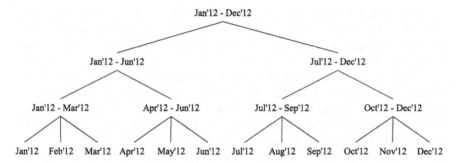

Fig. 5.12 An example of time hierarchy

02,Glam-03}). Assume now that two users $\mathscr{U} = \{$*Alice, Barbara*$\}$ subscribe to the magazine for the first trimester of 2012 ([Jan'12,Mar'12]), and for the first issue of the year ([Jan'12,Jan'12]), respectively. The subscription-based policy grants *Alice* access to all the issues of the magazine in $\mathscr{O}$, while it grants *Barbara* access only to the first issue *Glam-01*.

5.8 Graph Modeling of the Subscription-Based Policy

Our idea to enforce the subscription-based policy consists in defining a key derivation structure so that each resource is encrypted only once with a single key, and each user receives only one key from which she can derive all and only the keys used for encrypting the resources that she can access according to the subscription-based policy. To fix ideas and make the discussion clear, we consider the system at a specific point in time when some resources have been published and some users have subscribed to the service offered by the resource provider. We first discuss how resources are encrypted and then describe how to model users' subscriptions.

Traditional techniques developed for enforcing an access control policy in the data outsourcing scenario build a key derivation structure on the basis of the sets of users that can access resources (like our solution illustrated in the previous sections of this chapter, building the key derivation structure on the access control lists of the resources of the system). In our extended scenario, such sets of users vary frequently over time, and therefore it is not convenient to exploit them for building the key derivation structure. We then use the time hierarchy $\mathscr{H}_{\mathscr{T}}$ defined by the resource provider as a key derivation structure where each time window is associated with a key, and each edge corresponds to a token. The timestamp associated with a published resource, therefore, identifies the time window in the time hierarchy representing the key used to encrypt the resource itself. The keys associated with time windows including more than a time instant (i.e., internal vertices) are not used for encrypting resources, but only for derivation purposes. Clearly, not all the time windows in the time hierarchy are necessary for enforcing the subscription-based policy, but only those corresponding to the timestamps of published resources along with all the time windows dominating them. For instance, with respect to Example 5.7, the time windows that must be represented in the key derivation structure are Jan'12, Feb'12, and Mar'12, which are the timestamps of the three published resources, and all the time windows dominating them in the time hierarchy in Fig. 5.12, that is, [Jan'12,Mar'12], [Jan'12,Jun'12], and [Jan'12,Dec'12]. In this way, from the knowledge, for example, of the key associated with [Jan'12,Mar'12] we can derive the keys used for encrypting all the resources published during the first trimester of 2012.

For each user in the system, the resource provider generates a new key and communicates it to the user. With this unique key, the user should be able to access all and only the resources for which she is authorized according to her subscriptions. The idea is to "hook the user" through a token on each time window T for which she subscribed. In this way, the user can adopt her key to directly derive the key associated with time window T. From this key she can directly or indirectly derive the keys used to encrypt all and only the resources whose timestamp is included in T. For instance, according to the subscriptions in Example 5.7, *Alice* can access all the resources published in the first trimester of 2012. The resource provider then creates a token from *Alice*'s key to the key associated with [Jan'12,Mar'12]. By construction, all resources published in Jan'12, Feb'12, and Mar'12 will be encrypted with a key derivable from the key associated with [Jan'12,Mar'12], which *Alice* can derive. Note that it may happen that a user subscribes for a time window for which no resource has been published (e.g., a user subscribes to a magazine for April'12 and the issue of April has not been published yet). The key derivation structure must then include also the time windows representing users' subscriptions, along with their ancestors in $\mathcal{H}_{\mathcal{T}}$. The resulting key derivation structure, which we call *user and resource graph*, can be formally defined as follows.

Definition 5.4 (User and Resource Graph). Let $\mathcal{H}_{\mathcal{T}}(\mathcal{T}, \succeq)$ be a time hierarchy on time domain $(\mathbb{TS}, \leq)$, $\mathcal{U}$ be a set of users with $u.\mathcal{S} \subseteq \mathcal{T}$ for all $u \in \mathcal{U}$, and $\mathcal{O}$ be a set of resources with $o.t \in \mathbb{TS}$ for all $o \in \mathcal{O}$. A *user and resource graph* over $\mathcal{U}$, $\mathcal{O}$, and $\mathcal{H}_{\mathcal{T}}$ is a graph $G(V, E)$, with:

- $V = \mathcal{T}_r \cup \mathcal{T}_s \cup \mathcal{T}_p \cup \mathcal{U}$, with $\mathcal{T}_r = \bigcup_{o \in \mathcal{O}} [o.t, o.t]$, $\mathcal{T}_s = \bigcup_{u \in \mathcal{U}} u.\mathcal{S}$, and
  $\mathcal{T}_p = \{T \in \mathcal{T} \mid \exists T' \in \mathcal{T}_s \cup \mathcal{T}_r \text{ such that } T \succeq T'\}$
- $E = \{(u,T) \mid u \in \mathcal{U} \wedge T \in V \setminus \mathcal{U} \wedge T \in u.\mathcal{S}\} \cup$
  $\{(T_i, T_j) \mid T_i, T_j \in V \setminus \mathcal{U} \wedge T_i \succeq T_j \wedge (\nexists T_z \in V \setminus \mathcal{U}, T_i \succeq T_z \succeq T_j \wedge T_z \neq T_i \neq T_j)\}$

The vertices in the user and resource graph represent the keys of the system, while the edges represent the tokens in the *token catalog* $\mathcal{D}$ stored at the external cloud storage server together with the encrypted resources.

Example 5.8. Consider the time hierarchy in Fig. 5.12 and the subscription-based policy in Example 5.7. Figure 5.13a shows the corresponding user and resource graph, where dotted triangles represent subtrees of the time hierarchy that are not associated with a vertex in the graph. For the sake of clarity, vertices in the graph are associated with a label that is used to refer to the time windows of

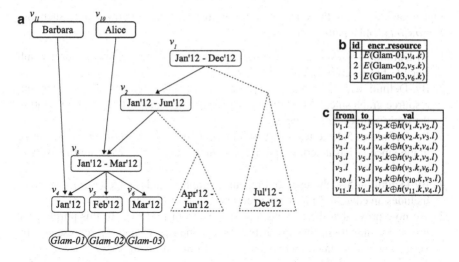

Fig. 5.13 An example of user and resource graph (**a**), published resources (**b**), and token catalog (**c**)

interest. Hence, for instance, [Jan'12,Dec'12] is associated with label v_1, its key is indicated with $v_1.k$, and its label with $v_1.l$. The figure also reports the published resources, represented as ovals connected with the vertices in the graph representing their timestamp and whose keys are used to encrypt them. Figure 5.13b shows the encrypted resources stored at the external cloud storage server, with **id** the resource identifier and **encr_resource** the encrypted resource ($E(r,k)$ denotes the encryption of o with k), and Fig. 5.13c illustrates the token catalog resulting from the user and resource graph in Fig. 5.13a.

The user and resource graph in Definition 5.4 guarantees the correct enforcement of the subscription-based policy since each user can decrypt all and only the resources with a timestamp included in at least one of the time windows in the user's subscriptions. This is formalized by the following theorem.

Theorem 5.4 (Correct Enforcement of Subscription-Based Policy). *Let $\mathcal{H}_{\mathcal{T}}(\mathcal{T}, \succeq)$ be a time hierarchy on time domain $(\mathbb{TS}, \leq)$, $\mathcal{U}$ be a set of users with $u.\mathcal{S} \subseteq \mathcal{T}$ for all $u \in \mathcal{U}$, and $\mathcal{O}$ be a set of resources with $o.t \in \mathbb{TS}$ for all $o \in \mathcal{O}$. The user and resource graph $G(V,E)$ correctly enforces a subscription-based policy $\mathcal{A}$ on $\mathcal{U}$ and $\mathcal{O}$ when $\forall u \in \mathcal{U}$, $\forall o \in \mathcal{O}$:*

$$\exists [t^s, t^e] \in u.\mathcal{S} \text{ s.t. } t^s \leq o.t \leq t^e \iff \langle u, [o.t, o.t] \rangle \text{ is a path in } G.$$

Proof. We first prove that, if $\exists T = [t^s, t^e] \in u.\mathcal{S}$ s.t. $t^s \leq o.t \leq t^e$, then u can decrypt o. User u knows the key of vertex v_u representing herself in G, while o is encrypted with the key of vertex v_r representing $[o.t, o.t]$ in G. User u can derive the key with which a resource o is encrypted (and then access its content) only if there exists a path in G from v_u to v_r. The path connecting v_u to v_r is composed of two parts: an edge connecting v_u to the vertex v_T representing the time window in $u.\mathcal{S}$ such that $T \succeq [o.t, o.t]$, and a path from v_T to v_r.

1. By Definition 5.4, vertex v_u representing u belongs to the user and resource graph since G has a vertex v_u for each $u \in \mathcal{U}$.
2. By Definition 5.4, vertex v_r representing $[o.t, o.t]$ belongs to the user and resource graph since G has a vertex for each time window $[o.t, o.t]$ representing the timestamp of a resource $o \in \mathcal{O}$.
3. By Definition 5.4, vertex v_T representing T belongs to the user and resource graph since G has a vertex v_T for each time window in $u.\mathcal{S}$ for all the users in $u \in \mathcal{U}$.
4. By Definition 5.4, the user and resource graph includes edge (v_u, v_T), since G includes an edge (u, T) for each user u and each time window $T \in u.\mathcal{S}$.
5. We now prove that there exists a path in G from v_T to v_r. To this purpose we prove, by induction, that given two time windows T_i and T_j represented by vertices v_i and v_j in G, there exists a path from v_i to v_j iff $T_i \succeq T_j$.
   Base: $T_i \succeq T_j$ and $\nexists T_z \in \mathcal{H}_\mathcal{G}$ s.t. $T_i \succeq T_z \succeq T_j$ and $T_i \neq T_z \neq T_j$. By Definition 5.4 edge (v_i, v_j) belongs to G.
   Induction: let us suppose that, given sequence of n time windows $\{T_{z_1}, \ldots, T_{z_n}\}$ such that $T_{z_1} \succeq \ldots \succeq T_{z_n}$ and $\nexists T_k \in \mathcal{H}_\mathcal{G}$ s.t. $T_{z_i} \succeq T_k \succeq T_{z_j}$ and $T_{z_i} \neq T_k \neq T_{z_j}$, $i, j = 1, \ldots, n$, G includes a path from v_{z_1} to v_{z_n}. Let us now consider a sequence of $n + 1$ time windows $\{T_{z_1}, \ldots, T_{z_n}, T_{z_{n+1}}\}$ such that $T_{z_1} \succeq \ldots \succeq T_{z_n} \succeq T_{z_{n+1}}$ and $\nexists T_k \in \mathcal{H}_\mathcal{G}$ s.t. $T_{z_i} \succeq T_k \succeq T_{z_j}$ and $T_{z_i} \neq T_k \neq T_{z_j}$, $i, j = 1, \ldots, n+1$. By assumption, there exists a path from v_{z_1} to v_{z_n}. Also, there exists an edge $(v_{z_n}, v_{z_{n+1}})$ for the base of the induction. As a consequence, there exists a path from v_{z_1} to $v_{z_{n+1}}$.

We now prove, by contradiction, that if $\nexists T = [t^s, t^e] \in u.\mathcal{S}$ s.t. $t^s \leq o.t \leq t^e$, then u cannot decrypt o. Let us assume that u can decrypt o, that is, there exists a path from v_u to v_r. Since $\nexists T = [t^s, t^e] \in u.\mathcal{S}$ s.t. $t^s \leq o.t \leq t^e$, then for all (v_u, v_T) in G, time window T represented by v_T does not include $o.t$ by Definition 5.4. As a consequence, u can access o only if there exists a path in G from vertex v_i representing T_i to vertex v_j representing T_j such that $T_i \nsucceq T_j$. Let us assume that the path is composed of a sequence of edges $(v_i, v_{z_1}), \ldots, (v_{z_n}, v_j)$. By Definition 5.4, $T_i \succeq T_{z_1}$, $T_{z_n} \succeq T_j$, and for each edge $(v_{z_i}, v_{z_{i+1}})$ in the sequence, $T_{z_i} \succeq T_{z_{i+1}}$. Therefore, we obtain that $T_i \succeq T_j$, which contradicts the initial hypothesis. $\qquad\square$

5.9 Management of Resources and Subscriptions

Whenever there is a change in the subscription-based policy (e.g., a new resource is published, a user subscribes to a service for a specific time window, or a user decides to withdraw from a subscription), the user and resource graph has to be updated accordingly. In the following, we discuss how changes to the policy can be managed in a transparent way for the users.

PUBLISH_RESOURCE(o)

1: $\mathcal{O} := \mathcal{O} \cup \{o\}$
2: $v := $ **Get_Vertex**($[o.t,o.t]$) /* retrieve the vertex representing the timestamp of the resource */
3: **Encrypt**($o,v.k$)
4: publish the encrypted resource

GET_VERTEX(T)

5: **if** $T \in V$ **then** /* T already belongs to G */
6:     let $v \in V$ be the vertex with $v = T$
7:     **return**(v)
8: generate vertex $v := T$
9: generate encryption key $v.k$
10: generate public label $v.l$
11: $V := V \cup \{v\}$ /* insert the vertex into the user and resource graph */
12: let $T_i \in \mathcal{T}: T_i \succeq T \land \nexists T_j: T_i \succeq T_j \succeq T, T_j \neq T_i \neq T$ /* determine the direct ancestor of T in $\mathcal{H}_\mathcal{T}$ */
13: **if** $T_i \neq $ NULL **then**
14:     $v_i := $ **Get_Vertex**(T_i) /* retrieve the vertex in G that represents T_i */
15:     $E := E \cup \{(v_i,v)\}$ /* insert the edge connecting T_i to T in G */
16:     $\mathcal{D} := \mathcal{D} \cup \{v.k \oplus h(v_i.k,v.l)\}$ /* publish the corresponding token */
17: **return**(v)

Fig. 5.14 Pseudocodes of procedure **Publish_Resource** and function **Get_Vertex**

5.9.1 Resource Publishing

At initialization time, the user and resource graph is empty (no key is necessary for resource encryption) and it is dynamically built as resources are published. Figure 5.14 illustrates the pseudocode of procedure **Publish_Resource** that the resource provider calls whenever it needs to publish a resource. The procedure takes a resource o as input and publishes its encrypted representation. The procedure first calls function **Get_Vertex** on time window $T=[o.t,o.t]$ (line 2). This function checks whether the vertex representing $[o.t,o.t]$ is in the user and resource graph, since its key has to be used for encrypting o. If such a vertex exists, the function returns it (lines 5–7). Otherwise, the function first creates a vertex v representing T, along with the corresponding encryption key $v.k$ and public label $v.l$, and inserts v into the set V of vertices of the user and resource graph (lines 8–11). To guarantee that the time window T_i directly dominating T in the time hierarchy is represented in the user and resource graph, function **Get_Vertex** recursively calls itself on T_i, obtaining the vertex v_i representing T_i in the graph (lines 12–14). The function inserts into G edge (v_i,v) and publishes the corresponding token (lines 15–16). We note that the recursive nature of function **Get_Vertex** guarantees that all the ancestors of T in $\mathcal{H}_\mathcal{T}$ are represented by a vertex in the user and resource graph, and that each vertex is connected to all its direct descendants represented in the graph. The function then returns vertex v representing $[o.t,o.t]$

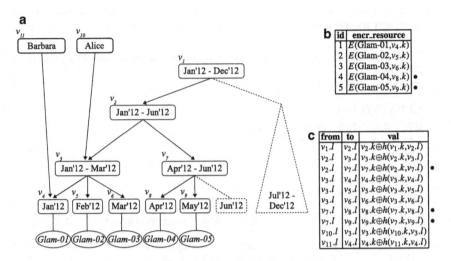

Fig. 5.15 User and resource graph (**a**), published resources (**b**), and token catalog after *Glam-04* and *Glam-05* are published (**c**)

(line 17). Finally, procedure **Publish_Resource** encrypts o with $v.k$ and publishes the resulting encrypted resource (lines 3–4).

Example 5.9. Consider the user and resource graph, published resources, and token catalog in Fig. 5.13 and assume that Condé Nast publishes the fourth issue of *Glamour* in April'12. The resource provider calls procedure **Publish_Resource** on resource *Glam-04* that in turn calls function **Get_Vertex** on [Apr'12,Apr'12]. The function inserts vertex v_8 representing [Apr'12,Apr'12] and its direct ancestor v_7 representing [Apr'12,Jun'12]. Procedure **Publish_Resource** then encrypts *Glam-04* with the key of vertex v_8. Assume now that Condé Nast publishes the fifth issue of *Glamour* in May'12, calling procedure **Publish_Resource** on resource *Glam-05*. Function **Get_Vertex** inserts vertex v_9 representing [May'12,May'12] and directly connects it to [Apr'12,Jun'12], since it is already included in the graph. Resource *Glam-05* is encrypted with the key of vertex v_9. Figure 5.15 illustrates the resulting user and resource graph, published resources, and token catalog, where new resources and tokens are denoted with a bullet •.

5.9.2 New Subscription

Both new and existing users can subscribe to a service for a time window at any point in time (i.e., before the beginning, during, or even after the expiration of the window). Figure 5.16 illustrates procedure **Subscribe** that manages new subscriptions. The procedure takes a user u and a time window T as input and works as follows. If u is a new user, the procedure creates a vertex v_u representing u,

SUBSCRIBE(u,T)

1: **if** $u \notin \mathscr{U}$ **then** /* u is a new user in the system */
2:   $\mathscr{U} := \mathscr{U} \cup \{u\}$
3:   generate vertex $v_u := u$
4:   generate encryption key $v_u.k$
5:   generate public label $v_u.l$
6:   $V := V \cup \{v_u\}$
7: **else** let $v_u \in V$ be the vertex with $v_u = u$
8: $u.\mathscr{S} := u.\mathscr{S} \cup \{T\}$
9: $v_T := \textbf{Get\_Vertex}(T)$
10: $E := E \cup \{(v_u,v_T)\}$
11: $\mathscr{D} := \mathscr{D} \cup \{v_T.k \oplus h(v_u.k,v_T.l)\}$
12: let $T_i \in \mathscr{T}$: $T_i \succeq T \wedge (\nexists T_j: T_i \succeq T_j \succeq T, T_j \neq T_i \neq T)$ /* determine the direct ancestor of T in $\mathscr{H}_{\mathscr{T}}$ */
13: $\mathscr{T}' := \{T_j \in u.\mathscr{S} \mid T_i \succeq T_j \wedge (\nexists T_z \in \mathscr{T}: T_i \succeq T_z \succeq T_j, T_i \neq T_z \neq T_j)\}$
14: **if** $\bigcup_{T_j \in \mathscr{T}'} T_j = T_i$ **then**
15:   $u.\mathscr{S} := u.\mathscr{S} \setminus \mathscr{T}'$
16:   $E := E \setminus \{(v_i,v_j) \mid v_i = u \wedge v_j = T_j, T_j \in \mathscr{T}'\}$
17:   $\mathscr{D} := \mathscr{D} \setminus \{v_j.k \oplus h(v_i.k,v_j.l) \mid v_i = u \wedge v_j = T_j, T_j \in \mathscr{T}'\}$
18:   **Subscribe**(u,T_i)

Fig. 5.16 Pseudocode of procedure **Subscribe**

her encryption key $v_u.k$, and public label $v_u.l$ (lines 1–6). Otherwise, the procedure identifies the vertex v_u representing the user in G (line 7). The procedure then inserts T into $u.\mathscr{S}$, calls function **Get_Vertex** on T so that the vertex v_T representing T and its ancestors are possibly added to the graph, and inserts edge (v_u,v_T) in the user and resource graph, publishing the corresponding token (lines 8–11). Through this token, the user can directly derive from her key the key of the time window to which she is subscribing.

To keep the number of tokens under control, the procedure verifies whether the set $u.\mathscr{S}$ of subscriptions includes all the time windows directly dominated by T_i that in turn directly dominates T in $\mathscr{H}_{\mathscr{T}}$ (e.g., a user may be subscribed for three issues of a magazine that correspond to a trimester). In this case, instead of maintaining a token from u to all the direct descendants of T_i, it is possible to replace them with a single token from vertex u to T_i. To this purpose, procedure **Subscribe** identifies the direct ancestor T_i of the time window T to which u is subscribing and checks if $u.\mathscr{S}$ includes all the descendants $T_j, \ldots, T_l$ of T_i (lines 12–14). In this case, it removes $T_j, \ldots, T_l$ from $u.\mathscr{S}$, the edges connecting v_u to the vertices representing them, and the corresponding tokens (lines 15–17). The procedure then recursively calls itself to subscribe u to T_i to possibly propagate up in the graph this factorization (line 18).

Example 5.10. Consider the user and resource graph, published resources, and token catalog in Fig. 5.15, and assume that *Alice* renews her subscription to *Glamour* for trimester [Apr'12,Jun'12]. Since both *Alice* and [Apr'12,Jun'12] are already in the graph (vertices v_{10} and v_7, respectively), procedure **Subscribe** only inserts edge (v_{10},v_7) and publishes the corresponding token. Renewing her subscription,

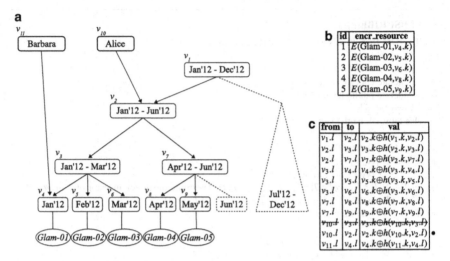

Fig. 5.17 User and resource graph (**a**), published resources (**b**), and token catalog after *Alice* subscribes for [Apr'12,Jun'12] (**c**)

Alice is now subscribed for the first semester of year 2012. Procedure **Subscribe** factorizes the two subscriptions for [Jan'12,Mar'12] and [Apr'12,Jun'12] in a unique subscription for [Jan'12,Jun'12]. Figure 5.17 illustrates the resulting user and resource graph, published resources, and token catalog (removed tokens are ~~crossed out~~). Assume now that *Carol* joins the system and subscribes for [Apr'12,Jun'12]. Procedure **Subscribe** first inserts vertex v_{12} representing *Carol* in the graph, and communicates her the corresponding key. It then inserts edge (v_{12}, v_7) in the graph. Figure 5.18 illustrates the resulting user and resource graph, published resources, and token catalog.

5.9.3   Withdrawal from a Subscription

As our system provides high flexibility in defining the time windows available for subscription, withdrawal from a subscription represents an exception in the working of the system and must be managed as a special case. In fact, no action is needed when a subscription naturally expires. When a user withdraws from a subscription for time window $[t^s, t^e]$, starting from time instant t, the resource provider must guarantee that: (1) she cannot access the resources with timestamp in $(t, t^e]$ (backward protection), and (2) she continues to access the resources with timestamp in $[t^s, t]$. For instance, consider Example 5.10. In May'12 *Alice* could decide to withdraw from her subscription for the first semester of year 2012. In this case, she should not be able to decrypt the issue of June of the magazine, while she will continue to access the issues of January, February, March, April, and May.

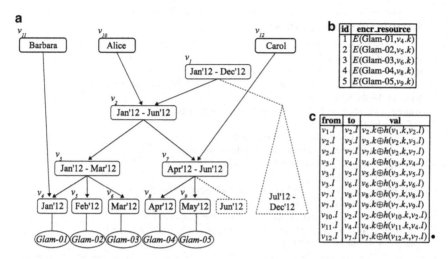

Fig. 5.18 User and resource graph (**a**), published resources (**b**), and token catalog after *Carol* subscribes for [Apr'12,Jun'12] (**c**)

Clearly, a user can withdraw from her subscription at time t only if no resource with timestamp in $(t,t^e]$ has been published yet, since otherwise she could have accessed it before withdrawal. To guarantee that withdrawals are transparent for all the users and cause a limited overhead to the resource provider, our approach avoids re-keying and re-encryption operations.

Figure 5.19 illustrates procedure **Withdraw_Subscription**, which takes a user u and a time instant t as input, and updates the user and resource graph. The procedure first identifies the vertex v_u representing the user in G and the time window $[t^s,t^e]$ in $u.\mathscr{S}$ that includes t (lines 1–2). If such a time window does not exist or if at least a resource with timestamp in $(t,t^e]$ has been published, the procedure terminates notifying the problem to the resource provider (line 3). Otherwise, procedure **Withdraw_Subscription** removes the subscription by first substituting $[t^s,t^e]$ with $[t^s,t]$ in $u.\mathscr{S}$ (line 4). Since user u already knows the keys of the vertices along the path from vertex $[t^s,t^e]$ to t if they are represented in the user and resource graph, the resource provider must guarantee that all the resources with a timestamp following t will be encrypted with a key that is not derivable from the keys along this path. To this purpose, the procedure updates the time window $[t_i^s,t_i^e]$ that each of these vertices represents by setting t_i^e to t, creates a new set of vertices representing the time windows that has been changed, and connects them in a path of the user and resource graph. Also, the procedure inserts an edge between each new vertex $[t_i^s,t_i^e]$ to vertex $[t_i^s,t]$ since $[t_i^s,t_i^e]$ clearly dominates $[t_i^s,t]$. Finally, for each user u such that $[t_i^s,t_i^e]\in u.\mathscr{S}$, the procedure substitutes the token (and corresponding edge) between u and $[t_i^s,t]$ (i.e., the vertex that represented $[t_i^s,t_i^e]$ before the change performed by procedure **Withdraw_Subscription**) with

---

WITHDRAW_SUBSCRIPTION(u,t)

1:   let $v_u \in V$ be the vertex with $v_u = u$
2:   let $T=[t^s,t^e] \in u.\mathscr{S}$ s.t. $t^s \leq t \leq t^e$
3:   **if** T=NULL $\vee$ ($\exists o \in \mathcal{O}$ s.t. $t < o.t \leq t^e$) **then exit**
4:   $u.\mathscr{S} := u.\mathscr{S} \setminus \{T\} \cup \{[t^s,t]\}$ /* update the time window in user subscriptions */
5:   let $v_T \in V$ be the vertex with $v_T = T$
6:   **while** $t^e \neq t \wedge t^s \neq t^e \wedge T \in V$ **do** /* visit the path from T to $[t,t]$ */
7:     $T_{new} := [t^s,t^e]$
8:     $v_T := [t^s,t]$ /* update the label of the vertex */
9:     $v_{new} := $ **Get_Vertex**(T_{new}) /* create a vertex representing T_{new} */
10:     $E := E \cup \{(v_{new},v_T)\}$ /* $[t^s,t^e]$ dominates $[t^s,t]$ */
11:     $\mathscr{D} := \mathscr{D} \cup \{v_T.k \oplus h(v_{new}.k,v_T.l)\}$
12:     **for each** (v_u,v_T) s.t. $v_u \in \mathscr{U} \setminus \{u\}$ **do** /* update users' subscriptions */
13:       $E := E \cup \{(v_u,v_{new})\} \setminus \{(v_u,v_T)\}$
14:       $\mathscr{D} := \mathscr{D} \cup \{v_{new}.k \oplus h(v_u.k,v_{new}.l)\} \setminus \{v_T.k \oplus h(v_u.k,v_T.l)\}$
15:     let $T=[t^s,t^e] \in \mathscr{T}$ s.t. $T_{new} \succeq T \wedge t^s \leq t \leq t^e \wedge \nexists T_j: T_{new} \succeq T_j \succeq T, T_j \neq T_{new} \neq T$
16:     let $v_T \in V$ be the vertex with $v_T = T$

Fig. 5.19 Pseudocode of procedure **Withdraw_Subscription**

the token (and corresponding edge) between u and the new vertex representing $[t_i^s,t_i^e]$, to preserve her ability to derive all the keys of the time windows dominated by $[t_i^s,t_i^e]$.

Note that the keys along the path from T to t, whose time windows have been updated by procedure **Withdraw_Subscription**, are not affected. Therefore, users who have already computed these keys can still use their local copy. The number of additional vertices and edges in the user and resource graph is limited and is at most $h - 1$ and $2(h - 1)$, respectively, where h is the height of the time hierarchy. The number of updated edges is $|\mathscr{U}| - 1$ in the worst case.

Example 5.11. Consider the user and resource graph, published resources, and token catalog in Fig. 5.18, and assume that *Alice* withdraws from her subscription in May'12. Procedure **Withdraw_Subscription** updates her subscription for [Jan'12,Jun'12] to [Jan'12,May'12], and visits the path from vertex v_2 (representing [Jan'12,Jun'12]) to the vertex representing [May'12,May'12]. First, it visits vertex v_2, updates its time window to [Jan'12,May'12], creates a new vertex v_2' for time window [Jan'12,Jun'12], and inserts edge (v_2',v_2) in the user and resource graph. The procedure executes the same operations when visiting v_7. Since *Carol* should still be able to access all the issues of *Glamour* published in [Apr'12,Jun'12], the procedure substitutes edge (v_{12},v_7) with edge (v_{12},v_7'). From her key *Alice* can derive, after this update, the keys used to encrypt the issues published in [Jan'12,May'12], while *Carol* can still derive keys used to encrypt issues published in [Apr'12,Jun'12]. Figure 5.20 illustrates the user and resource graph, published resources, and token catalog after *Alice*'s withdrawal.

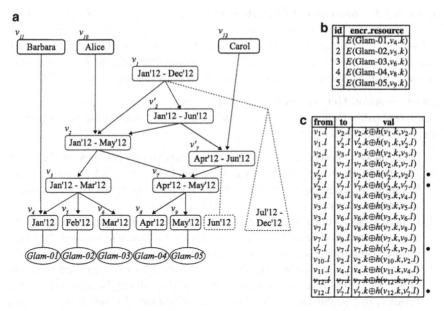

Fig. 5.20 User and resource graph (**a**), published resources (**b**), and token catalog after *Alice* withdraws from her subscription in May'12 (**c**)

5.9.4   Correctness

The procedures described in this section correctly enforce changes to the subscription-based policy. This is formally stated by the following theorem.

Theorem 5.5 (Correct Enforcement of Policy Updates). *Let $\mathcal{H}_{\mathcal{T}}(\mathcal{T},\succeq)$ be a time hierarchy on time domain* $(\mathbb{TS},\leq)$, $\mathcal{U}$ *be a set of users with* $u.\mathcal{S}\subseteq\mathcal{T}$ *for all* $u\in\mathcal{U}$, $\mathcal{O}$ *be a set of resources with* $o.t\in\mathbb{TS}$ *for all* $o\in\mathcal{O}$, *and* $G(V,E)$ *be the user and resource graph over* $\mathcal{U}$, $\mathcal{O}$, *and* $\mathcal{H}_{\mathcal{T}}$.

1. *Procedure* **Publish_Resource**(o) *generates a user and resource graph that correctly enforces the subscription-based policy on* $\mathcal{U}$ *and* $\mathcal{O}\cup\{o\}$.
2. *Procedure* **Subscribe**(u,T) *generates a user and resource graph that correctly enforces the subscription-based policy on* $\mathcal{U}\cup\{u\}$ *and* $\mathcal{O}$, *with* $u.\mathcal{S}\cup\{T\}$.
3. *Procedure* **Withdraw_Subscription**(u,t) *generates a user and resource graph that correctly enforces the subscription-based policy on* $\mathcal{U}$ *and* $\mathcal{O}$, *with* $u.\mathcal{S}\setminus\{[t^s,t^e]\}\cup\{[t^s,t]\}$.

Proof. To prove Theorem 5.5, we first need to prove that function **Get_Vertex**, which possibly inserts vertices and edges in the user and resource graph, guarantees that the resulting graph is still a user and resource graph (Definition 5.4) correctly enforcing the subscription-based policy.

Lemma 5.3 (Correctness of Function Get_Vertex). *Let $\mathcal{H}_{\mathcal{T}}(\mathcal{T},\succeq)$ be a time hierarchy defined on time domain $(\mathbb{TS},\leq)$, $\mathcal{U}$ be a set of users with $u.\mathcal{S}\subseteq\mathcal{T}$ for all $u\in\mathcal{U}$, $\mathcal{O}$ be a set of resources with $o.t\in\mathbb{TS}$ for all $o\in\mathcal{O}$, and $G(V,E)$ be the user and resource graph over $\mathcal{U}$, $\mathcal{O}$, and $\mathcal{H}_{\mathcal{T}}$. Given a time window T, the user and resource graph generated by function $\boldsymbol{Get\_Vertex}(T)$ satisfies Definition 5.4.*

Proof. Function **Get_Vertex** is correct if: (1) it terminates; (2) when it returns, graph G satisfies Definition 5.4; and (3) when it returns, graph G correctly enforces the subscription-based policy.

1. Function **Get_Vertex** terminates since its recursive call operates on the direct ancestor of time window T in the time hierarchy $\mathcal{H}_{\mathcal{T}}$ and $\mathcal{H}_{\mathcal{T}}$ is a finite hierarchy. As a consequence, $\mathcal{H}_{\mathcal{T}}$ includes at least a root vertex $T_{\top}$ (i.e., a vertex with no ancestors).
2. If there exists a vertex in G representing T, the function does not modify G. As a consequence, if G satisfies Definition 5.4 when the function is called, the graph satisfies Definition 5.4 also when the function returns. If T is not represented by a vertex in G, function **Get_Vertex** inserts into G a vertex v representing T. To satisfy Definition 5.4, its direct ancestor T_i in $\mathcal{H}_{\mathcal{T}}$ should be represented by a vertex v_i in G, connected by an edge to v. Function **Get_Vertex** recursively calls itself on T_i, obtaining vertex v_i representing T_i, and inserts edge (v_i,v). Since function **Get_Vertex** correctly connects v to its ancestor, also each ancestor of v is correctly connected to its ancestor because they are all generated by function **Get_Vertex**. We conclude that, when function **Get_Vertex** returns, the user and resource graph satisfies Definition 5.4.
3. Since function **Get_Vertex** does not modify the subscription-based policy of the system, users should not gain/lose their ability to decrypt resources. Function **Get_Vertex** does not insert, remove, or modify edges incident to vertices representing users and timestamps of existing resources; it does not modify the time windows represented by vertices; and the resulting graph satisfy Definition 5.4. As a consequence, if G correctly enforces the subscription-based policy when function **Get_Vertex** is called, it correctly enforces the policy also when the function returns.   □

We are now ready to prove Theorem 5.5, as follows. We prove each of the statements in the theorem separately. For each procedure, we prove that: (1) it terminates; (2) when it returns, G satisfies Definition 5.4; (3) when it returns, G correctly enforces the subscription-based policy.

1. Let us first analyze procedure **Publish_Resource**, which inserts o into $\mathcal{O}$.

   a. Procedure **Publish_Resource** terminates since function **Get_Vertex** terminates (Lemma 5.3).
   b. When the procedure returns, the graph satisfies Definition 5.4, since the procedure does not modify the graph and function **Get_Vertex** is correct (Lemma 5.3).
   c. Procedure **Publish_Resource** inserts o into $\mathcal{O}$. Since the procedure calls function **Get_Vertex** on $[o.t,o.t]$, vertex v representing the timestamp of

the resource belongs to G. Also, o is encrypted with the key of v. As a consequence, since G satisfies Definition 5.4, it correctly enforces the subscription-based policy also after o is published.

2. Let us now consider procedure **Subscribe**, which grants user u access to the resources in time window T.

   a. Procedure **Subscribe** terminates since function **Get_Vertex** terminates (see Lemma 5.3) and its recursive call operates on the direct ancestor of time window T in the time hierarchy $\mathcal{H}_{\mathcal{T}}$, which is a finite hierarchy.
   b. The procedure possibly inserts a vertex representing u and calls function **Get_Vertex** over T, which preserves the correctness of the graph (Lemma 5.3). The procedure inserts an edge from vertex v_u, representing u, to vertex v_T, representing T, according to the fact that T is inserted into $u.\mathcal{S}$ (Definition 5.4). The procedure modifies the graph by removing all the edges connecting vertex v_u to the vertices representing all the descendants of a time window T_i, according to the fact that all these time windows are removed from $u.\mathcal{S}$. The resulting graph then satisfies Definition 5.4.
   c. Procedure **Subscribe** inserts T into $u.\mathcal{S}$. Since it possibly inserts the vertex representing u into G, the user's key is correctly defined. If all the direct descendants of a time window T_i belong to $u.\mathcal{S}$, the procedure removes these time windows from $u.\mathcal{S}$. However, it recursively calls itself on T_i and therefore T_i is inserted into $u.\mathcal{S}$. Since T_i covers the same time instants as the union of its descendants, a subscription to T_i is equivalent to a set of subscriptions to all its descendants. As a consequence, since G satisfies Definition 5.4, it correctly enforces the subscription-based policy also after u subscribed to T.

3. Finally, let us now consider procedure **Withdraw_Subscription**, which enforces the leave of user u at time t.

   a. Procedure **Withdraw_Subscription** includes a **while** loop, with a nested **for each** loop. The **for each** loop terminates, since the number of time windows in a user subscription is finite, as well as the set of users in the system. The **while** loop includes, besides the **for each** loop, a call to function **Get_Vertex** that, as already proved, terminates. The **while** loop stops when either $t=t^e$, $t^s=t^e$ or $T \notin V$, reaching in the worst case a leaf in G. Since G is acyclic and the **while** loop visits a path in the graph, the **while** loop, and therefore also procedure **Withdraw_Subscription**, terminates.
   b. The user and resource graph obtained when the procedure returns is based on a different time hierarchy than the original one, $\mathcal{H}_{\mathcal{T}}'(\mathcal{T}', \succeq)$, defined on a different set $\mathcal{T}'$ of time windows $\mathcal{T}'=\mathcal{T} \cup \mathcal{T}_{new}$, with $\mathcal{T}_{new}=\{[t^s,t]: \exists[t^s,t^e]\in\mathcal{T} \wedge t^s \leq t \leq t^e\}$. To guarantee that G is defined on $\mathcal{H}_{\mathcal{T}}'$, procedure **Withdraw_Subscription** changes the time window associated with vertices representing a time window $[t^s,t^e]\in\mathcal{T}$ with $t^s \leq t \leq t^e$ by substituting t^e with t. For each of these vertices, the procedure calls function **Get_Vertex** on $[t^s,t^e]$. As a consequence, G includes a proper subset of time windows

in $\mathcal{T}$ and all the time windows in $\mathcal{T}_{new}$. The **while** loop in procedure **Withdraw_Subscription** changes the end time of all the time windows along a path, reducing these time windows to a subset of the time instants of the original ones. Hence, the edges along this path correctly reflect the dominance relationship among the time windows represented by the vertices. As already proved, function **Get_Vertex** guarantees the correct representation of dominance relationships. Also, $[t^s,t^e]$ clearly dominates $[t^s,t]$, therefore the edge connecting the new vertex representing $[t^s,t^e]$ with the existing one representing $[t^s,t]$ correctly reflects a direct dominance relationship. The procedure also substitutes edge $(v_u v_T)$ with $(v_u,v_{T'})$, where v_u represents user u, v_T represents time window $[t^s,t^e]$ and is updated to $[t^s,t]$, and $v_{T'}$ is inserted and represents $[t^s,t^e]$. This update is not performed for the user who is withdrawing from a subscription, since her subscription is updated to $u.\mathscr{S}\setminus\{[t^s,t^e]\}\cup\{[t^s,t]\}$. We can then conclude that, when procedure **Withdraw_Subscription** returns, the user and resource graph satisfies Definition 5.4.

c. Procedure **Withdraw_Subscription** updates $u.\mathscr{S}$ to $u.\mathscr{S}\setminus\{[t^s,t^e]\}\cup\{[t^s,t]\}$. Since no resource has been published with timestamp greater than t and the user and resource graph satisfies Definition 5.4, when the procedure returns G correctly enforces the subscription-based policy.   □

5.10 Chapter Summary

In this chapter, we presented an approach for enforcing read and write authorizations in data release scenarios. Our solution does not require intervention of the data owner for filtering query results and/or access requests, and efficiently supports updates in the access control policy, minimizing the overhead of the data owner and resulting transparent to the final users. Data integrity can be easily verified by the data owner and by the users authorized to write resources, thus providing guarantees on the fact that resources externally stored have not been tampered with by unauthorized parties without being detected. The proposed solution relies on the use of symmetric encryption, hashing, and HMAC functions for enforcing access control and integrity checks in an efficient and effective way. We have then complemented our solution with a subscription-based policy, proposing a technique for effectively restricting access to published resources based on the subscriptions of the users to a service, to take into account scenarios in which user subscriptions and released resources change dynamically over time. Changes in the subscription-based policy due to the addition of new users and resources, and to the withdrawal of users from their subscriptions are efficiently enforced updating the key derivation structure, again in a transparent way to the final users. Our proposal then performs a step toward the development of solutions actually applicable in real-world scenarios where efficiency and scalability are mandatory.

Chapter 6
Conclusions

In this book, we have addressed the problem of protecting sensitive information in scenarios of data release (e.g., in cloud/outsourcing contexts). After some introductory remarks and a discussion of related works, we focused on three specific aspects: the protection of data explicitly published, the protection of information not explicitly included in a release but possibly exposed to privacy breaches by the release itself, and the enforcement of access restrictions. In this chapter, we summarize the contributions of this book and we outline possible directions for future works.

6.1 Summary of the Contributions

The contribution of this book is threefold.

Protection of Data Explicitly Involved in a Release We proposed our solution for protecting privacy of sensitive information included in a release. The technique is based on the fragmentation approach, which vertically splits the original data collection in disjoint fragments satisfying both confidentiality and visibility constraints, respectively modeling requirements for privacy protection and information visibility. We provided a novel OBDD-based formulation of the fragmentation problem, and proposed two efficient algorithms (exact and heuristic) for computing a minimal fragmentation. The efficiency of our OBDD-based approach has been testified by our experimental results, showing also that the heuristic well approximates the optimal solutions computed by the exact algorithm while requiring limited computation time. To further increase the utility of the released data for final recipients, we complemented fragments with loose associations, specifically extended to operate on arbitrary fragmentations (thus removing the limiting original assumption of operating on a pair of fragments).

© Springer International Publishing Switzerland 2015
G. Livraga, *Protecting Privacy in Data Release*, Advances in Information
Security 57, DOI 10.1007/978-3-319-16109-9_6

Protection of Data Not Explicitly Involved in a Release We provided a solution for capturing and counteracting the risk that the release of a collection of non sensitive data can expose sensitive information that, despite not appearing in the released dataset, can be derived observing peculiar distribution of the values of the released dataset. We identified and modeled a novel inference scenario, raised from a real case study that needed consideration. We introduced several metrics to assess the inference exposure due to a data release, we formally defined a safe release with respect to the modeled inference channel, and we illustrated the controls to be enforced in a scenario where data items are released one at a time, upon request. Our solution has been experimentally evaluated to assess both inference exposure and information loss.

Access Control Enforcement We defined an access control solution for enforcing dynamic write authorizations in data release scenarios. Our proposal is based on selective encryption, originally designed to enforce read privileges over outsourced data, to fit the emerging cloud computing paradigm where the storage server is not trusted to enforce access restrictions. Our technique supports grant and revoke of write authorizations and results appealing for its efficiency and flexibility, as it avoids expensive re-keying and re-encryption operations. We also proposed an integrity check technique to verify that modifications to a resource have been produced only by authorized users. We complemented our solution with the definition and enforcement of a subscription-based authorization policy, to consider emerging real-world scenarios where users pay for a service and need to access the resources released during their subscriptions at any time. Our proposal avoids to the users the burden of downloading resources, allowing them to maintain the right to access such resources without the worry that they will lose this right after the expiration of their subscriptions.

6.2   Future Work

The research illustrated in this book can be extended along several directions, as we outline in the following.

6.2.1   Protection of Data Explicitly Involved in a Release

Dynamic Datasets In line with traditional protection techniques, our fragmentation and (extended) loose associations presented in Chap. 3 make the implicit assumption that the original dataset is static (i.e., it does not change over time). In particular, it assumes that no tuple (attribute, respectively) be inserted into/removed from the original relation (relation schema, respectively). In particular, updating the schema adding or removing attributes might cause the violation of one or more constraints: removing attributes from fragments might violate visibility constraints, while adding attributes to fragments might reveal sensitive associations among attributes that have not been considered. On the other hand, adding or removing tuples might compromise the protection degree offered by the published loose associations: removing tuples from fragments decreases the size of the groups in fragments, while adding a tuple might allow an adversary to recombine it by concatenating its sub-tuples in each of the fragments (as the heterogeneity properties might be violated). A future line of work will consist in the definition of protection techniques able to handle updates at both the schema and instance levels.

Multiple Input Relations A common assumption of traditional protection techniques, which we also adopted, is that data to be released are organized in a single universal relation. However, real-world datasets can be composed of several relations, possibly belonging to different domains, thus complicating the definition of confidentiality constraints for computing a fragmentation. Intuitively, defining constraints for a relation without consideration of the other ones might be insufficient for capturing all sensitive associations. Besides, these relations might be related though integrity constraints (e.g., since they include some common attributes whose values are related by a dependency) that might be used for re-joining the fragments in which the relations have been split, possibly enabling the recomposition of sensitive associations. To address this issue, it is necessary to define a technique for managing multiple input relations.

6.2.2 Protection of Data Not Explicitly Involved in a Release

Different Metrics The metrics adopted to counteract the risk of sensitive information disclosure have been specifically devised to capture deviations between an observed value distribution (in the released dataset), and an expected one. They therefore well suit our inference scenario, where inferences on sensitive information are drawn by observing differences between value distributions. However, in other scenarios inferences might be enabled by other peculiarities of the observed distributions (e.g., by observing similarities, rather than differences, with peculiar/specific value distributions, or by observing specific values in the released dataset). It is important therefore to define other metrics, able to handle different peculiarities of the released distributions, to address more variegate scenarios.

Different Inference Channels The inference channel modeled in this book is based on the assumption that the background knowledge of a recipient is the baseline value distribution, which is then considered typical and expected. This is indeed reasonable in real-world scenarios, in which a given value distribution can be considered publicly available as, for instance, being released by its owners for statistical purposes. However, a recipient might possess different knowledge she can exploit to derive sensitive information, such as the expected order in which tuples are requested, or the typical time between two subsequent releases. For instance, knowing the order in which tuples are requested and comparing it with the order in which tuples are actually released, a recipient might infer that delayed requests refer to sensitive information. A future line of work will investigate other kinds of knowledge a recipient might exploit to draw inferences of sensitive information.

6.2.3 Access Control Enforcement

Multiple Owners Our access control system based on selective encryption operates with the implicit assumption that all data to be stored at the external server are of the same owner, who can therefore define a single authorization policy to regulate read and write privileges on the entire dataset. However, in some collaborative scenarios different owners might be responsible for different portions of the resources to be made selectively available. A naive solution to enforce access control in this scenario adopting our technique can require each data owner to define her own key derivation structure modeling authorizations for her resources. This, however, would require users to manage one key for each owner authorizing them. Besides, different owners might control overlapping portions of the same dataset, requiring their policies to be collectively enforced. A possible direction for future works will explore how to solve these two issues, by defining techniques able to handle the cases of multiple owners.

Exposure Evaluation The integrity control technique complementing our access control system assumes the server, in case of resource updates, to never overwrite resources but to maintain all their versions. This allows, whenever the owner or the users identify an illegal update, to discard it and restore the previous genuine version of the resource. To avoid the need of keeping all the different versions of every resource in the system, it will be necessary to define a technique able to identify an update as illegal before it is enforced, so that it can be discarded without the need of resorting to previous versions of the resources.

Subscriptions Flexibility In our subscription-based authorization policy, subscriptions are defined based on their beginning and ending time. It therefore fits wells emerging scenarios in which users pay for a service, and are allowed to access all and only those resources released during their subscriptions. Our selective encryption strategy might however be adapted to different scenarios, where subscriptions to a service can be defined on the basis of different criteria (e.g., topic of interest, geographical region) as the hierarchy of subscriptions is not pre-defined, but it is dynamically created depending on users' requests. An interesting direction for future research would extend our technique to allow for more flexibility in the definition of user subscriptions.

References

1. N.R. Adam, J.C. Wortmann, Security-control methods for statistical databases: a comparative study. ACM Comput. Surv. **21**(4), 515–556 (1989)
2. C. Aggarwal, P.S. Yu (eds.), *Privacy-Preserving Data Mining: Models and Algorithms* (Springer, New York, 2008)
3. G. Aggarwal, M. Bawa, P. Ganesan, H. Garcia-Molina, K. Kenthapadi, R. Motwani, U. Srivastava, D. Thomas, Y. Xu, Two can keep a secret: a distributed architecture for secure database services, in *Proceedings of CIDR 2005*, Asilomar, CA, 2005
4. S. Akl, P. Taylor, Cryptographic solution to a problem of access control in a hierarchy. ACM TOCS **1**(3), 239–248 (1983)
5. M.J. Atallah, K.B. Frikken, M. Blanton, Dynamic and efficient key management for access hierarchies, in *Proceedings of CCS 2005*, Alexandria, VA, 2005
6. M. Atallah, M. Blanton, N. Fazio, K. Frikken, Dynamic and efficient key management for access hierarchies. ACM TISSEC **12**(3), 18:1–18:43 (2009)
7. M. Barbaro, T. Zeller, A face is exposed for AOL searcher no. 4417749. *New York Times*, August 9 2006
8. L. Batina, B. Gierlichs, E. Prouff, M. Rivain, F. Standaert, N. Veyrat-Charvillon, Mutual information analysis: a comprehensive study. J. Cryptol. **24**(2), 269–291 (2011)
9. R.J. Bayardo, R. Agrawal, Data privacy through optimal k-anonymization, in *Proceedings of ICDE'05*, Tokyo, Japan, 2005
10. M. Bellare, R. Canetti, H. Krawczyk, Keying hash functions for message authentication, in *Proceedings of CRYPTO 1996*, Santa Barbara, CA, 1996
11. E. Bertino, C. Bettini, E. Ferrari, P. Samarati, An access control model supporting periodicity constraints and temporal reasoning. ACM TODS **23**(3), 231–285 (1998)
12. C. Bettini, C. Dyreson, W. Evans, R. Snodgrass, X.S. Wang, A glossary of time granularity concepts, in *Temporal Databases: Research and Practice*, LNCS 1399, ed. by O. Etzion, S. Jajodia, S. Sripada (Springer, Berlin, 1998), pp. 406–413
13. M. Bezzi, S. De Capitani di Vimercati, G. Livraga, P. Samarati, Protecting privacy of sensitive value distributions in data release, in *Proceedings of STM 2010*, Athens, Greece, 2010
14. M. Bezzi, S. De Capitani di Vimercati, S. Foresti, G. Livraga, P. Samarati, R. Sassi, Modeling and preventing inferences from sensitive value distributions in data release. JCS **20**(4), 393–436 (2012)
15. J. Biskup, M. Preuß, Database fragmentation with encryption: under which semantic constraints and a priori knowledge can two keep a secret? in *Proceedigs of DBSec 2013*, Newark, NJ, 2013

© Springer International Publishing Switzerland 2015
G. Livraga, *Protecting Privacy in Data Release*, Advances in Information
Security 57, DOI 10.1007/978-3-319-16109-9

16. J. Biskup, M. Preuß, L. Wiese, On the inference-proofness of database fragmentation satisfying confidentiality constraints, in *Proceedings of ISC 2011*, Xi'an, 2011
17. E. Brier, C. Clavier, F. Olivier, Correlation power analysis with a leakage model, in *Proceedings of CHES 2004*, Cambridge, MA, 2004
18. A. Brodsky, C. Farkas, S. Jajodia, Secure databases: constraints, inference channels, and monitoring disclosures. IEEE TKDE **12**(6), 900–919 (2000)
19. R.E. Bryant, Graph-based algorithms for Boolean function manipulation. IEEE TC **35**(8), 677–691 (1986)
20. F. Cayre, C. Fontaine, T. Furon, Watermarking security: Theory and practice. IEEE TSP **53**(10), 3976–3987 (2005)
21. B.-C. Chen, R. Ramakrishnan, K. LeFevre, Privacy skyline: privacy with multidimensional adversarial knowledge, in *Proceedings of the VLDB 2007*, Vienna, 2007
22. P.E. Cheng, J.W. Liou, M. Liou, J.A.D. Aston, Data information in contingency tables: a fallacy of hierarchical loglinear models. JDS **4**(4), 387–398 (2006)
23. V. Ciriani, S. De Capitani di Vimercati, S. Foresti, S. Jajodia, S. Paraboschi, P. Samarati, Fragmentation and encryption to enforce privacy in data storage, in *Proceedings of ESORICS 2007*, Dresden, 2007
24. V. Ciriani, S. De Capitani di Vimercati, S. Foresti, P. Samarati, k-anonymity, in *Secure Data Management in Decentralized Systems*, ed. by T. Yu, S. Jajodia (Springer, New York, 2007)
25. V. Ciriani, S. De Capitani di Vimercati, S. Foresti, P. Samarati. Microdata protection, in *Secure Data Management in Decentralized Systems*, ed. by T. Yu, S. Jajodia (Springer, New York, 2007)
26. V. Ciriani, S. De Capitani di Vimercati, S. Foresti, S. Jajodia, S. Paraboschi, P. Samarati, Fragmentation design for efficient query execution over sensitive distributed databases, in *Proceedings of ICDCS 2009*, Montreal, Canada, 2009
27. V. Ciriani, S. De Capitani di Vimercati, S. Foresti, S. Jajodia, S. Paraboschi, P. Samarati, Keep a few: outsourcing data while maintaining confidentiality, in *Proceedings of ESORICS 2009*, Saint Malo, 2009
28. V. Ciriani, S. De Capitani di Vimercati, S. Foresti, S. Jajodia, S. Paraboschi, P. Samarati, Combining fragmentation and encryption to protect privacy in data storage. ACM TISSEC **13**(3), 1–33 (2010)
29. V. Ciriani, S. De Capitani di Vimercati, S. Foresti, G. Livraga, P. Samarati. Enforcing confidentiality and data visibility constraints: An OBDD approach, in *Proceedings of DBSec 2011*, Richmond, VA, 2011
30. V. Ciriani, S. De Capitani di Vimercati, S. Foresti, G. Livraga, P. Samarati. An OBDD approach to enforce confidentiality and visibility constraints in data publishing. JCS **20**(5), 463–508 (2012)
31. G. Cormode, M. Procopiuc, D. Srivastava, T. Tran, Differentially private publication of sparse data, in *Proceedings of EDBT/ICDT 2012*, Berlin, 2012
32. J. Crampton, K. Martin, P. Wild, On key assignment for hierarchical access control, in *Proceedings of CSFW 2006*, Venice, 2006
33. T. Dalenius, Towards a methodology for statistical disclosure control. Statistik Tidskrift **15**, 429–444 (1977)
34. S. Dawson, S. De Capitani di Vimercati, P. Lincoln, P. Samarati, Minimal data upgrading to prevent inference and association attacks, in *Proceedings of PODS 1999*, Philadelphia, PA, 1999
35. S. Dawson, S. De Capitani di Vimercati, P. Lincoln, P. Samarati, Maximizing sharing of protected information. JCSS **64**(3), 496–541 (2002)
36. S. Dawson, S. De Capitani di Vimercati, P. Samarati, Specification and enforcement of classification and inference constraints, in *Proceedings of S&P 1999*, Oakland, CA, 1999
37. S. De Capitani di Vimercati, S. Foresti, S. Jajodia, S. Paraboschi, and P. Samarati, Encryption policies for regulating access to outsourced data. ACM TODS **35**(2), 12:1–12:46 (2010)

38. S. De Capitani di Vimercati, S. Foresti, S. Jajodia, S. Paraboschi, and P. Samarati, Fragments and loose associations: Respecting privacy in data publishing. PVLDB **3**(1), 1370–1381 (2010)

39. S. De Capitani di Vimercati, S. Foresti, S. Jajodia, S. Paraboschi, P. Samarati, Support for write privileges on outsourced data. in *Proceedings of SEC 2012*, Heraklion, 2012

40. S. De Capitani di Vimercati, S. Foresti, S. Jajodia, G. Livraga, Enforcing subscription-based authorization policies in cloud scenarios, in *Proceedings of DBSec 2012*, Paris, 2012

41. S. De Capitani di Vimercati, S. Foresti, S. Jajodia, G. Livraga, S. Paraboschi, P. Samarati, Enforcing dynamic write privileges in data outsourcing. Comput. Secur. **39**, 47–63 (2013)

42. S. De Capitani di Vimercati, S. Foresti, S. Jajodia, G. Livraga, S. Paraboschi, P. Samarati, Extending loose associations to multiple fragments. in *Proceedings of DBSec 2013*, Newark, NJ, 2013

43. S. De Capitani di Vimercati, S. Foresti, S. Jajodia, G. Livraga, S. Paraboschi, P. Samarati, Fragmentation in presence of data dependencies. IEEE TDSC **11**(6), 510–523 (2014)

44. S. De Capitani di Vimercati, S. Foresti, S. Jajodia, G. Livraga, S. Paraboschi, and P. Samarati, Integrity for distributed queries, in *Proceedings of CNS 2014*, San Francisco, CA (2014)

45. S. De Capitani di Vimercati, S. Foresti, S. Jajodia, G. Livraga, S. Paraboschi, P. Samarati, Loose associations to increase utility in data publishing. JCS **23**(1), 59–88 (2015)

46. A. De Santis, A.L. Ferrara, B. Masucci, Cryptographic key assignment schemes for any access control policy. IPL **92**(4), 199–205 (2004)

47. H.S. Delugach, T.H. Hinke, Wizard: a database inference analysis and detection system. IEEE TKDE **8**, 56–66 (1996)

48. W.J. Dixon, Analysis of extreme values, Ann. Math. Stat. **21**(4), 488–506 (1950)

49. W.J. Dixon, Ratios involving extreme values. Ann. Math. Stat. **22**(1), 58–78 (1951)

50. C. Dwork, Differential privacy, in *Proceedings of ICALP 2006*, Venice, 2006

51. C. Dwork, A. Smith, Differential privacy for statistics: What we know and what we want to learn. JPC **1**(2), 135–154 (2009)

52. C. Dwork, F. Mcsherry, K. Nissim, A. Smith, Calibrating noise to sensitivity in private data analysis, in *Proceedings of TCC 2006*, New York, 2006

53. C. Dwork, A. Nikolov, K. Talwar, Using convex relaxations for efficiently and privately releasing marginals. in *Proceedings of SOCG 2014*, Kyoto, 2014

54. R.M. Fano, *Transmission of Information; A Statistical Theory of Communications* (MIT University Press, New York, 1961)

55. Federal Committee on Statistical Methodology. Statistical policy working paper 22, May 1994. Report on Statistical Disclosure Limitation Methodology

56. K.B. Frikken, Y. Zhang, Yet another privacy metric for publishing micro-data, in *Proceedings of WPES 2008*, Alexandria, 2008

57. B. Gierlichs, L. Batina, P. Tuyls, B. Preneel, Mutual information analysis - a generic side-channel distinguisher. in *Proceedings of CHES 2008*, Washington, 2008

58. J.A. Goguen, J. Meseguer, Unwinding and inference control, in *Proceedings of S&P 1984*, Oakland, 1984

59. P. Golle, Revisiting the uniqueness of simple demographics in the US population, in *Proceedings of WPES 2006*, Alexandria, 2006

60. V. Goyal, O. Pandey, A. Sahai, B. Waters, Attribute-based encryption for fine-grained access control of encrypted data, in *Proceedings of CCS 2006*, Alexandria, 2006

61. M. Hay, V. Rastogi, G. Miklau, D. Suciu, Boosting the accuracy of differentially private histograms through consistency. PVLDB **3**(1–2), 1021–1032 (2010)

62. T. Hinke, Inference aggregation detection in database management systems. in *Proceedings of S&P 1988*, Oakland, 1988

63. T.H. Hinke, H.S. Delugach, A. Chandrasekhar, A fast algorithm for detecting second paths in database inference analysis. JCS **3**(2/3), 147–168 (1995)

64. T.H. Hinke, H.S. Delugach, R. Wolf, A framework for inference-directed data mining, in *Proceedings of DBSec 1996*, Como, 1996

65. T.H. Hinke, H.S. Delugach, R.P. Wolf, Protecting databases from inference attacks. Comput. Secur. **16**(22), 687–708 (1997)
66. S. Jajodia, C. Meadows, Inference problems in multilevel secure database management systems, in *Information Security: An Integrated Collection of Essays*, ed. by M. Abrams, S. Jajodia, H. Podell (IEEE Computer Sociery Press, Los Alamitos, 1995)
67. D. Kifer, A. Machanavajjhala, Pufferfish: A framework for mathematical privacy definitions. ACM TODS **39**(1), 3:1–3:36 (2014)
68. D.E. Knuth, *The Art of Computer Programming, Volume 4, Fascicle 1: Bitwise Tricks & Techniques; Binary Decision Diagrams* (Addison-Wesley Professional, Upper Saddle River, 2009)
69. K. LeFevre, D.J. DeWitt, R. Ramakrishnan, Incognito: Efficient full-domain k-anonymity, in *Proceedings of SIGMOD 2005*, Baltimore, 2005
70. K. LeFevre, D.J. DeWitt, R. Ramakrishnan, Mondrian multidimensional k-anonymity, in *Proceedings of ICDE 2006*, Atlanta, 2006
71. F. Li, J. Sun, S. Papadimitriou, G.A. Mihaila, I. Stanoi, Hiding in the crowd: Privacy preservation on evolving streams through correlation tracking, in *Proceedings of ICDE 2007*, Istanbul, 2007
72. N. Li, T. Li, S. Venkatasubramanian, t-closeness: privacy beyond k-anonymity and ℓ-diversity, in *Proceedings of ICDE 2007*, Istanbul, 2007
73. C. Li, M. Hay, V. Rastogi, G. Miklau, A. McGregor, Optimizing linear counting queries under differential privacy, in *Proceedings of PODS 2010*, Indianapolis, IN, 2010
74. T.F. Lunt, Aggregation and inference: facts and fallacies, in *Proceedings of S&P 1989*, Oakland, 1989
75. A. Machanavajjhala, D. Kifer, J. Gehrke, M. Venkitasubramaniam, ℓ-diversity: Privacy beyond k-anonymity. ACM TKDD **1**(1), 3:1–3:52 (2007)
76. A. Machanavajjhala, J. Gehrke, M. Götz, Data publishing against realistic adversaries. PVLDB **2**(1), 790–801 (2009)
77. D.G. Marks, Inference in mls database systems. IEEE TKDE **8**(1), 46–55 (1996)
78. D.G. Marks, A. Motro, S. Jajodia, Enhancing the controlled disclosure of sensitive information. in *Proceedings of ESORICS 1996*, Rome, 1996
79. D.J. Martin, D. Kifer, A. Machanavajjhala, J. Gehrke, J.Y. Halpern, Worst-case background knowledge for privacy-preserving data publishing, in *Proceedings of ICDE 2007*, Istanbul, 2007
80. C. Meinel, T. Theobald, *Algorithms and Data Structures in VLSI Design* (Springer, Berlin, 1998)
81. G. Miklau, D. Suciu, Controlling access to published data using cryptography, in *Proceedings of VLDB 2003*, Berlin, 2003
82. Minnesota Population Center. IPMUS-USA (Integrated Public Use Microdata Series). http://www.ipums.org
83. I. Mironov, O. Pandey, O. Reingold, S.P. Vadhan, Computational differential privacy, in *Proceedings of CRYPTO 2009*, Santa Barbara, 2009
84. M. Morgenstern, Controlling logical inference in multilevel database systems, in *Proceedings of S&P 1988*, 1988
85. A. Narayanan, V. Shmatikov, Robust de-anonymization of large sparse datasets, in *Proceedings of IEEE S&P 2008*, Berkeley/Oakland, 2008
86. M.E. Nergiz, C. Clifton, A.E. Nergiz, Multirelational k-anonymity, in *Proceedings of ICDE 2007*, Istanbul, 2007
87. P.R.J. Östergård, A new algorithm for the maximum-weight clique problem. Nordic J. Comput. **8**, 424–436 (2001)
88. P.R.J. Östergård, A fast algorithm for the maximum clique problem. Discret. Appl. Math. **120**, 197–207 (2002)
89. J. Pei, Y. Tao, J. Li, X. Xiao, Privacy preserving publishing on multiple quasi-identifiers, in *Proceedings of ICDE 2009*, Shanghai, 2009

90. W.H. Press, S.A. Teukolsky, W.T. Vetterling, B.P. Flannery, *Numerical Recipes: The Art of Scientific Computing*, 3rd edn. (Cambridge University Press, Cambridge, 2007)
91. X. Qian, M.E. Stickel, P.D. Karp, T.F. Lunt, T.D. Garvey, Detection and elimination of inference channels in multilevel relational database, in *Proceedings of S&P 1993*, Oakland, 1993
92. M. Raykova, H. Zhao, and S.M. Bellovin. Privacy enhanced access control for outsourced data sharing, in *Proceedings of FC 2012*, Bonaire, February-March 2012
93. S. Ruj, M. Stojmenovic, A. Nayak, Privacy preserving access control with authentication for securing data in clouds, in *Proceedings of CCGrid 2012*, Ottawa, 2012
94. P. Samarati, Protecting respondents' identities in microdata release. IEEE TKDE **13**(6), 1010–1027 (2001)
95. P. Samarati, S. De Capitani di Vimercati, Access control: Policies, models, and mechanisms, in *Foundations of Security Analysis and Design*, LNCS 2171, ed. by R. Focardi, R. Gorrieri (Springer, Berlin, 2001)
96. R.S. Sandhu, On some cryptographic solutions for access control in a tree hierarchy, in *Proceedings of FJCC 1987*, Dallas, 1987
97. R.S. Sandhu, Cryptographic implementation of a tree hierarchy for access control. IPL **27**(2), 95–98 (1988)
98. G.W. Smith, Modeling security-relevant data semantics. IEEE TSE **17**(11), 1195–1203 (1991)
99. F. Somenzi, Cudd: Cu decision diagram package – release 2.4.2, 2009. Department of Electrical and Computer Engineering – University of Colorado at Boulder
100. Y. Tao, J. Pei, J. Li, X. Xiao, K. Yi, Z. Xing, Correlation hiding by independence masking, in *Proceedings of ICDE 2010*, Long Beach, 2010
101. M. Terrovitis, N. Mamoulis, P. Kalnis, Privacy-preserving anonymization of set-valued data. PVLDB **1**(1), 115–125 (2008)
102. M.B. Thuraisingham, Security checking in relational database management systems augmented with inference engines. Comput. Secur. **6**(6), 479–492 (1987)
103. TSP 8 - Age distribution of UK regular forces, Edition - 01 Apr 2006
104. Ubuntu: Intel Q6600 one core – computer language benchmarks game. http://benchmarksgame.alioth.debian.org/u32/performance.php?test=nbody
105. N. Veyrat-Charvillon, F. Standaert, Mutual information analysis: How, when and why? in *Proceedings of CHES 2009*, Lausanne, 2009
106. Z. Wan, J. Liu, R.-H. Deng, Hasbe: A hierarchical attribute-based solution for flexible and scalable access control in cloud computing. IEEE TIFS **7**(2), 743–754 (2012)
107. K. Wang, B.C.M. Fung, Anonymizing sequential releases, in *Proceedings of KDD 2006*, Philadelphia, PA, 2006
108. H. Wang, R. Liu, Privacy-preserving publishing data with full functional dependencies. in *Proceedings of DASFAA 2010*, Tsukuba, 2010
109. K. Wang, Y. Xu, R. Wong, A. Fu, Anonymizing temporal data. in *Proceedings of ICDM 2010*, Sydney, 2010
110. B. Waters, Ciphertext-policy attribute-based encryption: an expressive, efficient, and provably secure realization. in *Proceedings of PKC 2011*, Taormina, 2011
111. X. Xiao, Y. Tao, Anatomy: simple and effective privacy preservation. in *Proceedings of VLDB 2006*, Seoul, 2006
112. X. Xiao, Y. Tao, Personalized privacy preservation, in *Proceedings of SIGMOD 2006*, Chicago, 2006
113. X. Xiao, Y. Tao, *m*-invariance: towards privacy preserving re-publication of dynamic datasets, in *Proceedings of SIGMOD 2007*, Beijing, 2007
114. X. Xiao, G. Wang, J. Gehrke, Differential privacy via wavelet transforms. IEEE TKDE **23**(8), 1200–1214 (2011)
115. K. Yang, X. Jia, K. Ren, Attribute-based fine-grained access control with efficient revocation in cloud storage systems, in *Proceedings of ASIACCS 2013*, Hangzhou, 2013

116. S. Yu, C. Wang, K. Ren, W. Lou, Achieving secure, scalable, and fine-grained data access control in cloud computing, in *Proceedings of INFOCOM 2010*, San Diego, CA, 2010

117. F. Zhao, T. Nishide, K. Sakurai, Realizing fine-grained and flexible access control to outsourced data with attribute-based cryptosystems, in *Proceedings of ISPEC 2011*, Guangzhou, 2011

118. B. Zhou, Y. Han, J. Pei, B. Jiang, Y. Tao, Y. Jia, Continuous privacy preserving publishing of data streams, in *Proceedings of EDBT 2009*, Saint Petersburg, 2009

119. S. Zhou, K. Ligett, L. Wasserman, Differential privacy with compression, in *Proceedings of ISIT 2009*, Coex, Seoul, 2009

Printed in the United States
By Bookmasters